HIT THE GROUND *LEADING!*

Angela Mondou

Library and Archives Canada Cataloguing in Publication
Mondou, Angela, 1963-
Hit the ground leading!: seize your leadership potential and do incredible things / Angela Mondou.
Includes bibliographical references and index.
ISBN-10: 0-9780225-1-3
ISBN-13: 978-0-9780225-1-8
1. Leadership. I. Title.
HD57.7.M634 2006 658.4'092 C2006-903717-5

Editor and book consultant: Fina Scroppo
Assistant editor: Leslee Mason-Gomes
Copy editor: Nancy Howden
Chief visionary and creative director: Angela Mondou
Cover design: Sasha Carreiro
Design consultation: Vellone Design
Cover/Inside photography: Stan Switalski
Marketing and events director: Lindsay Gibson
Fact-checkers: Tara Brouwer, Nancy Howden and Elaine Sung

We are a highly creative team and would love to work with you! Our company delivers a leadership and growth experience. If you are interested in purchasing volume orders of the book, developing a co-branded program or interested in our keynotes and workshops, please contact us.

All inquiries should be addressed to:

LEADERSHIP
integrate • communicate • execute

ICE Publishing
2036 Hidden Valley Cres., Suite 1A
Kitchener, Ontario N2C 2R1
1-866-397-3826
www.iceleadership.com angela@iceleadership.com lindsay@iceleadership.com

Printed and bound in Canada

The information presented in this book is based on the research, training, and professional experience of the author, and is true and complete to the best of her knowledge.

Dedication

To my Irish Granny, Suzie Crymble, who has spread her positive 'make it happen' energy around the world for 96 years.

Top entrepreneurial schools are endorsing *Hit the Ground Leading!*

"This leadership handbook is now required reading in the most enterprising campus in Canada! Action plans and practical tools will help you hit the ground leading, whatever your enterprise or business venture!"

– Steve Farlow, Schlegel Centre for Entrepreneurship, Wilfrid Laurier University School of Business and Economics

"To be an entrepreneur in a technology venture you must be prepared to hit the ground leading! This leadership guide, packed with fast-action examples, delivers on three principles in which our entrepreneurship program is based: it's unique, innovative and creative."

– Dr. Paul Doherty, Centre for Business, Entrepreneurship and Technology (CBET), University of Waterloo

"Being a start-up entrepreneur is like being a special forces commando. The mission of the start-up entrepreneur is to quickly identify a market opportunity and exploit it using the resources at hand. ***Hit the Ground Leading!*** is essential basic training for any aspiring entrepreneur. Angela Mondou provides a field guide packed with practical tools and techniques for the entrepreneur to build and lead a venture that is equipped to profit in market forces."

– Dr. Brent Mainprize, Entrepreneurship Faculty, Faculty of Management, Royal Roads University

"***Hit the Ground Leading!*** is 'leadership innovation' and it strikes new ground in leadership development. At McMaster's Xerox Centre for Engineering Entrepreneurship & Innovation, we believe in creating innovative, opportunity-oriented leaders. Angela's book provides entrepreneurs and leaders in any enterprise the skills to seize every leadership opportunity."

– Mohan Nadarajah, McMaster University, Xerox Centre for Engineering Entrepreneurship & Innovation

Foreword

We all have a choice in life.

We can get up every morning, step outside and go through the motions of life, guided by the caprice of fate. Or we can see life as an adventure, one in which we can mold our destiny, set challenging goals and live a life of energy, integrity and conviction.

All of us make this choice, and in fact, we renew this choice every day of our lives. This is what struck me most when I read Angela's book, ***Hit the Ground Leading!***

It's not just a 'playbook' for leadership; it's a playbook for life. This is a book for anyone who is looking to put more meaning and purpose into their life. If you want to lead and live the adventure, this book will help you do that in a refreshing and profoundly tangible way.

This is not a book about leadership theory. It's a powerful and practical guide based on hard-learned experience that goes way beyond the boardroom. Angela draws on the very visible and real experience of both her military background from the war zone and her experience working within one of the fastest-growing and sustaining companies in the history of Canada. As part of Research In Motion's senior management team, Angela had numerous meaningful opportunities to practice what she preaches, leading and executing in a mission-critical environment. She has demonstrated a unique leadership talent, combined with marketing savvy and creative energy, all of which have led to some successful one-of-a-kind programs with RIM. She has a knack for creating a loyal following as a leader, and, with the energy she brings to this book, I'm certain she will have the same effect on her readers.

Over the last several years, we have seen a paradigm shift on the attributes of effective leadership, including an environment of accountability, a team focus and personal empowerment, just to name a few. Angela's book does an outstanding job of illustrating these attributes. The book's presentation style is practical and captivating. Each chapter stands on its own merit. Each leadership attribute is fully explored. Its cadence moves with ease and energy. Every chapter begins with exciting real life insight and is followed by leadership principles and no-nonsense advice. Action plans and tools and tips provide the reader with simple access to convert the learning into practical advice that can be immediately applied to one's own life.

This won't be a book you put aside or place on a bookshelf. You'll want to keep it close by and revisit it every time you have to hit the ground – ***leading!***

Don Morrison
Chief Operating Officer, BlackBerry
Research In Motion

You've got to believe...

One more adventure to add to my list. I can't believe that I actually accomplished this one! Writing this book has been quite a journey, and it has put me in touch, in a profound way, with what I think is one of the most powerful gifts you can give to someone. A gift that will influence a person's life: A belief – in YOU.

I've always been somewhat of a free spirit, so when I announced to my family, friends and colleagues that I was going to leave behind a lucrative executive position in a skyrocketing, high-tech company to start my own consulting and marketing business, and later write a book, let's just say I found out very quickly that there are those who believe in you and those who don't. And they stand out pretty quickly.

One thing I can tell you with absolute certainty is that it's tough, maybe even impossible, to follow your free spirit without people who believe in you.

I remember the vote of confidence I got from my youngest son, Liam, after he and my older son, Daniel, had evaluated my latest "great" book title, for which they both gave me a big hearty thumbs-down. Looking back, they were both right. It was really bad. Liam must have felt badly for the thumbs-down vote because he looked at me with such sincerity and said, "Don't worry, Mommy, your book is going to sell millions." Not to be outdone by his younger brother, Daniel piped up with: "Yeah, Mom, you've already sold thousands, right? That's what I'm telling everybody." You've got to love it. My book was only half complete and apparently my title needed some work, but my sons, both such enthusiastic participants throughout this entire journey, sure believed in me.

Then there is Tom, my partner, who couldn't have been in a tougher position throughout this entire book-publishing venture. Let me tell you, after you spend months and months writing that first draft, let's just say you feel utterly exposed, like you're walking around in public in your underwear (and not necessarily your best Victoria's Secret gear) when you allow someone to read your work. Poor Tom bravely walked into the lion's den, month after month, offering to read my draft chapters and give me some much-needed feedback. If he could read a chapter in an hour or less, and it was able to keep his undivided attention (darn near impossible), I knew I was on the right track. Unfortunately, his smallest critiques brought out the worst in me, and I was usually ready to bite heads off – Tom's in particular. He was in a high-risk, lose-lose situation. But, I was lucky, because Tom survived my wrath and continued to believe in me. And I can assure you, this book is much better for it! Tom, you deserve a medal.

Even before others can believe in you, you have to believe in yourself. And that's where I've been really lucky. My parents brought me up to do exactly that. I know it was probably tough for my parents (Carl and Erica) to accept my latest career

you've got

choice, which meant leaving what I was really good at to become an author – something I didn't know much about, as my mother quickly pointed out. But then again, my parents are the ones who have always told me that "the world is your oyster, it's yours to experience." I could not have written this book without believing that, right down to the core. See, Mom, I actually listen to some things you tell me! And Brendan, my little brother, who has always been my cornerstone, believed in me before I believed in myself. He taught me how to fly gliders, trained me on obstacle courses for boot camp, pep-talked me when the going got tough in my career challenges, and was the first one to encourage me to write a book. All those years of sticking up for my little brother during his 'sand box battles' with the neighborhood bullies have paid off. What goes around really can come around.

This book-publishing journey has been all about belief. Believing in myself. Believing in others. And, most of all, being surrounded by incredible people who believed in me. There is no greater gift. Without any of you, I could not have done this.

But next time I come up with yet another great 'life-changing' plan, could one of you PLEASE remind me, before I head off on my next adventure, that I will no doubt be asking myself, yet again, "What the hell was I thinking?!"

"You're a shining star, no matter who you are
Shining bright to see what you can truly be."

– *"Shining Star," Earth Wind & Fire*

PART 1: SEIZE YOUR POTENTIAL

PART 2: 13 PRINCIPLES TO LEAD INCREDIBLE THINGS!

table of

contents

PART ONE

SEIZE YOUR POTENTIAL

SEIZE THE DECADE

Look, if you had one shot, or one opportunity
to seize everything you ever wanted – one moment
Would you capture it or just let it slip? *Lose Yourself,* Eminem

OPPORTUNITY

Realize your potential

Be careful what you wish for

The ultimate skill

Your most powerful opportunity

The new leadership era

No-man's-land

MARCH 1992. I THOUGHT I HAD LANDED in the middle of the Wild, Wild West, but it was actually the former Yugoslavia. Crazy-looking soldiers were everywhere. I say crazy because these guys had mismatched uniforms and unrecognizable or 'missing' rank insignia. Although I had no prior war-zone experience, one thing I did understand was that in the military, rank represents chain of command, authority, decision-making, leadership – all those good things you might think are necessary in this sort of environment. So what would lack of rank represent? Or even worse, what did missing rank on an AK-47 gun-wielding soldier mean? My gut was telling me that this might not be a good thing!

As we slowly approached no-man's-land in our United Nations (UN) convoy, preparing to explore this great unknown, I couldn't get over the devastation around us. What used to be buildings were now heaps of colored bricks and rubble. Bridges were bombed and blown apart, and roads were completely destroyed. I will never forget the sight of an elderly couple, sitting at the side of the road on a pile of rubble. Clinging desperately to some plastic bags – probably with the only remaining contents of their homes, lives and dreams – I couldn't imagine what was next for them. How do you pick up and march on when your entire life – your home, your workplace, and very likely, family and friends – has been wiped away, just like that?

I was quickly getting a clear sense of the kind of desperation and feelings of absolute helplessness that accompany a war zone. I snapped back to reality. But what kind of reality was this? As I heard a machine gun rattling in the distance, I found myself asking a question that I have asked many times before, and will ask many times again: What the hell am I doing here?

FRIDAY THE 13TH

I think Brigadier General Lewis MacKenzie, leader of the Canadian contingent, and Canada's most famous peacekeeper, might have been asking himself the same question. "March 13. Friday the 13th appropriately turned into a wild day…I got an idea of how spies must have felt when they were exchanged at checkpoint Charlie in Berlin during the Cold War. We crossed at Novska – where the JNA [Jugoslovenska narodna armija, Yugoslav People's Army] and the Croatian army were separated by no-man's-land – 100 metres in the middle of the town, devastated by the recent fighting. We dismounted from our cars and formed up on the Croatian side of the line… Weighted down with our suitcases and bulging briefcases, our two parties slowly approached each other at a walking pace. As we entered no-man's-land, we could see that the ditches were lined with anti-surface-laid anti-tank mines. Several destroyed fighting vehicles, including one tank, provided ample encouragement for us to pick our way carefully down the very middle of the road."[1]

What the hell am I doing here? The good news is that if you're asking yourself that question, then you're at least living in the now. And right here, right now is what really matters!

So what are you doing right now? Maybe you're taking on your first big job, or shifting your career path to an entirely new industry, or heading up a planning committee for a charity benefit or moving across the country to start a new life. Whatever giant leap you're making, maximizing on your leadership potential will help you succeed.

The past two decades have provided me with lots of opportunities to ask this question – from surviving military boot camp to deploying fighter squadrons to the Gulf War (Operation Desert Storm) to a UN mission in the former Yugoslavia to orphanage projects and traveling the world for the high-tech industry to marketing programs with the Oprah Winfrey Show and the National Football League. I find myself asking that question, oh, at least once a year. It has become an attitude to live by!

oppor

> Our troops will have a delicate mission at hand, for which they are very well prepared. Along with our UN partners, Canada intends to make every effort possible to end the bloodshed in Yugoslavia.[2]
>
> *– Marcel Masse, then federal minister of National Defence, 1992*

NO EASY TASK

What I was doing in the former Yugoslavia was "no easy task," according to news reporter Jane Howard on CBC's and the BBC's international radio broadcast. "More than 1,000 Canadian troops will be arriving in Yugoslavia within the next month. But getting them there is no easy task. Road and rail links between Serbia and Croatia have been cut and Croatian airspace is still closed. Vital bridges have been blown up, and in some cases, troops may have to negotiate their way through minefields. Working out the best routes and the means of transport for the Canadians is the job of Captain Angela Mondou, a movement control officer attached to the main infantry battalion."[3]

I had decided to take a leap of faith and put my leadership skills to the ultimate test: I volunteered for a high-risk, fast-paced environment – a war zone, as a matter of fact. And I was going to learn more about leadership and life in a shorter amount of time than I could ever have imagined. But isn't that how it goes? You usually learn the most from your greatest challenges.

As a trained international movement control officer (in business terms, a global supply chain leader), my mission was to go on site with the army battalions' special advance task force (reconnaissance team) and come up with a rapid plan to deploy the UN's then-largest deployment in history – about 1,200 troops from two battalions and everything to support them. This included millions of pounds of equipment (Jeeps, armored recovery tanks, cars, tents, ammunition, mine-clearing equipment, etc.) and anything else we required to live – water, clothing, rations, bedding and combat boots. You name it.

> Leaders don't wait. They shape their own frontiers. The bigger the challenge, the greater the opportunity. *– Unknown*

This large mandate in the business world would equate to moving a town of 1,200 families, tons of equipment, trainloads of heavy vehicles, the contents of entire office buildings and temporary housing, from one side of North America to the other…into a war zone. One other small detail – we had 10 days to make this happen!

ASK FOR IT — YOU JUST MIGHT GET IT!

"Delicate" might be the last word that comes to mind when I think of this mission, although Canada's then-minister of National Defence saw it that way. Newspaper headlines around the world added more realistic details of my new job description: "Peacekeepers told of danger as Yugoslav missions starts" and included further warnings heeded by General Nambiar, the Indian Army General: "Don't take chances. There are minefields and booby-traps."[4] I learned very quickly to walk only on paved ground.

The general was addressing the newly formed UN force formerly known as the United Nations Protection Force or UNPROFOR comprised of peacekeepers from 22 different countries. Nambiar had been appointed as the First Force Commander and would head up the entire UN mission. In his best-selling book, *Peacekeeper: The Road to Sarajevo,* our own General MacKenzie would later describe Nambiar as a phenomenal leader. (To this day, I still wonder where my life would have taken me had I accepted Nambiar's offer to stay on as one of his staff officers responsible for providing deployment leadership to the many other nations on their way to this war zone.)

Naturally, even under great leadership, the troops were apprehensive about this mission. One newspaper described the danger: "Eight people were killed and more than 20 wounded Saturday in battles with artillery, rockets, machine guns and mortars…(O)ne peacekeeper, Finnish Major Sepp Koponen, said his group was ready for troubles and would shoot if neces-

tunity

sary. 'I may be nervous but I'm not afraid…We have flak jackets and helmets.'"[5]

Well, I had a flak jacket and a helmet. I was nervous and becoming more afraid by the day, in particular, when our commanding officer assigned two personal 'shower escorts' because of a new concern – I happened to be the only female in uniform among thousands of men. So this is what it was like to be a trailblazer or at least part of this reconnaissance team. I wasn't one to ever keep a personal journal, but now seemed like a better time than any!

"I learned that courage was not the absence of fear, but the triumph over it. The brave man is not he who does not feel afraid, but he who conquers that fear." – *Nelson Mandela, South African revolutionary*

JOURNAL ENTRY

March 14: *What the hell was I thinking? Why didn't I leave this high-profile UN mission to the army guys? I'm an air force officer for God's sake! I should be staying in hotels and deploying fighter squadrons instead of staying in a condemned communist barrack block and watching where I step because there are land mines everywhere. Worst of all, I'm sitting here surrounded by a few thousand men from 22 other countries, all of whom look like they've never seen a woman in uniform before. And apparently no other women are due in for weeks. I had no idea how ugly this was going to be. Last night, I actually dragged the only two pieces of furniture I had across the disgusting floor in this filthy room to barricade my door. We're staying in this decrepit, old JNA barrack block that must have been condemned years ago. Hopefully my barricade and the loaded pistol under my pillow (which I have every intention of using should I need to) should, at least, help me get some sleep. All this because I want to be a major. When I get home, no more heroics or ego-driven, high-profile jobs for me. Who cares about getting promoted? Maybe it's time to have a real life: puppies, babies, a good glass of wine....*

RED FLAG **Things could be worse**

You've decided to take the leap. You're heading into unknown territory and taking on something you've really wanted to do for some time. But you're nervous and there is no turning back.

I once got some profound advice when I headed into a war zone that puts any daunting situation in perspective. With his usual charisma and optimism, Major General Lewis MacKenzie wrote the following in this former classified military message: **Classification: For Canadian eyes only**. "Combat clothing is the best solution. Following the principles of never separating oneself from his 'snowshoes' I'd have unit personnel bring battle order less weapons and a suitcase…don't be discouraged by the apparent shoestring operations. We have no budget, few staff and a potential powder-keg; however, it's spring in the Balkans and the people want us here. Things could be worse."[6]

Heading into the unknown, one thing remains constant – you don't know what you don't know. But when the going gets tough you can always keep this in mind: things could be worse!

THINGS GOT WORSE

The realities of the war zone set in quickly. At night, I would awaken to the sounds of bombs blowing up houses down the street from the half-destroyed Hotel Daruvar, where I was staying. Senseless bombing for an even more senseless reason – the "ethnic cleansing" of Serbians or Croatians, depending on which side of the border they lived. I kept thinking of the Brigadier General's advice – things could be worse. Really? How? I couldn't wait to meet him to tell him how I really felt!

Things got worse by the hour. My two-man team and I had 10 days to come up with the deployment strategy and an on-site execution plan. "No big deal, Captain," my major told me from Germany. "Get in there, find a runway where we can land our transport aircraft, and you'll be home in 10 days!" It all sounded so doable at the time, that is, until I arrived and the intelligence started rolling in. There wasn't a usable runway that wasn't mine-ridden or blown up anywhere in this war zone. Yep, things were definitely getting worse. On to Plan B.

Leaders at every level

This leadership mandate has been one of the most challenging of my life. I learned more about myself as a leader in what was to become a seven-week mission than I may ever learn again. But sometimes there's a reason for that: the greatest challenges you face, the ones that force you to really face fear and stretch your limits, become the greatest opportunities for growth.

I experienced, saw, tasted and felt the impact of great leadership in an 'extreme' environment – where everything was mission critical. Incredible leaders in an incredible time. Leaders at all levels, all ranks, all nationalities, all involved in one heroic duty – to establish peace in a warring nation. I witnessed generals leading by example in the midst of confusion, corporals making critical decisions because they were the closest to the action, captains 'making it happen' despite insurmountable challenges. And facing fear brought all of this to light.

The success of this mission depended on leadership at every level. Success depended on these leaders taking action, on applying simple but critical leadership principles, such as leading by example. It also required accountability and ownership.

> "You can gain strength, courage, and confidence by every experience in which you really stop to look fear in the face…You must do the thing which you think you cannot do." – *Eleanor Roosevelt, influential First Lady*

JOURNAL ENTRY

March 22: *I'm convinced there is someone out there watching over me! Today, the first train arrived with the 'advance party' of our Canadian contingent. I got down, kissed the ground and I didn't care who was watching! I haven't slept in days – I keep having nightmares of exploding trains and BBC reporters telling the world about a Canadian captain who failed the UN deployment. But I guess Marion [my translator] did his job because the railway officials obviously got the message to minesweep the tracks every hour if necessary before that first train arrived. I still can't believe the train actually arrived in one piece…well sort of. The kitchen car caught fire somewhere between Slovenia and Croatia because of the change in electrical current going from Western European to Eastern European tracks… but hey, what's a little fire in the grand scheme of what could have gone wrong?!*

Tonight, we [the small team of reconnaissance officers] had a celebration 'mess dinner' with Brigadier General MacKenzie [who was later promoted to Major General MacKenzie]: a five-course meal, complete with wine and PIVA [big bottles of beer]. Considering that we are living in the midst of a bombed-out hotel, walls scattered with bullet holes and shattered windows held together by gun tape, the mess dinner was like a weird glimpse of the normal world I lived in a few days ago! That glimpse didn't last too long. Halfway through our meal, the building seemed to vibrate a bit, we started to hear strange noises, and then the air-raid sirens went off. We got confirmation on the radio from November Company [the advance troops that had just arrived] that we were, in fact, under mortar attack! It was like in the movies, except this time I was in it. I will never forget the general's response when all eyes around the table turned to him, wondering what we were to do. Army or not, it's not every day one comes under mortar attack. He gave us the most practical direction a leader could have given amid the confusion: "Put on your helmets and flak jackets and grab your PIVAs. Let's head down to the basement bunker where we can carry on our conversation."

I was nervous and confused about what was happening to us. But one thing was for sure: I suddenly felt a whole lot better after getting such practical advice from the general. The last thing I wanted to do was leave that beer on the table!

So I followed the general's orders. When I hurried into the lobby looking for Jodoin and Henderson (my small team of two), I was almost knocked over by some other panicked soldiers who asked me, "Ma'am, what do we do?" The sounds of air-raid

> "The greater danger for most of us lies not in setting our aim too high and falling short, but in setting our aim too low, and achieving our mark." – *Michelangelo*

sirens and mortar explosions have that sort of effect on people. So I gave them the best advice I could think of at that particular moment: "Grab your helmets, your flak jackets and your PIVAs, and head down to the bunker!" I still remember a small smirk replacing the look of panic on one of the privates' faces, as if he was thinking, "Yeah, now why didn't I think of that?"

There is nothing like a leader with a calm, cool approach in the face of danger to keep one's head on straight. The general displayed that very approach – he was leading by example. Despite my own fear of what was really happening, I followed the general's example and was able to have the same impact with these young soldiers.

Reality Check: Be cool

Troops need someone to look up to. If you happen to be the leader, at least look like you know what you're doing! Looking like you know what you're doing is half the battle.

Hot seat: A new era

Leading in this 'hot seat' meant I was making rapid decisions – planning and then ripping up my plans because priorities were changing fast and furious – and communicating with global headquarters by mobile satellite or with local business leaders on hand-scratched notes, whatever it took to carry through with my mission. I was pulling a multinational team together in a matter of days to accomplish our goals in an environment with little access to information. Twenty-one other countries were watching closely to see how Canada was going to figure this out. This was leadership in a mission-critical environment and I was definitely in the hot seat.

▶▶ **Fast forward** *to Chapter v, "Mission Critical NOT Mission Impossible," for more on mission-critical leadership.*

So, you're probably wondering, is this kind of leadership approach unique to military missions? Not a chance. After working 10 years in the high-tech industry, I can tell you that it seems to be the norm. Powerful communications technology, instant access to information and the shrinking global marketplace have created a new 'speed' with which leaders need to lead.

Remove the war zone, and leading in high tech and other industries requires a similar leadership approach:

- Thinking, planning, leading and executing can all be required at the same time;
- Making rapid decisions and delegating decisions to whoever is close to the action;
- Communicating at the highest levels with global organizations and on the street with local business.

Leadership experience of any kind can be life-defining. The powerful principles I learned throughout my experiences, from Operation Desert Storm, to the UN mission, to hot high-tech marketing or meaningful humanitarian projects, have been transferable to so many aspects of my life and career. And these are principles that I want to share with you throughout this book.

> "No limits but the sky...within our reach lies every path we ever dream of taking...within ourselves lies everything we ever dream of being." – *Unknown*

LEADERSHIP: THE OPPORTUNITY

Phenomenal leadership and how we can attain it continues to be researched, explored, documented and written about. It has been called an art, a skill, a science, a tool. But I like to think of leadership as something even more intriguing: a powerful opportunity. Like no other. And now is the time to seize it.

A new era is about to unfold and you are standing right in front of it. Leadership is about to take on a whole new look and a

oppor

whole new feel in a brave new world. Many exciting and powerful changes are happening in society, in the business world, in demographics and in people's attitudes. You might even consider it a revolution. The age of downsizing, re-engineering, axe men and ruthlessness is moving over to make room for a new kind of leadership.

I envy this new opportunity for graduates and younger generations as they surf the crest of this leadership wave. More than ever before, the next few years are going to open more doors of opportunity for those of you who want to lead:

> CEOs around the world are retiring or being removed at the youngest average age ever – 57.8 years old – creating more room at the top.[8]

> Baby boomers will be retiring in masses, creating a vacuum of management and leadership positions for anyone who wants to step up to the plate.

> The new generations (generations X and Y, born 1965-1994), armed with great attitude and skepticism for authority, are a self-empowered force moving into entrepreneurship with the ease and confidence to lead.

> Instant global communication and information available at your fingertips is providing anyone who is up for the adventure visibility to career opportunities anywhere in the world.

> The glamour of big business and corporate suits seems to be shifting to a different life purpose – global humanitarian efforts, increased education for Third World countries or running your own show instead of someone else's.

> Transparency, credibility, integrity, ethics, trust, commitment to employees and customers, honesty and accountability – no longer words we use to pay lip service; rather, they are words to act upon – all the characteristics that leaders should expect their teams to hold them accountable for.

What's next?

Being a leader with accountability for a team of people on an incredible mission has had a major impact on me. Any powerful leadership experience will be a tremendous, life-changing eye-opener for anyone.

One thing is clear – great leaders have a built-in way of being, knowing and doing. They take their roles very seriously – and they approach their roles with solid principles and a desire to take action when necessary. Without action there are no results, and without principles, there is no accountability.

Some of you might have leadership experience or you might be contemplating leading an exciting project or a team for the first time. Wherever you are on your leadership path, this book is designed to help you get to the next level and take advantage of the incredible leadership opportunities that are expected to come your way.

With a focus on leadership principles and some simple actions to help you start leading exciting opportunities, this book will help you create an effective leadership game plan. Your game plan will help you create and execute your vision of success and enable you to realize your potential. Great leadership is definitely within your reach.

This book is written for people like you – people who want to lead, lead with the right mindset, the right approach and the right stuff to really make a difference in the world.

Now it's your turn. Jump in – with both feet! No matter where you are in your career, no matter what life-changing event is causing you to consider leadership, consider this: leadership can be your life-changing opportunity.

It's time to make that difference. It's time to seize the decade. Seize your leadership potential.

"Knowing that we can make a difference in this world is a great motivator. How can we know this and not be involved?" – *Susan Jeffers, best-selling author*

tunity

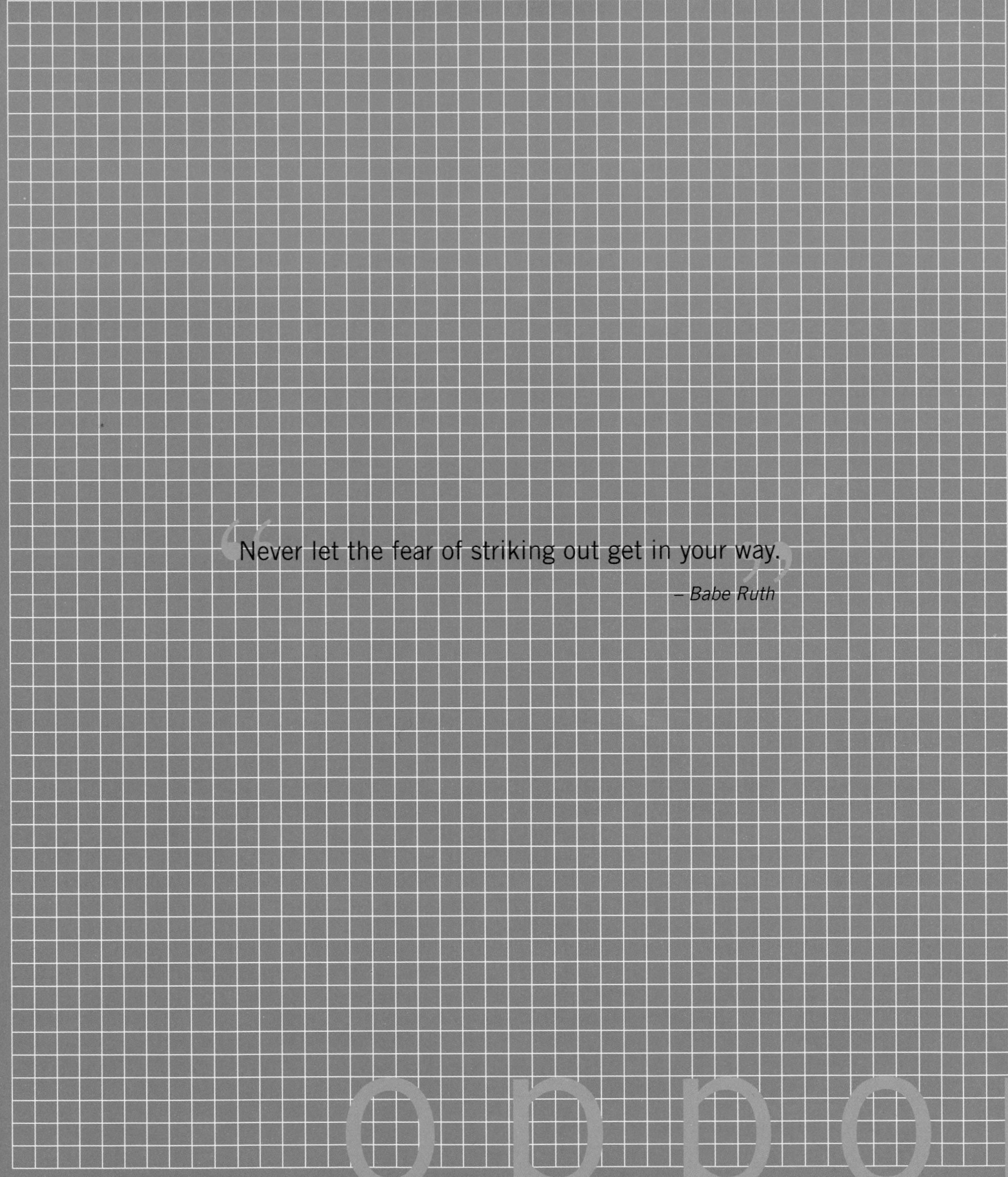

> "Never let the fear of striking out get in your way."
>
> – *Babe Ruth*

oppor

ACTION PLAN

Explore the unknown

1 WHAT THE HELL AM I DOING HERE?

- It's a question you should ask yourself frequently

2 REMEMBER, when you seize your potential and things seem tough, things could always be worse!

3 PLAN TO HAVE AN IMPACT.

- Make a difference

tunity

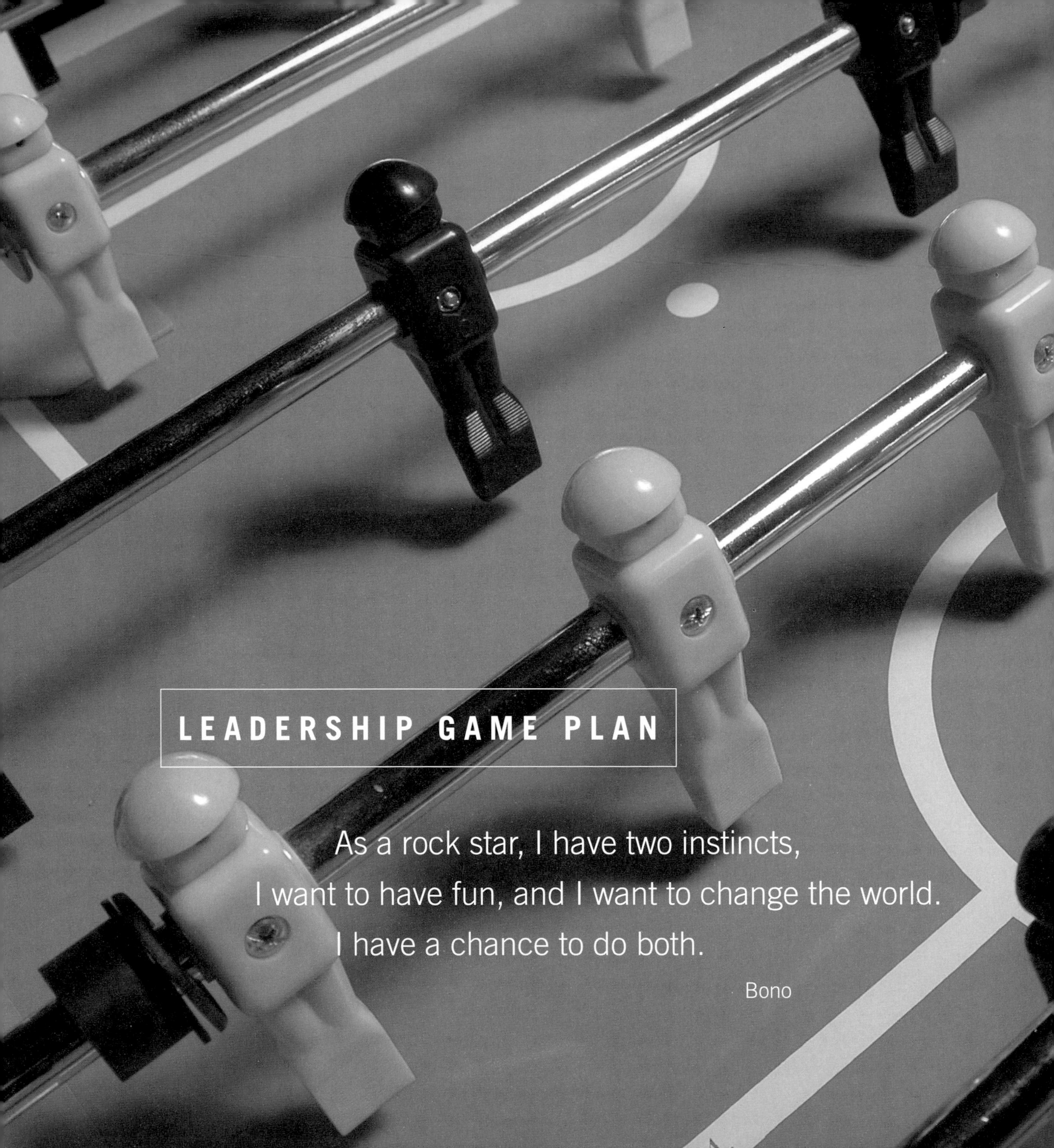

LEADERSHIP GAME PLAN

As a rock star, I have two instincts,
I want to have fun, and I want to change the world.
I have a chance to do both.

Bono

TARGET

The bare essentials

Create your own doctrine

Taking action

Dynamic is in

Leadership backbone

Skin in the game

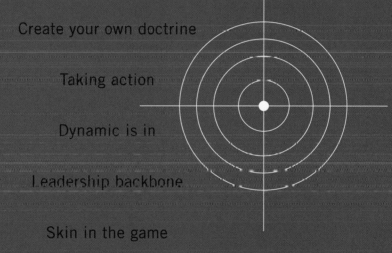

Get on your mark...

It's race day and, after a year of training, you finally find yourself among thousands of runners at the starting line. The energy is high. The pressure is intense. And all of the runners are anxious to get going, jogging on the spot to keep their muscles warm. The tension is building and your mind is filling up with nervous thoughts: "Am I going to make it to the finish line? How are my legs going to hold up? Will I be able to manage the heat? How tough is that hill that I've heard so much about really going to be?" This is your first marathon and you're pretty anxious about your ability to finish all 26 miles. The fear of not making it is staring right at you.

A year ago, you could barely run a five-mile race. One of your closest friends had inspired you to set this incredible goal – to actually run a marathon – and now here you stand!

So how did you get here? Not by accident. You prepared well for this day. You didn't just get up one morning and decide to start running in the hopes that you could pull off the 26 miles on race day. You wouldn't have that much success if you did.

To hit your target, you came up with a plan and targeted key goals and objectives. You got the scoop on what it takes to run a marathon. You became familiar with different physical training programs and referenced how-to guides to understand what personal monthly goals you should be setting. You joined a running group to connect with some experienced marathoners and understand how they've approached this lofty goal. You applied some key principles of success – eating healthy so you could sustain the long training phase, building muscle, increasing endurance, and training properly to minimize injuries. You prepared yourself mentally for this challenge to make sure you have the drive, energy and passion to get through the highs and lows of it. Through this entire experience, you have been taking care of yourself – mind, body and spirit. You made it to the start line because you had a game plan and you targeted some goals and objectives. And now you're putting your dream into action!

Maybe your 'race day' doesn't look anything like running a marathon. But I'll bet you have either a lifetime dream or a special challenge you want to pursue. Maybe you've always wanted to learn how to fly an airplane, or you'd like to plan a global trek that takes you to exotic, foreign countries, or write a book? I can't tell you how many people have confided in me in the past year about their dream to write a book!

Achieving goals, living dreams and taking on new challenges requires preparation, planning and an understanding of yourself – your strengths, weaknesses and the courage and confidence to go out and pursue those challenges.

And it's no different with your next incredible leadership opportunity – in business or otherwise. You've got to have a plan!

> "If you are failing to plan, you are planning to fail."
>
> – *Tariq Siddique*

How do you prepare for leadership?

Simply put, you need a game plan. Like any big event you might prepare for, you need to be in shape for leadership. It doesn't have to be fancy, but having a plan is essential for success. You need a road map to help you get started and show you where you might want to go (a big picture), so you know which building blocks and basic principles you should apply throughout your leaderhip journey.

Then comes the really fun part. You need to put your plan into action.

Consider this scenario: you're about to climb onto the latest and greatest airbus jet heading to your dream destination (or maybe just to your customer's headquarters across the country or continent). Most of us take for granted the well-planned approach that a captain and first officer will follow to fly across the ocean, or maybe even as far as the other side of the world. Can you imagine if they didn't? In fact, these pilots have an 'approach plate' for every destination in the world, so that they can fly with a plan, have goals and milestones of where they need to be, by when, with an understanding of potential obstacles on their

tar

approach, as well as alternate runways to land successfully at the right destination if they need to for certain reasons. There are also clear unwritten guidelines, or rules of engagement, between the captain, first officer, air traffic control, ground crew and in-flight personnel on how to communicate and who makes decisions at certain times. There are some basic principles that underlie the success of the crew and the entire team that supports them. These tried-and-true best practices are the right way of achieving success.

Finishing a marathon race or reaching your dream destination requires the following:

- ✓ A big picture plan…a game plan
- ✓ Some targets and goals along the way…an action plan
- ✓ Best practices for success…basic principles
- ✓ Conviction and commitment…accountability

TAKING IT SERIOUSLY!

Why not approach leadership in the very same way? Why not give it the same scrutiny and attention? Committing to a project, leading a team of people and, ultimately, impacting your team and their life experiences – not to mention the ability to attain your project's goals – is something to take very seriously!

When leading a project, we should apply the same elements for success as we would most other things we would prepare for. To keep things simple, I'm nailing it down to three bare essentials:

- Principles
- Action
- Accountability

These bare essentials will prepare you for your leadership adventure, whether it's a small volunteer project, a political campaign or a big leap like starting your own company. You have to start somewhere and getting the experience that is essential to success takes a lot of time and work. You've got a great starting point with these essentials, so get to it.

get

WHAT ARE YOU WAITING FOR?

By preparing yourself for leadership, you're taking a huge step in the right direction – you're making a commitment, taking on accountability for your own career and, ultimately, your life. Why would you want to leave that in anyone else's hands?

The reality is that people and many businesses tend to approach leadership with a more laissez-faire attitude than they might approach other less important goals, such as pursuing a hobby or going on a big trip. What's with that?

> "The 20-somethings of the 1980s should be poised to replace their baby-boomer superiors just about now, yet very little investment has been made in their leadership development.[1]"
>
> – *Catherine Mossop, president, Sage Mentors*

Leaders are often thrown into their roles with little, if any, training and very little coaching from more experienced leaders. New leaders are often left on their own – to fly by the seat of their pants or, as I like to put it, to lead from the hip.

It doesn't make sense. Why would you leave the people who impact your company revenue or influence your customer-facing front lines to jump into a leadership role without a game plan? Why would you start up your own company or take over a team without a clear approach, some big picture idea of where you want to go and what you want to impact?

Leadership needs to be taken seriously.

> "When it comes to translating a company's strategy into results, there's no denying the importance of first-level leaders – those who manage others who do not manage others… managers on the front line are critical to sustaining quality, service, innovation, and financial performance.[2]"
>
> – *Harvard Business Review*

FRONTLINE INTELLIGENCE

Bottom-line impact

Leading from the front lines means big impact on the bottom line!

- 70 to 80 percent of company employees report to frontline leaders; that means frontline leaders lead a large group of people who impact everything from a company's customer service to its revenue – and future business.
- Entrepreneurs, small-medium enterprises (SMEs) and new company owners are accountable for billions of dollars of revenue in North America – pretty big clout!

Bottom line:

You have a large impact from any front line.

3 bare essentials for leadership backbone

Principles. Action. Accountability. These three essentials are powerful building blocks for good leadership – and form a great game plan.

"In matters of style, swim with the current. In matters of principle, stand like a rock." – *Thomas Jefferson, third president of the United States*

Principles will provide a great point of reference – guidance and direction on where to start and what action to consider. An action plan will detail the necessary steps to move things forward. And personal accountability means you're taking ownership and responsibility for what you're about to step into. And leadership is a big step.

Here's why they will help you make a difference:

1 Leadership principles

"Money won't create success, the freedom to make it will." – *Nelson Mandela, South African revolutionary*

Leadership and principles go hand in hand. As a military officer, I was bombarded with principles in the earliest phase of my career – in boot camp training. Many other organizations also have a very solid grounding in principles. Humanitarian organizations build their foundations on them. Without them, the humanitarian world could not attract enough funds or donations to continue operating. Sports teams are trained and conditioned for success against major competitors with powerful team principles. Billion-dollar empires have been driven into the ground when they've failed to apply them. Heroic movie characters are quoted and remembered by them for years. Selfless leaders focused on the troubles of the Third World, such as Nelson Mandela, Mahatma Gandhi and U2's Bono, continue to make a huge difference to humanity by applying principles of leadership. We are entering a leadership era where principles are a hot topic – and those organizations leading without them are being held accountable for any lack of integrity, ethics, honesty and, most recently, transparency. But they need to be more than just a hot topic. Today, they need to be part of your leadership reality.

Leadership principles *unplugged*

What are principles? Principles are the attitudes, core values or beliefs of an individual or an organization demonstrated through actions, behaviors and ideologies. So we're talking about what you say and how you do things.

Principles are like an internal compass – when you need to know in which direction to go, they can provide you with a frame of reference, or guide, for what actions you might take, and what road you might choose to get there. Do you ever wonder why some of the leaders you've been around have a certain innate leadership style? Part of what you see comes down to their principles and how they apply them.

> If you have a sense of purpose and a sense of direction, I believe people will follow you.
>
> *– Margaret Thatcher, first female British Prime Minister*

Think about how you, or other people you know, describe leaders you've worked with: "that person is firm but fair," "they stand up for their team players," "they really take care of their people," "they drive a hard ship," or "they're ruthless." Principles make up your fabric as a leader, what you believe in, what you stand for and, ultimately, how you are defined. Because we're all unique individuals, we'll each be influenced by different principles and leaders. So what works for you, what attracts you and empowers you, will be very different from one leader to the next.

Create your own doctrine

Unique leaders represent outstanding leadership principles from all walks of life. You'd be wise to stay open-minded. Principles can come from any experience, any organization, any industry. Anywhere.

I'm now more inspired by unique leaders doing incredibly different things – people who are leading 'outside the corporate box;' leaders who might come from the far corners of the Earth with any background – the military, sports, business, religion, movies, business, politics, music. The more I learn and understand from these unique individuals, the more I realize that many of their success stories have some common denominators – a foundation of core principles, a willingness to take action and move things forward and, ultimately, accountability to own what they are responsible for. There are a lot of people in business who will go to the moon and back when their own personal interest is at stake. But the leaders who will stick their neck out for others – for the team, the organization and the mission – now those are the leaders who are a real inspiration and the type of leader you should aspire to become. Look to whatever incredible examples might energize and excite you and start creating your own leadership doctrine! It keeps going back to the three bare essentials.

get

Outside the corporate BOX

PASSION TO PRINCIPLES

Military

Principle: Lead by example.

Who: Canadian Armed Forces, Marine Corps and most other military teams

What it means: Be the role model for your team.

Movies

Principle: Failure is not an option![3]

Who: Flight director Gene Kranz in *Apollo 13*

What it means: Your goal as a team is to succeed.

Sports

Principle: One die. All die.

Who: National Football League coach Bill Belichick

What it means: The team is in this together. If one player fails, the whole team fails.

Music

Principle: "I always thought the world was mine, that it was a stomping ground for me, full of opportunities."

Who: Pop diva Madonna

What it means: An infinite amount of possibilities

Business

Principle: Just do it!

Who: Sports gear company Nike slogan

What it means: Get out there and make it happen.

Spirituality

Principle: Thought into action.

Who: Spiritual leader Yehuda Berg

What it means: We are often inspired by brilliant thoughts, innovative ideas and lofty goals. But we need to follow through and 'close the deal.'

History

Principle: Assess your opponents.

Who: Sun Tzu, *The Art Of War*

What it means: Make sure you know what the competition is doing!

▶▶ **Fast forward** *to Section 2 for a review of 13 exciting leadership principles, such as Chapter 05: "What Goes Around Comes Around." This section will inspire you to identify key principles for your own game plan and best practices for your action plan.*

Insight from outside

This book is full of outside-the-corporate-box insight and principles. Having an open mind and educating yourself on the many different leadership models will make you a far stronger leader. But you will have to decide what works best for you so you can define your own personal approach.

For example, take the principle "assess your opponent." This principle is highlighted in Sun Tzu's *The Art Of War* and seems to have become somewhat of a mantra in the high-tech industry. And so it should be in a business world where the slimmest of competitive edges could be the difference between the life and death of your product. I learned how useful this principle could be from a savvy sales manager who applied this principle when working with his team. He made a point of staying closely in touch with the competition, their range of products and even the structure of their sales force because he understood the importance of knowing what the competition was doing, and what they were not doing.

He was able to incorporate this big-picture information into his team's sales strategy and build proactive steps into its action plan to stay well ahead of the competition. The result: a well-prepared sales team who could deal with any questions on how its programs compared to the competition, and who was able to stay two steps ahead in developing more unique, differentiated offerings – a great way to mitigate competition issues before they happen.

Knowing your enemy can provide both strategic and tactical advantages. And it's far better than being blindsided! Principles like this are an essential element of good leadership and a great catalyst that can inspire leaders to take great action.

The bottom line: you should have some fundamental principles to lead with. Without your own set of core principles, you'll lack direction. And that means you'll lack the internal guidance you need to put your leadership into action with a commonsense approach that your team can follow.

2 Action plan

Leaders who can 'make things happen' tend to stand out. But they don't stand out because they are 'lucky.' There's a good chance they approach their world with energy, to get things accomplished and to act on their objectives. Many things are made feasible with a good action plan.

There really is no situation where a good plan of action can't add value. For example, an action plan can support a project that introduces change by including a project team to support the new work, establishing important milestones, aligning team members with key tasks, or defining your department's or company's vision.

Injecting energy and action into a team or a project is one of the most valuable things a leader can do. Action is a bare essential of leadership.

Action plan *unplugged*

Simply put, it doesn't matter what you do, formalizing actions and assigning ownership will move goals and objectives forward. Moving things forward is a large part of successful leadership.

An action plan will enable you to:

- ✓ Create energy within your team
- ✓ Drive momentum on the project
- ✓ Deliver impact to your end goal

Energy and how to create it is one of my favorite topics. It's such a powerful concept in life *and* in leadership. Creating the right energy will depend on how well you work with your people and help them align in such a way that they're adding value and feel valued. With value comes the passion and enthusiasm to drive momentum and, once you have that, you're on your way to achieving your goals and objectives.

> The ancient Romans had a tradition: whenever one of their engineers constructed an arch, as the capstone was hoisted into place, the engineer assumed accountability for his work in the most profound way possible: he stood under the arch!
>
> *– C. Michael Armstrong, former chairman and CEO of AT&T Inc.*

And then there's change. Today's business leader faces lots of change – from starting up new teams to working on new projects to launching new products or services to joining forces with other companies to be more competitive. Nothing can move forward without change – no goals will be achieved, no plans turned into reality. How can you best lead through any change? A plan of action!

▶▶ **Fast forward** *to Chapter 08, "Link Your Team to the Mission" for more insight on how to get the most out of your team.*

Leading with karma

Karma is a belief based on Eastern philosophies (Hinduism and Buddhism) that says our actions and the force of energy behind them have consequences – that there is a cause and an effect in what we do. In other words, what goes around comes around, or you reap what you sow. This philosophy is an interesting consideration in leadership. How can you test the effects of your actions? The answer is summed up by looking at: (1) the intention behind your action, (2) the effects of the action on you, and (3) the effects of your action on others.[4] Here's how you might apply the karmic way of thinking when leading in your next project: Not only will your actions have an impact, but the energy you create, good or bad, will also have a cause and an effect. Share the spotlight and let the team participate in the success and you will energize your team players on an even greater scale. But use people to your advantage and keep the success and spotlight to yourself, and it won't be long before you will lose momentum – and valuable team players. Not good karma. Who's going to stick around with that kind of energy?

get

3 Accountability as part of your game plan

Along with principles and an action plan, accountability is the third essential piece of becoming an effective leader who can make a real difference.

You can't make a difference if you're not willing to be accountable and responsible.

Accountability *unplugged*

Accountability = ownership = responsibility for your mandate... and all that goes with it. Good and bad. Accountability is putting your own 'skin in the game.' It's about taking responsibility for the people on your team and ownership for the risks, actions and success or setbacks you may experience. Until you're ready and willing to step up to the plate and take on the responsibility of leadership, and all the good and the bad that goes with it, you aren't really leading. Sure, you might be getting promotions and acquiring titles, but all you're really doing is acting as a figurehead versus someone who is taking on a leadership challenge.

The entrepreneur is a great example of a highly accountable leader. Imagine starting up a project, a company or a new venture with nothing but your own funding, your own personal belief that you'll succeed in the marketplace and your own drive and initiative. No one else's. Now that takes confidence! That demands a willingness to take risks and ownership of the ensuing successes and failures. The "entrepreneur" is described in Wikipedia, the online encyclopedia, as someone who accepts responsibility and is "morally, legally, and mentally accountable for their ventures." Yes, as an entrepreneur, I definitely feel 'mental accountability' – certainly sleepless nights and grinding my teeth seem to be a common entrepreneurial side effect. But I wouldn't have it any other way.

Reality Check: Reality bites

If you've watched the hit reality show *The Apprentice,* you'll know what I mean by finger-pointing. The 'it wasn't my fault we failed' attitude often displayed by some of the project managers makes you wonder why some of these individuals are leading at all. But as 'The Donald' himself has pointed out, leadership comes with responsibility and accountability. Before handing out the pink slip, he has questioned departing project managers how they can consider themselves a project manager or leader when they don't feel accountable for the team's actions. Like Donald says: "You're fired!"

> First rule of leadership: everything is your fault, Princess. It's a bug-eat-bug world out there.[5]
>
> – *Hopper in Disney's* A Bug's Life

Remember: No one ever said it would be easy. Leadership is not just about the glory, the privilege that goes with the title or rank, the corner office, the global travel, the big meetings or the big bucks – a theme you might hear throughout this book. Although, if you find someone offering you a corner office in the near future, I would say take it – quickly. Office space is hard to come by these days! Beyond any privilege or perks that we all enjoy, being a leader needs to go hand in hand with being accountable – to both your team and the mission you are leading. Leaders who do not accept accountability have a hard time maintaining credibility, respect, loyalty and, ultimately, performance of their team.

There is no question – you've got to really want to be a leader to be a leader. Owning your leadership is important. Accepting responsibility for your mandate is important. If these essentials are not part of your leadership game plan, you won't have the impact or effectiveness you need as a leader.

Connecting the essentials

How do all three essentials – principles, action and accountability – all come together to help you create a powerful game plan that you can apply to your leadership?

By applying fundamental leadership principles, you're taking action to create energy and momentum within your team to meet goals and objectives. Ultimately, as a leader, you're also taking accountability of the outcome of your team's work.

It always helps to have a game plan. So why not add some powerful components to get started?

What's next?

Now that you're familiar with the three key leadership essentials, it's time to look in the mirror.

One of the most important things you must do to lead successfully is to know yourself first. What makes you tick? What are your strengths? What areas do you need to work on? What do you believe is important when you're working with people? Understanding these things about yourself will help you understand more about the principles you'll use to lead.

It's time to tune into yourself because YOU and no one else will drive your leadership behavior. We'll examine some quick tips and powerful tools to help you better understand yourself, your personality and your dynamics with others so you can start to understand what might drive your leadership style.

Get ready to go solo.

> Naturally I'm worried if I do it alone.
> Who really cares cuz it's your life
> You never know, it could be great.
> Take a chance cuz you might grow
> What you waiting for?
>
> – *"What you waiting for?" Gwen Stefani*

tar

ACTION PLAN

Create a playbook

1 GET YOUR LEADERSHIP GAME PLAN TOGETHER.

- What's your big picture? Where do you want to go as a leader?
- What do you want to accomplish now? In the next year or two?

2 THINK ABOUT PRINCIPLES.

- What leadership attitudes or beliefs inspire you?

3 IT'S ALL ABOUT ACTION.

- Without action it's tough to get results
- Recognize the need to create energy and momentum through people and projects
- Injecting energy will become a big part of what you do

4 ACCOUNTABILITY – GET READY TO STEP UP TO THE PLATE.

- What difference do you want to make?
- Where do you want to have impact?

get

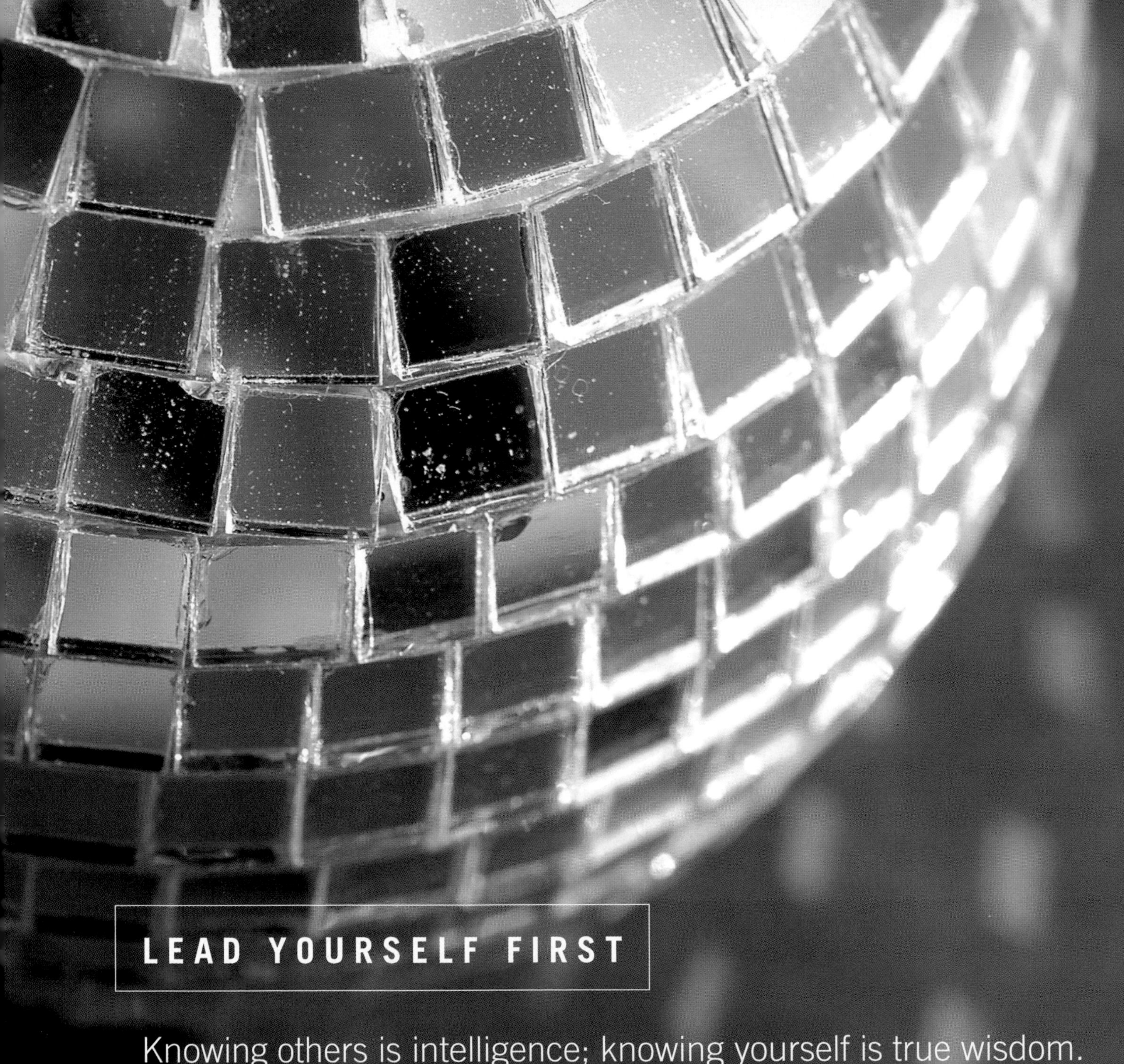

LEAD YOURSELF FIRST

Knowing others is intelligence; knowing yourself is true wisdom.
Mastering others is strength; mastering yourself is true power

Lao Tzu, *Tao Te Ching*

GOING SOLO

Lead yourself first

Attitude defines leadership

Look in the mirror

Think big. Do big things

Embrace the extreme

Test of an adventure

Oh…my…God! Now my heart was thumping. My flying instructor had just given me the nod and said three life-defining words to me. Words that every fledgling pilot wants to hear, dreams of hearing, but you're never quite sure how you're really going to feel when you do finally hear them. "You can tie down the safety straps on that pax seat, Angela. You're on your own today." Then he said it. "You're going solo!" With that he closed the passenger door, gave C-GKIF (the aircraft call sign), my Cessna 172, a smack on the fuselage and yelled, "Have fun!" as he walked back to the flying club.

At that moment, I was feeling many things. Exhilaration and excitement because I was finally going to take this airplane up into that 'wild blue yonder' all by myself. Well, at least around this airport for some solo circuits. But there was also a slight feeling of panic, an oh-my-God, can I really do this by myself? I wasn't sure I could actually take the airplane up in the sky and be completely responsible for getting it (and me) back safely on the ground.

Before I knew it, I was rolling down the taxiway, talking to ground control with my David Clark Headset (the Mont Blanc of aviation headsets) and then stopping to do the usual pre-takeoff routine, but this time with some extra due diligence. *Brakes – HOLD. Flight controls – CHECK. Instruments – SET. Mixture – RICH. Throttle – 1900 RPM.*

"GKIF – you are cleared for takeoff on runway 26. Have a good flight," said ground control. Yikes! My heart was pounding in my throat now. In my very small Cessna 172, I lined up on the active runway. There was 10,000 feet of runway ahead of me at this international airport. I felt small, squeezed in for takeoff between an Air Canada DC-9 that just took off for Toronto and a couple of air force fighters who were coming in for final approach. Ready or not it was my turn to go. As I looked way down the rubber-streaked tarmac ahead of me, I took a deep breath, got the engine to full throttle and released my brakes. Yahoo! I was going solo.

As the daughter of an air force officer, I grew up around runways, airplanes, air shows and the smell of JP4 (kerosene jet fuel) in the air. I was intrigued with flight, airplanes and the pilots who flew them – in fact, maybe in 'awe' is a better description. I just knew that one day I had to learn to fly. So I did. That's not to say that flying and I are a match made in heaven! Quite the opposite. I was lucky to have survived some of my really, really bad landings. There were even times when I thought that flying airplanes as pilot-in-command was one of those dreams I might have been better off not pursuing. But the bad landings didn't stop me and the exhilaration I felt after flying in gliders, going solo in a single-engine Cessna or doing a day-long cross-country flight on my own was very powerful. All of this flying experience added up to one thing – it was life-defining. Life-defining because it built character and equipped me with the attitude and principles for the challenges I would meet later in my life.

> "There is an art, or rather, a knack to flying. The knack lies in learning how to throw yourself at the ground and miss…You will then learn all sorts of things about how to control your flight, your speed, your maneuverability, and the trick usually lies in not thinking too hard about whatever you want to do, but just allowing it to happen as if it was going to anyway.[1]"
>
> – The Hitchhiker's Guide to the Galaxy, *Douglas Adams*

Reality Check: Bad landings = big attitude

In the early stages, flying for me was more about facing my fear than exploring the clouds above. But over time I gained confidence, experienced the world from an incredible perspective at 5,000 feet and felt like there wasn't anything on the 'ground' that I couldn't tackle. Bad landings led to a whole new attitude. Go ahead and feel the fear, maybe even experience some bad landings, and do it anyway!

going

> The test of adventure is that when you're in the middle of it, you say to yourself, 'Oh, now I've got myself into an awful mess; I wish I were sitting quietly at home.' And the sign that something's wrong with you is when you sit quietly at home wishing you were out having lots of adventure.[2]
>
> – The Matchmaker, *Thornton Wilder*

Your experience. Your principles

How did I get here? Hurtling small airplanes through the sky and actually finding the chutzpah to land them with some occasional skill definitely had an impact on shaping my attitude, inner strength and principles that drove many of my career and life decisions. Just by 'doing' I learned to think big and have the confidence to take on things that were larger than me.

I can now look back to several events that have helped define my attitude in life. In turn, that attitude has influenced certain choices I've made along the way and the experiences that I've gained. And all of these things have had a big impact on the principles I live and lead by. It's all a cycle.

For instance, as an eight-year-old, I recall looking out my bedroom window and my new view in a small farm town in southern Germany, where my father had been stationed in the 1970s. There were pigs, roosters and other barnyard animals, along with a new and distinct aroma of cow manure that I was not familiar with after living in a high-rise apartment in downtown Toronto for a few years. My little friends across the street had names I couldn't pronounce and they spoke a language I did not understand.

I had the feeling I had just moved into a Disney cartoon movie as I looked out onto a scene that could have been in *Snow White and the Seven Dwarfs*. I wondered, in amazement, at how absolutely different this new world was from the bedroom window I looked out of just one week before in Toronto. But despite the pigs, the noisy animals, the new language and food, I could still hear my mom blasting her favorite Neil Diamond and Creedence Clearwater Revival albums on the stereo in the background as she shouted for me to come and have some macaroni and cheese. At that very moment, as I stood there taking this all in, a brave new awareness came over me. I headed to the kitchen for my Kraft Dinner, and I just knew that this new 'unknown' was going to be okay.

My lust for new beginnings, global travel and the unknown started right there in that German barnyard. Red Square, Angkor Wat, Mount Kilimanjaro. It didn't matter – it was now within my reach. The unknown was no longer something to fear, but something to seek. And that was the beginning of many more life-defining moments to come.

LIFE-DEFINING MOMENTS

The great thing about life-defining moments is that they keep on coming. Like the time I was 16 years old and ran into the house after school to share some great news with my father. I had been selected for the high-school cheerleading squad after weeks of tryouts among dozens of athletic girls and I was pretty proud of myself. "A cheerleader?" my father blurted out. "You're not serious are you? You should be a quarterback, not a cheerleader!" You have got to love a father who believes in you so much that he doesn't see anything standing in your way, not even a 250-pound linebacker! But he was a man who questioned the status quo for himself so his reaction was almost predictable for his children. And it instilled in us a certain life attitude – to think big, to think out of the box that the world sometimes tries to fit us all into. He believes in defining your own destiny, not what others define for you…all opportunity is available to everyone.

Did I want to play football? Not a chance. But my father's question had an impact that made me stop to think for minute. What are my choices? What other options are really out there beyond what I perceive as my choices, beyond the status quo?

solo

Reality Check: Think big. Define your own destiny

Don't let others define it for you. It's easy to get caught in the trap of doing what's expected and what pleases others instead of yourself. But be aware – before you know it, you might wake up 10 years later to find that you still haven't done what you want to really do.

> "It's my life
> Don't you forget
> Caught in the crowd
> It never ends."
>
> – *"It's My Life," Talk Talk*

Our defining moments are the shapers of our soul. It's through such tests and challenges that our personal beliefs and attitudes are created. Your defining moments will highlight the core values that are important to you, or the real nature of your character. Sooner or later, you'll face a big "aha" that you'll carry with you throughout your life.

So why are life-defining moments so important? They influence the choices you make, the actions you take and your leadership abilities. Ultimately, the defining moments that shape your attitude and beliefs can become your business drivers. What better template could you ask for?

Who do you think you are?

> "Control is not leadership; management is not leadership; leadership is leadership. If you seek to lead, invest at least 50% of your time in leading yourself – your own purpose, ethics, principles, motivation, conduct. Invest at least 20% leading those with authority over you and 15% leading your peers." – *Dee Hock, founder and CEO emeritus, VISA*

In the HOT SEAT

"LOSING MY VIRGINITY"

Cheeky. Bold. In your face. Words that might be used to describe Virgin Atlantic advertising. If you haven't seen it, you might make a point of catching it on TV or in print ads. The airline company's brand is incredibly innovative, very hip and even a little controversial. Phrases like 'jetrosexual' describe Virgin's services, and humorous but provocative commercials feature a man dreaming that he was sharing first-class bed space with another man. In fact, never mind the ads, go for a flight. The in-flight massages and a door-to-door limo service in a Range Rover take the hot hand towels and mixed nuts service up a notch!

And how does Virgin remain competitive in the extremely competitive industry of world travel? Well, when you think big, the universe is the limit and intergalactic destinations are all within the realm of possibilities. So it only makes sense that Virgin will be offering the first commercial space flights on their new Virgin Galactic service. Talk about being 'out there.'

What kind of mastermind leads such a mind-bending, successful operation? Sir Richard Branson, founder of the Virgin Atlantic empire (records, airplanes, travel, cell phones, you name it). And he attributes his powerful business savvy to some life-shaping events that began as early as 12 years old. In his recent autobiography, *Losing My Virginity*, he says his "mum" woke him up in the dark one January morning because she had decided he should cycle to Bournemouth – a mere 50 miles away – to help him build stamina and a sense of direction. After he accomplished this long and arduous feat, he received a quick "well done" from his mother and then got tasked with some household chores![3]

Branson's story points to family upbringing and childhood experience as a key influencer in developing the principles that have influenced his own leadership:

- Live through a sense of adventure
- Believe in yourself
- Challenge yourself and embrace the unknown

going

Before you can lead others, you'll need to lead yourself. And that means you have to know yourself. You should be able to tune into the life principles that you really connect with and understand what really drives you – what makes you tick. Your life principles, your beliefs and your values stand for your own personal ideology. And this very ideology will become the basis on which you will build your leadership principles.

So, who are you and what makes you tick? Are you an adventurer who loves to try new things and believes that if you want something you go for it? Maybe you're a science buff who believes in black and white solutions. Or a creative genius who loves spontaneity. Here are a few things to ask yourself to help you with your soul-searching:

How would you describe yourself?

- A thrill seeker always looking for a new adventure
- A homebody who enjoys routine and comfort

How do you look at things?

- As a detail-oriented or big-picture person
- As a creative thinker who enjoys radical approaches
- With the cup half full or half empty

How would you describe your personality?

- Introverted or extroverted
- A people person or a loner
- Methodical or free-flowing

How do you manage challenging or stressful situations?

- Pack things in and head for the hills
- Let someone else take over
- Go with the flow
- Grab the bull by the horns

What are you passionate about outside of work?

- Traveling to different countries
- Exploring art galleries
- Learning new sports

What dreams do you have?

- Writing a book
- Getting an MBA
- Learning how to scuba dive
- Starting your own business

solo

What dreams have you turned into reality?

- Earned a special certification
- Worked for a top-notch company
- Skied the Alps

Guess what? There are no or right or wrong answers to these questions. Your answers are a quick reflection of who you are.

This is just a brief snapshot of what things mean the most to you, how you might make choices and what principles might emerge from this personality overview. Who you are on the inside will influence every relationship you have, how you perceive things, actions you take, choices you'll make. It will influence who you become on your life journey and what you choose to lead.

As you climb the corporate ladder, you'll be working with different people, different personalities, different styles, different principles. All types of people and perspectives are valuable and necessary for your success. This is where knowing yourself comes in. As a leader, you need to understand your strengths, weaknesses, the complementary skills you share with team members, where the gaps might be, and how you might – or might not – work well together based on your personalities. Think about how much more successful you can be as a leader by embracing the different people on your team who bring with them an entirely different set of skills.

See how it makes sense to know a bit more about yourself before leading others?

LOOK IN THE MIRROR

Now, I have to admit, it's not always easy to be objective about yourself! Trying to look 'within' to know yourself better can be a tough process. If objectivity is a challenge, your job just got easier: there are some insightful tools, as well as personality and leadership tests, which are easily accessible on the Internet or in books. You don't have to take a course to get this information. No matter what your preference – science, psychology or spirituality – there is a tool out there to help you look at yourself in the mirror and understand what makes you tick.

To get an idea of your own 'personality intelligence,' I've listed a few of my personal favorite tests. All of these tests have been tremendously helpful to me. They have helped me define who I am and what I am passionate about. They also offer insights into how I might be perceived by others around me and how I might work with other personality types.

> "Most beer execs are marketers. I like numbers because they don't listen. They tell you the truth."
> – *Carlos Brito, Labatt president and engineer,* Report on Business *magazine*

Get to know yourself

Here are four credible personality tests to help you get to know yourself:

1. Herrmann Brain Dominance Instrument

"The HBDI is changing the world...one brain at a time."

• This 'whole brain technology' takes the right brain-left brain research to a whole new level: it will help you optimize your ability to adapt your thinking, decision-making, communication and management styles.

• As a team leader, I found this to be a great self-awareness tool to help you better understand your personality, in terms of creativity, leadership, team-building and many other areas.

www.hbdi.com

2. True Colors Personality Assessment Program

"Valuing differences, creating unity."

• Complex psychological theory is transformed into a powerful career and life tool, helping people understand their strengths and differences. Participants are asked to identify their color spectrum, using four cards that identify their personality type.

• The key is to not just understand the strengths of the colors but also the differences; if these are not well understood, they can become barriers to communication.

www.truecolors.org

3. Myers-Briggs Type Indicator Instrument

"Whatever the circumstances of your life, the understanding of type can make your perceptions clearer, your judgments sounder, and your life closer to your heart's desire."
– *Isabel Briggs Myers*

• When making decisions, do you prefer to first look at logic and what might make analytical sense, or do you prefer to first look at people and circumstances?

• A psychological profile tool to assess personality type, it will also identify leadership scenarios your personality will favor and scenarios where other skills should be considered.

• Introvert, extrovert, thinker, feeler, intuitive, perceiver or judger...these traits will be evaluated, both as a team player and a leader.

www.myersbriggs.org

4. TAIS – The Attentional and Interpersonal Style Inventory

"Skills that allow you to perform at a very high level in one situation can destroy you in another!"

Used by business leaders, Olympic athletes and coaches, this inventory assesses 20 different performance and behavioral attributes in the context of 'pressure placed on an individual.' Consider knowing this about yourself!

• Behavior control – which measures an individual's willingness to think outside the box and, at times, bend the rules.

• Speed of decisions – measures the extent to which an individual is likely to obsess or overanalyze situations before making a decision.

www.taisdata.com

RED FLAG

Not everyone needs to think like you

Rise above the notion that great minds think alike. Instead, embrace different styles of leading, views and personalities. For example, if you're the marketer who likes to think 'blue sky' and 'big picture,' it might be very wise to have a numbers guy on board who can present the facts, not only a creative person to help with the visuals.

going

> It all came down to choice. I had the choice between lying to myself and pretending that I could turn on a switch and become a details person, or accepting the fact that I'm not, and partnering with someone who is. Continuing to lie meant I would probably lose my business... What choice will you make?
>
> *– Mark Cuban, billionaire and owner of the Dallas Mavericks NBA basketball team*

DON'T LIE TO YOURSELF

Think back to when you were a teenager or in your early 20s. Think of the times when something big happened to you, perhaps something that was said to you that had a powerful impact, or a sudden realization that would change how you view things and the choices you would make. Here are a few life defining moments that may have shaped your life:

- A lesson on respect. Your teacher pointed out one of your flaws in front of the whole class and you vowed that no one would ever single you out again – and that you would never put someone through that same humiliation.
- Defining drive. You trained hard to make the high-school track team, only to discover that the hard work had only just begun!
- The value of support. Someone went to bat for you...and you learned the importance of standing up for people around you – everyone needs someone to believe in them.

Reality Check: Launchpad

Tuning in to who you are and what has shaped your perceptions, values and principles is an important starting point for leaders. But don't let who you are limit where you might want to go. Think of this process in terms of standing on a launching pad instead of standing in a box. Where you come from is a platform upon which you will grow in leaps and bounds – it doesn't define where you'll end up. The more you tune into who you are, the more prepared you'll be to move around beyond these barriers.

solo

Connect principles with passion

So why is leading yourself first so important? Your life principles, beliefs and values will be tied directly to the things you're passionate about. By knowing yourself and what drives you, you'll also start to understand your personal passion.

Sadly enough, we can all think of a few people who stroll through their lives and careers without understanding what really drives them. Even worse, they're aware of their passion, but they don't have the time or the energy or courage to really focus on it. In other words, they live and work in mediocrity.

It's up to you to seize your leadership potential and do incredible things.

> My job and mission in life as I travel around this great world of ours is connecting the head with the heart of entrepreneurship...A lot of people don't like to talk about passion, it makes them nervous. But that's the future – how passionate are you?[1]
>
> *– Frank Maguire, business and employee relations guru*

CLOSET ENTREPRENEUR

If you're like me, it might take you a decade or even two to understand what you really should be doing, and where your passion really lies. For instance, the other day I found myself describing my career path to a successful business owner. In doing so, I realized that I had spent the first 18 years of my career working for very big business – defence and high tech at an early age – yet I had always been tuned in to a couple of very important life principles that had guided me in my work and my personal goals:

- Sense of adventure
- Lust for travel
- Ability to influence my own show

I realized I had always been a 'closet entrepreneur.' Almost two decades later, I was finally living out my dreams.

Would you want to ignore something as important as *who* you are and *what* you are passionate about on your quest to lead? It might take you a few years to really understand who you are but, in the meantime, you can do one thing: connect with your passion and your principles.

PASSION IS MAGNETIC

Your passion is your energy and drive, and it creates enthusiasm. Having a zest for life is the difference between those who love getting up to go to work and those who just mark time. Not only does drive inspire, but it's magnetic and creates action.

◄◄ **Rewind** *to Chapter ii, "Leadership Game Plan," for a review of the three essentials you will want to have in your game plan: principles, action and accountability.*

An old university friend I know went off to study his MBA at Harvard after graduating summa cum laude and was studying as a future leader at one of the top corporate business schools in the world. Partway through his second year, he realized that he actually had no desire to lead a team of 10 people, never mind 10,000! Instead, he had a passion for teaching and coaching. He went on to graduate in the top 10 percent of his class, but after several years and a few more life-defining moments, he decided to mix experience with passion and become

Outside the corporate BOX

"BAD ASS BARBIE" LOVES RACE CARS

Her car is hot pink, her website is hot pink and her racing suit is, you guessed it, pink. Sherri Heckenast, a professional race car driver, has been tuned into her passion and principles since the early age of five. Heckenast was practically brought up at Santa Fe Speedway outside Chicago before learning the ropes of the race car circuit and taking the plunge herself. Fast Company (my favorite business mag) recently featured her intriguing success story:

"When [Sherri Heckenast] was just five, she was using an electric wrench to help change the tires on her father's No. 99 race car. At 16, she bought a cheap 1986 Ford Mustang, stripped off the glass and chrome and painted 99 on the doors."

Now a late-model race car driver, she drives a hot-pink car with "Bad Ass Barbie" on the hood and "U Go Girl" on the rear spoiler. And that's just her hobby. Her day job is CEO of her dad's $30-million company, A-Reliable Auto Parts, and she now owns and runs Kentucky Lake Motor Speedway, which is considered a miniature NASCAR-caliber speedway. Heckenast describes herself as someone who likes to take the leap:

"I've always been the kind of person who wants to do something big, or I don't want to do it."

At 30-something years old, she is one of the few race track operators who wears pink lipstick. Lucky for her, she was able to tune in at a really young age to some valuable principles that have helped her lead an exciting career:

- Take the leap
- Do something big
- Make your mark!

None are surprising when you understand her childhood experience, influences and her dad's fatherly advice:

"Drive your own race, not anybody else's."[5]

going

an elementary school teacher who is now delivering the latest in technology integration across an education system.

This is a decade where many of us find ourselves asking, "What's it all for?" and "What's in it for me?" It might have taken years for my friend to discover his calling, but he has now discovered what really motivates him. Now, he's one of those people who jumps out of bed every morning and says to himself, "I really love what I'm doing!"

"You cannot be effective, you cannot be a leader, until you apply what you know, until you act and DO what you must. As with skills, you will learn more leadership actions as you serve in different positions. Leadership is about taking action, but there's more to being a leader than just what you do. Character and competence, the BE and the KNOW, underlie everything a leader does.[6]" – *The U.S. Army's leadership manual,* Army Leadership: Be, Know, Do!

Tying it all together

Different worlds, different leaders, different principles. It doesn't matter whose principles resonate with you – whether it's Richard Branson's, Bad Ass Barbie's, Mark Cuban's or your own friend's. One thing is for sure: if you can take your life principles and passion and incorporate them as you build your career path, you're setting yourself up for success and for great leadership.

Once you have connected passion and principles, your next step is to take action. Tie it all together and you'll be one step closer to creating your own powerful leadership...with attitude!

LEADERSHIP DRIVERS

Now that you know more about yourself and what drives you personally, think about how your principles and attitudes might impact how you lead. There is no question – who you are and what you believe in will define how you lead.

solo

"MY BUTT is big. And that's just fine and those who might scorn it are invited to kiss it. Just do it.[7]" – *www.nikewomen.com*

Take Nike's great tag line "Just do it." It was a buzzword in Nike's internal daily meetings at corporate offices for a long time. Whenever employees discussed a project or strategy, they were told to go ahead and do it.[7] Now a global corporate marketing strategy, this little tag line has taken on a life of its own. "Just do it" has become a motivational life philosophy, a principle that many people like to live by and it's definitely one heck of an attitude.

It's an attitude I personally believe in. It not only impacts the choices I make but also how I lead. And the more I'm aware of this internal driving attitude, the better I can choose how, where and when this particular attitude may or may not work well. On a project where deadlines are urgent, a 'just do it' leadership attitude can be very effective. Other times, when time is on your hands, a 'just do it' type may have to refocus efforts and dig deeper into the details before making decisions.

It's all about knowing yourself.

"A rock pile ceases to be a rock pile the moment a single man contemplates it, bearing within him the image of a cathedral.[8]"

– The Little Prince, *Antoine de Saint-Exupery*

What's next?

An infinite amount of possibilities. Take a look at your life and work experience from different perspectives. Where do you want to lead today? What do you want to do tomorrow? By taking the time to understand yourself, you have a great building block in place. But it's equally important to understand what drives others, so we'll look at some of the tried-and-true best practices and principles used by one of the most robust leadership models going – the military. Why re-invent the wheel, right?

Lead yourself first. Then you can lead others.

"Are you bored with life? Then throw yourself into some work you believe in with all your heart, live for it, die for it...and you will find happiness that you had thought could never be yours."

-*Audrey Hepburn, actress*

going

ACTION PLAN

Look in the mirror

1 KNOW YOURSELF: YOUR EXPERIENCE, YOUR LIFE.

- What experiences have you had that have had big impact?

A trip to Nepal, a tough relationship, a bad boss, winning an award?

- How has this experience impacted your outlook on life?

2 USE EXPERIENCE TO PINPOINT YOUR PRINCIPLES AND UNDERLYING ATTITUDE.

- Be more in-tune to the choices you make and actions you take

3 DO A GUT CHECK.

- Think about it. What can and can't you live without?
- Use your personal awareness to help guide you on what's important, going forward

4 THINK BIG. EXPECT BIG THINGS.

- Use your attitude to do great things
- Embrace the extreme

solo

GET INTO THE LEADERSHIP GROOVE

> Life shrinks and expands
> in proportion to one's courage
>
> Anaïs Nin

READINESS

Performance anxiety

Tried-and-true principles

Get a jump start

Walk the talk

Payback

Who said this was going to be easy?

I will never forget my first few hours as an 'official' leader. I recall vividly walking toward the large, army-green building where the majority of my new 75-member team and I worked. The military doesn't mess around with leadership – once you sign on the dotted line, you've made the commitment to tackle any leadership task, big or small. In my case, it meant leading a very large team almost immediately with very little experience. In fact, the extent of my credentials for leading this team was surviving three months of boot camp basic training, and a sliver of a 'gold bar' attached to my epaulets that I had received when I was commissioned as second lieutenant.

As you can imagine, I was pretty nervous on this day. I really had no idea what was waiting for me, what challenges or opportunities lay ahead of me. Although I was vaguely familiar with my new role, I wasn't at all familiar with my team members or some of my responsibilities. There was no doubt about it, I was definitely stepping into the unknown.

What led me to this challenge was living out one of those life attitudes we talked about in the previous chapter: Think big. Don't let others define your destiny for you. I had decided after graduating university that I needed to live a life of adventure and excitement, and that I would not be able to realize that destiny by accepting one of the desk jobs being offered to many business graduates like me. Not that I'm knocking these jobs – some of my colleagues have had wonderful and lucrative careers in this regard. I just had different personal goals. With my fascination with aviation and recent flying lessons with gliders and power aircraft, despite several near crash landings, I still felt somehow that flying could lead to a very viable career path.

So I headed to the nearest military recruiting office to discuss my career options. Someone out there must have been looking out for me (or at least everyone else). It turned out flying airplanes would not be my destiny – the military was not accepting women pilots at that time. Either that or they had already heard about my bumpy landings.

But after spending an hour surrounded by walls plastered in exciting posters, watching videos of supersonic jet fighters, parachuters jumping out of aircraft, and hearing recruiters' promises of world travel and great adventures, how could a girl refuse? I was in! Well, that was if they could deliver on a couple of conditions: an air force-blue uniform (I could not do khaki-green garb) and could the recruiters kindly schedule my boot camp training around the upcoming trips I had planned? (I had a busy summer of travel to some lifelong dream destinations, including Red Square, St. Basil's Cathedral and the Hermitage. The intrigue of the iron curtain was calling.)

"Sure," the recruiters responded with a smirk on their faces. "We'll get right on that for you and be sure to make a note in your file." Looking back, I'm sure they were thinking, "Where did this chick come from?"

> "But sergeant, that's not the military I joined! I joined the military with the condos and the motor boats... I think there has been a terrible mistake![1]"
>
> – *Private Benjamin (Academy Award nominee Goldie Hawn) speaking to a recruiter in* Private Benjamin

After some discussion, I chose what I thought would be the next best thing to actually flying airplanes – working on them and with them, with mobile air movements (MAMs) teams. These were small teams of specially trained air force operators, responsible for moving gear around the world in transport aircraft to support military operations. I wasn't going to be a pilot after all, but the leader of large teams, traveling the world to the next military mission. And my uniform would be blue.

So there I was, walking up the steps to my brand new world as a leader! I was greeted by a group of team members and my warrant officer, one of the more senior members, who would become one of my right-hand men. His words of welcome still ring loudly in my ears: "Well, if it ain't the snot-nosed lieutenant!"

First day, first hour in the spotlight, and it already didn't feel good. I knew instantly that no amount of boot camp could prepare me for the realities of the military, the business world or

readi

> **BOOT CAMP INTELLIGENCE**
>
> **Leadership can be learned**
>
> If you still struggle with the question of whether or not leadership can be learned, consider this:
>
> - Every year, thousands of cadets graduate from North American military colleges and boot camps as second lieutenants – a rank that propels young officers into leadership roles such as peacekeeping missions, flying multimillion-dollar fighter aircraft or leading large teams almost immediately.
> - Thousands more non-commissioned officers are selected for combat leadership training for very serious leadership roles that Canada and the United States need filled, in order to face real challenges in operational theaters around the world.
>
> **Pretty powerful stuff considering we are talking about an average age of 22 years old for most graduating cadets!**

the trials and tribulations of being a leader. And one of my first profound leadership realities was setting in rapidly – leadership is not going to be easy.

Reality Check: Love what you're getting yourself into!

As glamorous as it might seem to be rising up through the ranks, leading teams and taking on a higher profile has many challenges. Sure, there will be some wonderful perks – rank does have its privileges. But it also comes with another reality: You will have to lead people – and yourself – through tough times. Downturns, downsizing, business crises, economic issues, social impact. You name it, you will have to lead through it. One thing is guaranteed, leadership is not easy. You've got to love what you're doing.

ness

> "The military takes people like me – a 21-year-old party animal – and turns them into officers."
>
> *– Angela Mondou,* Organizational Behavior, *3rd Canadian Edition (of all the things to be quoted for!)*

WHAT'S YOUR REALITY?

It's 7:30 a.m. You've just parked your car, straightened up your suit as you got out of the car, grabbed your briefcase from the backseat and are now heading up the stairs to the office building's front doors. Your heart is pounding, but you're trying to relax because you don't want to appear nervous. This is it – the job you've been waiting for. You finally did it! You've wanted to lead a team for more than a year, and now it's Day One as a customer service manager. But here's what might be going through your mind: "I have absolutely no idea what I'm doing! I sure hope nobody can tell."

Has reality set in for you yet? Are you asking yourself how you got yourself into this leadership challenge? Let me guess, you have no idea where to start, right?

Well, congratulations – you're actually headed in the right direction! By taking a leadership position, you're already putting a great life principle into practice – think big and expect big things. You're reaching out for the challenges and you're taking that big leap. Whether you're leading for the first time or you're a seasoned leader, you won't be successful unless you put some best practices in place.

Best practices

The right attitude can certainly drive you to be a better leader, but there's a powerful resource you can continually refer to throughout your leadership experience to give you an edge – leadership principles. And some of them come from one of the best training grounds in America – the military's leadership academies and training environments.

Leadership principles are a fundamental basic in the military world and there's a reason for them. Call them whatever you want – tried-and-true ground rules, a well-trodden path or best practices – certain fundamental principles are important to leadership. In fact, they're so important that military leadership schools (considered some of the best leadership factories) in North America instill these principles in every new leader, from the beginning of their career.

With heavy-duty traits like credibility, respect, trust and other important leadership qualities at stake, it's critical to get off on the right foot. And proven principles will help you take that first step in the right direction. The rest is up to you.

So if you're new at the game, why start from scratch? Consider putting some of the following military principles into your own best practices as a leader.

GETTING A JUMP START

Where did I learn about principles? Over my career, one of the best leadership learning forums I've experienced has been boot camp, where principles were drilled into trainees on a daily basis. And in good boot camp fashion, you don't learn about anything without having to put it into practice. The military is all about practice – you practice leadership, simulate missions and prepare for crises through war games. When you end up in a real-life situation, as shocking as it may be, you're extremely thankful for all of those opportunities you had to practice such an event. Practice is the next best thing to the real thing.

Motivating troops in the military is not as easy as it might be in the business world – as a military leader you don't necessarily have big financial rewards like bonuses, stock options, additional compensation or corner offices to motivate your team. No sir. So if you're not putting some of these principles into practice, which demand good leadership, you could have a real problem on your hands. Leadership principles help leaders focus on the two most important things in their role: (1) the people and (2) the mission. If you're not focusing on your resources and your end goal, then what?

Principles provide you with an excellent, best practices guide on the actions you need to take as a leader. Think of them as your call to action.

During my first few weeks of boot camp, things were fairly normal, given the environment. Sergeants were doing what sergeants do best – in-your-face hollering. And young cadets like us ran for miles at ungodly hours, marched endlessly, did push-ups on command, went through dreaded obstacle courses and even had ridiculous late-night chores like cleaning the bathroom grout with toothbrushes. But in the mix, with all the

Outside the corporate BOX

LEADERSHIP. WHERE DO YOU START?

Take a look at these military leadership principles to get you past the starting line:

1. Achieve professional competence.

2. Appreciate your own strengths and weaknesses.

3. Seek and accept responsibilities.

4. Lead by example.

5. Make sure that your followers know your meaning and intent, then lead until you've accomplished the mission.

6. Know your troops and promote their welfare.

7. Develop the leadership potential of your followers.

8. Make sound and timely decisions.

9. Train your soldiers as a team and employ them up to their capabilities.

10. Keep your followers informed of the mission, the changing situation and the overall picture.[2]

www.forces.gc.ca

readi

yelling, saluting and marching, were some valuable leadership lectures – that covered real leadership ground rules to live by, handed out on a small card with 10 fairly harmless phrases on it (see Outside the Corporate Box).

What I didn't realize at the time was that this lesson on principles would become an incredible resource for me as I took on teams, projects and exciting leadership challenges. I've been able to apply those same principles hundreds of times over as a leader, growing from a young, inexperienced officer-in-training to a high-tech executive.

As I stepped into my initial leadership role, performance anxiety and all, those same leadership principles provided me with an edge. I had an action plan to help me get beyond the starting line. And that's a great edge to have as you're stepping up to the plate.

Why reinvent the wheel when you have some tried-and-true best practices at your fingertips? I was lucky to have launched my leadership trajectory with some insight into military leadership principles. But if the military is not your thing, there are many unique leaders and diverse organizations that lead with their own proven principles. Whichever principles you decide to choose as your guide, I hope to inspire you throughout the upcoming chapters and stories with some exciting and practical leadership insights that I have found very helpful in my years of experience.

> "At least once a month, I pull out that little card they gave us back in boot camp with the 10 military leadership principles. After years of leading, I still see something on that card I should be reinforcing as a leader or applying with my team. It's like a continual reminder of some of the leadership basics. And I know that if I'm not applying even one of those principles, I'm probably not leading as effectively as I could be.
>
> *– Major Carolyn Boyd, Canadan Forces dental officer*

Walk the talk

Take a look at the list of principles in Outside the Corporate Box and you can't help but notice that it promotes some powerful actions. Simple actions like:

- Developing your team
- Communication
- Leadership accountability
- Decision-making

Actions like these will help you to walk the talk – help you put some action into what leadership is really about. These principles will take you beyond just being a figurehead or someone with a title, and prompt the kind of action that has a real impact on you, the team and the organization.

Think about how effective you'll be if you consistently work some of these actions into your leadership game plan. Maybe you're a new marketing coordinator and you're about to chair a team meeting for the first time but you're not sure what information you should be sharing. Need some help? Take Principle 10: Keep your followers informed of the mission, the changing situation and the overall picture. Perhaps you've just been advised by your product management team that there will be a delay in your company's hot new product hitting retailers because of production issues. The change in the delivery date will impact many things on the marketing end, from partners who've made a commitment to help you launch to the PR campaign. This is the type of change in the overall big picture that you'll want to pass along to your entire team. Now that's a great place to start!

Take another scenario: you're the son of a family-business owner and you've recently come into a senior position in the company with only a couple of years of leadership experience under your belt. How do you gain that much-needed respect so that you can start having some impact as a new leader? Principle 8: Make sound and timely decisions; or consider Principle 4: Lead by example. Making decisions is something all new leaders struggle with, but the sooner you realize everybody is watching you, the better; you need to take action instead of obsessing to the ninth degree!

In the HOT SEAT

SOUND AND TIMELY DECISIONS

When Andrew Pace left his role as project manager with one of the hottest high-tech companies in North America, he realized his new position as a senior leader in the family business did not come with automatic respect. In fact, quite the opposite: he had to start off with some fundamental leadership principles to begin earning that respect.

"To gain respect as a new leader there are a couple of things you must do. You have to be F&^ing organized! And you have to be able to make decisions. When operating in a fast-paced mission-critical environment, it is essential that leaders within an organization learn to take action in the absence of complete information. We can't always wait for all of the necessary information or direction from our managers before we decide to make a change that will benefit the organization, solve a problem, or help a customer situation. I encourage our people to assume authority when none is present and to add value to the company by doing more than what is outlined in their job description or project mandate. In a small company like ours this is the key to solving problems efficiently."*
– Andrew Pace, vice president, Pace Consulting Group Inc.

Sound familiar? The principles Andrew is referring to tie right into tried-and-true best practices:

- Take action
- Make decisions
- Delegate

PRINCIPLES. YOUR ACTION PLAN

In today's workplace, making sound and timely decisions is one of those abilities that most leaders need to develop. For example, in the high-tech industry where I've worked for the past decade, leaders at all levels in the company must make sound and timely decisions or they risk jeopardizing a product launch and possibly even a company's success. Applying this principle can be the difference between getting a product launched at the right time in the right place, or getting it stuck in analysis paralysis. Without effective decision-making, you can lose the momentum to move things forward; you might not launch your product on time and, ultimately, may not beat the competition. And in the high-tech world, maintaining a competitive edge is often the difference between success and failure.

This is a simple and proven leadership principle, yet it's often not put into action. Make leadership principles an important part of your leadership game plan.

PRINCIPLES. A SERIOUS BUSINESS

The one thing about belonging to an organization that bases its leadership philosophy on tried-and-true principles is that you can learn very quickly the impact of NOT applying principles. I got busted in the early days of boot camp and can remember a couple of other occasions where my lax behavior led to some very uncomfortable situations.

> "Soldiers represent what's best about our Army. Day in and day out, in the dark and in the mud and in faraway places, they execute tough missions whenever and wherever the Nation calls. They deserve our very best – leaders of character and competence who act to achieve excellence. That theme resounds throughout FM22-100, Army Leadership, and echoes our time-honored principles of BE, KNOW, DO.[3]" *– Eric K. Shinseki, general, United States Army, 34th chief of staff*

I admit I had a hiccup or two as I tried to transition myself from a footloose and fancy-free 20-something student who loved the European discos (this was the '80s after all) to an officer-cadet with combat boots and short hair who had to adhere to boot camp rules and regulations. One unfortunate Monday morning, I showed up to our cadet barracks after a well-deserved weekend of rest and relaxation with hot pink nail polish on my fingernails. I was still getting used to the fact that nail polish, makeup and other accessories that might be considered decorative were absolutely prohibited with any military uniform. And as luck would have it on that day, Captain Giffen, our platoon commander, was going to give us a lesson on leadership, and I was going to be the 'star.' Giffen was an army infantry officer (the army front lines who tended to think they were the be-all and end-all) and he had a real dislike for officer cadets – particularly female officer cadets. Showing up in my army-green combats and hot pink nail polish took his dislike to a whole new level.

There I sat in my preassigned seat, in the front row – not a good thing on this day. The cadet beside me took one look at my fingertips, cringed and made some under-the-breath comment like, "Geez, Ange, Giffen's going to kill you!" He was right, I didn't have a hope that I was going to get through that morning without Giffen noticing the polish.

I was busted within the hour, no longer maintaining a low profile – a position I was strongly advised to keep in boot camp so I wouldn't make the sergeant's hit list. Captain Giffen quickly marched me off to the Commandant's Office for a recorded warning on "dress and deportment." My actions would get documented in my personnel file – a file that would follow me for the rest of my military career, or so I was told by my superiors.

PINK NAIL POLISH, SO WHAT?

I learned an important lesson the day I received a warning about my appearance – the military takes its leadership principles very seriously. Wearing hot pink nail polish was in complete contradiction to the guidelines set out in the military manual and, specifically, to leadership Principle 4: Lead by example.

The uniform of an organization (police officers, firefighters, airline pilots, astronauts) represents many things, from achievement of rank, levels of professionalism, accomplishment of special training, awards and medals – in essence, it's a rite of passage. It's symbolic of important principles like professionalism, discipline, achievement and unity.

The message was clear from the commandant – as a new leader I was setting a poor example and dishonoring the uniform, which in turn, reflected on my professionalism and abilities. That's because everything you do as a leader is being watched by other members of the team and it sets the tone for how the team behaves. Sloppy dress, sloppy leader!

So it's not surprising that almost two decades later we are witnessing many big business leaders getting busted for their lack of ethics, integrity, honesty and professionalism. Bad behavior, bad principles. One way or another, without some solid leadership principles, you're going to get busted!

> "Sure, we will do market research, but in the end it comes down to you having to decide for yourself and being willing and ready to give it a go. Be willing to fall flat on your face if it doesn't work.[4]"
>
> *– Sir Richard Branson, Virgin*

Grooving, walking and talking

You've already read that I believe leadership principles should be a part of your game plan to give you an edge. Well, let me put that into perspective to demonstrate what I mean.

I had to deal with tough situations almost as soon as I began leading my first team. After boot camp, I was promoted to the rank of second lieutenant. In business terms, that means a leader, but one with virtually no experience. Despite my lack of experience, I was in charge of a large team – 75 people, of all ages and different levels of experience. In fact, many of my new team members had more years of experience than I had been living. At just 22 years old, I was leading a team that was two to three times the size of most teams I have led since. That meant I had to shift gears quickly, from learning the value of leadership principles to applying them.

You might remember me mentioning earlier how one of my new team members greeted me with a 'warm' and loud introduction to my new organization the first day I walked into the office ("Well, if it ain't the snot-nosed lieutenant."). I still remember his voice booming through the corridors as he mockingly snapped to attention and saluted me in front of at least 20 of my new team members. This was my introduction to that inevitable team member who would give me grief and, trust me, there will always be someone like him. Lucky me, I had a smart-ass on my team with years of experience who was going to challenge me, whether it was just because I was young, new to the team – or just because. I knew I either needed to start 'walking the talk' and gather the courage to start applying the principles I had learned months earlier in boot camp, or I would get bullied by a second-in-command who would undermine every bit of credibility I was trying to establish as a very new leader.

Tough choice, but after a few months, I made the right decision and took some action.

Reality Check: Trial by fire

Leading today often means trial by fire, learning the ropes on your own and at a very fast pace. You might be establishing your own start-up company or working in an organization where you don't get guidance or a buffer from your boss. Don't underestimate the power of a desktop reference guide like the military leadership principles I was given years ago. And remember, any tool is useless if you don't use it. Get a jump start by putting some tried-and-true principles into practice, and then leverage the confidence you will gain as you experience the results.

GETTING RESPECT

"If it ain't the snot-nosed lieutenant." Something about that comment hit me right in the gut – perhaps my second-in-command was trying to be funny but his sarcastic words just didn't feel right. First, this warrant officer was one of the more senior and experienced people who would be reporting to me. Second, the tone and gesture of his introduction of me to the team was disrespectful.

I already knew that people are boss-watchers. My team of 75 was watching everything this senior team member did and said. And they were watching me and my reactions to him.

I had to set the example. I had to demonstrate that this disrespectful behavior was not acceptable. But lacking experience and confidence at this point, I treaded a little too cautiously during my first few weeks in my role and decided to let the sarcastic comments slide. After all, maybe he really was joking? I now know that when you feel something right in your gut, there's no joking. The "snot-nosed lieutenant" comments didn't stop, the mocking salutes continued and, after a few months, I cringed every time I approached this individual.

The bad situation got worse. The more I witnessed this senior team leader in action, the more I realized I wasn't the only recipient of somewhat harassing comments. Some of the junior ladies on the team were being treated very disrespectfully and the lower-ranked men were being bullied. There was no doubt about it – this guy was way out of line and the team's morale was starting to sink.

PRINCIPLES = DIRECTION

I looked at my list of principles for guidance. I talked to my colleagues and other officers to see what they would do. It was becoming very clear – I needed to deal with the situation. I needed to set the example and start demanding respect for myself and for everyone else on the team.

I mustered up all of my confidence and took aside this senior team leader of almost twice my age. I explained to him what he was doing, the impact he was having on the team and potential actions I might have to take if his behavior didn't stop. I set expectations on how he needed to act and treat the team, me included. And in doing so, I was also demonstrating to the rest of the team that no one should accept this type of behavior.

The warrant officer got the message and the impact was immediate. He changed his behavior and the work environment quickly started improving. I was later approached by team members who came to see me in confidence to discuss some of their concerns and stress because of this individual's behavior. They were thankful that something had been done. Within a week, I was wondering what took me so long to set the example. I was getting into the leadership groove and it felt good.

The power in those somewhat lifeless principles given to me in boot camp was in applying them. I was finally getting it!

RED FLAG **Flexing muscles**
Acting on powerful principles can take confidence, courage and a willingness to face uncomfortable situations, such as frustrated team players, angry customers and difficult executives. Applying principles just takes guts. Who ever said leadership was easy?

> People are boss-watchers. The rank and file will always take their cues from their leader. It is therefore doubly important that the leader live with the values that he or she espouses. *– Colin Powell, former U.S. military top dog and joint chief of staff*

PAYBACK TIME

It is much easier to sit behind your desk and lead behind e-mail rather than getting out there with the troops and 'facing the music.' It takes confidence and courage to join your team on the front lines because once you step out of your cubicle, you have to start dealing with all of the issues.

But there's a big payback when you start leading from the front and leading by example. You'll be rewarded with:

- Credibility
- Trust and loyalty from the team
- Integrity
- Confidence
- Increased accountability and ownership
- An energized team
- Action

...all things a leader can't live without.

→ Apply principles → have an impact → make a difference = lead with confidence

▶▶ **Fast forward** *If you want to learn more about the payback you can expect with leadership principles, see Section 2 for 13 powerful, current principles and action plans to help you thrive in today's fast-paced environment.*

> The leader now has to emerge from the corner office, excite teams – energize them, lead them rather than manage them.[5] *– Dennis D. Dammerman, former vice chairman of the board, GE*

Sloppy principles mean consequences

Leaders in all industries can make a big impact on the teams they lead. When I say 'impact,' I mean a positive or a negative effect on a team. So, if you're not playing by the rules, you can expect the team to stretch the rules too. If you dress sloppily or unprofessionally, don't be surprised when a few members take some dress code liberties too. If you have a difficult time keeping regular office hours, plan on flex-hours being the norm. Like it or not, you're being watched, and the people who work with you vote in subtle ways – with respect, loyalty and credibility.

Just like the wrist-slapping I received in boot camp, when you apply principles sloppily, there's always a consequence to pay. I was reminded about this consequence recently while I was leading a professional team of marketing and technical sales staff at Research In Motion, one of the world's most successful producers of wireless data devices. A typical career woman with the added challenge of being a single mother of two, I was juggling a fast-paced job, global travel, high-powered projects, a house, a wonderful partner, and, thank God, a nanny. After a while, even though I have far more brainpower in the early hours of the day, I was finding it more and more difficult to get into the office before 9 a.m. Soon after my hours started to slide a little, I began to notice that two of my project managers were straggling in well after I arrived and leaving before I finished my workday. What these team players didn't realize was that, unlike their workday, mine did not end when I left the office. I was often on late-night conference calls with teams in other time zones, or working on project plans at home to meet deadlines.

But it didn't matter – 'optics' are important and these employees were taking their lead from me. And no one but me was to blame. I began to make a point of starting my workday at 8 a.m. again. And I had to 'reset' expectations on reasonable hours for our team members who did not have global roles and regular office hours.

> "Lead by example…always personally do what you learned in training even when exhausted, frozen or confused. Get up first, eat last, get on the first chopper into the LZ [landing zone], get on the last out…be a servant to your soldiers."[6]
>
> *– A U.S. retired general's advice to a lieutenant on his way to Afghanistan*

LEADING BY GREED

A quick word of caution: Just as I was paraded in front of my commandant for my hot pink nail polish, the business world has its own interesting way of holding leaders accountable who don't always practice what they preach – today more than ever before. Recent news reports are evidence of a new era of accountability in leadership, after a decade of business corruption, financial scandals and cheating innocent investors out of billions of dollars.

Think about how some of these companies and/or leaders have become household names, primarily because principles have been sorely lacking among leaders in their organizations.

- **Enron and its leaders** led the company to total meltdown and billions of dollars of losses to shareholders. Andrew Fastow, former chief financial officer, pleaded guilty to wire and securities fraud and sentenced to 10 years in prison.[7]
- **WorldCom's founder Bernard Ebbers** was convicted of fraud and conspiracy to the tune of $11 billion. Ebbers was sentenced to 25 years in a federal prison.[8]
- **Lord Conrad Black of Hollinger Inc.,** press baron of one of the top three newspaper publishers in the world,[9] has been accused by the U.S. Securities and Exchange Commission of transferring more than $400 million to himself and other execs.[10]
- **Former Canadian Prime Minister Jean Chrétien** was accused of the sponsorship scandal that led to millions of Canadian taxpayers' funds being handed out to loyal Liberal party supporters in Quebec – all during his leadership tenure.[11]

And, of course, there is always Martha Stewart. Everybody loves to hate Martha, with her stock scandal, subsequent jail time and now-cancelled NBC *The Apprentice*: *Martha Stewart* TV show. Whether she is the cut-throat, arrogant 'b' we so often hear about in the media, she was held accountable for acting unethically and without good business principles. Regardless, I'm not sure whether this decorating diva's lack of business principles is quite as extreme as some of the other corporate culprits we've heard about, but that's not the point.

The point is, however big or small her error in judgment, she was held accountable for not leading by example. In the end, she received fierce publicity, months of jail time and a company that plummeted in value, at least in the short term.

There's that principle again: lead by example. It just keeps coming up over and over again.

> "She sort of hits a common nerve in a lot of people. A friend of mine calls it homemaker porn. Essentially, it's aspiring to a lifestyle that you can't have…it's a fantasy world."[12]
>
> *– Diane Brady,* Business Week *magazine's associate editor*

CASE STUDY **Homemaker Porn**

Martha changed American culture and built a vision and an empire that brought many career women in North America to a guilt-wracked conundrum because they had essentially traded in home cooking, do-it-yourself decorating and cultivating herb gardens for the endless pursuit of the corner office. Martha re-engineered the housewife to a more glamorous profession, in the style of 'homemaker chic.' And she built that empire on willpower, guts and a work ethic she learned early in life. All of this became the foundation for some simple lifestyle principles that many of us were losing sight of in our career-path frenzy.

Despite her enormous success, principles and values, Martha chose to put at least one leadership principle on hold: leading by example. Some would say she allowed good corporate ethics to go by the wayside and chose instead to lead by greed, costing the homemaking diva dearly. Here was a woman who was worth close to a billion dollars who chose to save mere thousands on an insider stock-trading tip,[13] and she was caught and held accountable. By failing to lead by example, she became the example in corporate America of what not to do.

On release from prison, Martha debuted on *Forbes* magazine's billionaire list for the first time.[14] While *The Apprentice: Martha Stewart* wasn't renewed, Martha describes the show as a successful, calculated risk with "6 million eyeballs on your company in a very positive light every single week"[15] – a number that far exceeds the paid circulation of *Martha Stewart Living* magazine during a six-month period.[16] I'd say she has taken her failure and used it in a powerful way!

"The worst thing is just being held responsible. My legal problems for the last three years...could have crumbled the company. Sometimes, because you are so closely aligned with the company, (people) think there's no company without you. In fact, we have a really great company without me, but because I'm the face and the name, it could be a potential problem.[17]" – *Martha Stewart,* USA Today

What's next?

So you got over that performance anxiety and you're ready to get into that leadership groove. You're excited to be moving beyond being a team player or an independent contributor and leading a team, keen to put some of those leadership principles into practice.

There's something you need to be aware of. Business these days is moving fast – I mean at warp speed. And it doesn't seem to be slowing down in any way. That means you will have less time to accomplish your goals – with less time to execute.

Everything's moving at a whole new pace and it's having an impact on how we lead. What does this mean?

You're going to have to 'feel the need for speed!'

"Money, it's a gas
Grab that cash with both hands and make a stash
New car, caviar, four-star daydream
Think I'll buy me a football team
Money, it's a hit
Don't give me that do goody good bullshit
I'm in the high-fidelity first-class traveling set
And I think I need a Lear jet
Money, it's a crime
Share it fairly but don't take a slice of my pie
Money, so they say
It's the root of all evil today."

– *"Money," Pink Floyd*

readi

ACTION PLAN

Get the power

1 GET A HEAD START WITH LEADERSHIP PRINCIPLES.

- They're a great guide on how to get moving

2 YOU DON'T HAVE TO REINVENT THE WHEEL.

- Seek out some tried-and-true best practices

3 START WALKING THE TALK.

- The best way to get started is to start practicing
- Pick one principle and put it into action today

ness

MISSION CRITICAL NOT MISSION IMPOSSIBLE

Fast change is arriving
Slow changes are moving out
Here we are

Fast changes, Seal

SPEED

Leading in the hot seat

Fast. Changing. Complex

Feel the need for speed

No tribe has immunity

Thriving with a game plan

Ready. Aim. Lead

It was April 2000 and I was having one of those 'how did I get myself here' moments again. I had long ago replaced my combat boots for high-tech business garb (which could mean anything from Birkenstocks to Manolo Blahniks, depending on the business meeting). I was now responsible for strategic planning for the global logistics group in Nortel Networks, a very large company that produces telecommunications gear.

I had just returned from a very cool short-term assignment in Europe with my two sons when my boss, Sandi Pitcairn, called with some good news. "Angela, you know how you were a little concerned about being left out of the action back here in North America because you took on that European assignment? Well, you don't have to worry anymore. Have I got a job for you!" I could hardly wait to hear what it was.

At this time, the telecom industry was going absolutely gangbusters, and Nortel was in the thick of it. The company had been on a high-tech shopping spree to the tune of about $20 billion and had purchased numerous companies over a 12-month period – either to broaden its product portfolio or quite simply to buy up companies so the competition couldn't. Now we had a merger and acquisition (M&A) backlog since these new companies and their products needed to be integrated into the larger parent company. This highly competitive environment meant we had to get these newly acquired companies and their new products out into the marketplace before someone else did. And getting this expanded supply chain aligned was the job of our newly formed M&A integration team.

So that takes us to the exuberant call from my boss, as she had nominated me to be the global logistics leader on this team. I needed to be on a plane to the Silicon Valley in California, the land of high-tech start-ups, in a week. I barely had enough time to get over the jet lag, never mind unpack my bags.

So, off I went to California to meet my new 'dotted line' boss. This was the high-tech industry's clever way of getting everyone to do more with less: you report into two bosses – one solid line boss who is your full-time leader and one dotted line boss for special projects – so more work can be squeezed out of you since you have two areas of responsibility. Nothing like being a shared resource! My task during the first week was to get to know the new companies recently purchased, their products and people, and put together an efficient merger and acquisition plan for global logistics. My new mission and the new product terminology I was learning were coming at me fast and furious – ...time to market...photonic switching...rapid planning and integration...30-60-90-day plans...immediate market expansion...fast...turnaround...timelines.

My head was spinning.

▶▶ **Fast forward** *to Chapter 08: "Link Your Team to the Mission" for some great insight on how to get your team marching to the beat of the same drum and working together toward the same end goal. Chapters 08 to 10 provide a three-phased strategy on leadership readiness and how to integrate, communicate and execute your mission when things are moving at warp speed.*

RED FLAG **Do more with much less**

Many leaders are being forced these days to do more with less – less people, cash, time, facilities. You may end up leading a team with 'matrixed' resources – people who are on loan to you for a particular project from other departments and working with other leaders. Reality is these 'shared' resources already have a full-time job and may not respond to you and your project with the same urgency and attention, so you'll need to work hard to keep the team on the game and tied to the mission – with clear task alignment, accountability and most of all, motivation.

> "Moving an army into a war zone has a lot in common with the kind of challenges that arise in the technology business."[1] – *Angela Mondou,* The Record

It's all war

My eclectic career path has been covered on a couple of occasions in national newspapers and it never fails, the theme of the articles is always the same. It doesn't matter what type of work you're leading – it can end up feeling a lot like a war zone. Even though I traded in my combat boots years earlier, somehow I felt like my job in the high-tech industry put me right back into a war zone. The same words I used to describe a United Nations mission years earlier in these articles could easily be used to sum up my work (and anyone else's) in the business environment – you wouldn't know I was talking about two entirely different worlds. For me, today's business reality feels a lot like yesterday's missions:

- Thinking, planning, leading and executing all at once
- Tight timelines that feel almost impossible to deliver on
- Making important decisions with very little information
- Rapidly pulling a team together to make things happen

The same is true for almost any line of work today – whether we're talking about leading a UN mission, high-tech projects, big corporations, third-world projects or volunteer work. You'll be facing an inevitable sense of urgency to get results.

"There are, of course, differences in management between organizations – mission defines strategy, after all, and strategy defines structure. But the differences between managing a chain of retail stores and managing a Roman Catholic diocese are amazingly fewer than either retail executives or bishops realize. The differences are mainly in application rather than in principles.[2]"

– Peter F. Drucker, management guru

This new leadership pace is not all bad news. There is something about a tight deadline that can bring a team together quickly – the pace can force focus and a well-aligned team. Speed will push clear accountability to tasks. You certainly can't have things moving fast if people are tripping over each other and uncertain about their individual tasks. And a fast-paced, well-aligned team will be motivated through clear task ownership, impact and influence, and overall achievement on reaching the project's goal.

Reality Check: Leading at a new pace

If you think things are moving fast these days, you haven't seen anything yet. This is just the warm-up. The world is getting smaller, more connected, more complex by the day. No point banging your head against the wall – fast change is here to stay.

"This is a totally new world. We are operating in a totally new game, with new players and new challenges. This new world requires a new kind of leadership: fast, flexible, resourceful, savvy, strategic – and at every level of the company. No one person is capable of seeing everything, of seeing every problem, challenge and every opportunity. Leaders today must draw on the experience, smarts, capabilities, initiative and energy of all employees – and keep it all focused on achieving the mission, vision and strategy."

– www.ilead.com.au

THE NEW PACE

We've been talking about leadership at a new pace, on a whole new level – a level that demands readiness. Leadership where plans and action might happen at the same time; where people, tasks and timelines have to come together like a well-oiled machine. Before you know it, you'll feel like you're sitting in a very hot seat – making decisions more quickly, delivering projects at record speeds, or leading one of those matrixed teams who might be located in a different country.

This is what I call the mission-critical environment. And thriving at this new pace means you will have to get good at sitting in the hot seat. Now is the time to feel that need for speed.

Not to worry, however. With the right preparation, you don't need to fear this environment. It can be tough leadership and it will present some challenges. But it can bring about a real focus, and it can be exciting and very energizing.

Readiness is key.

Mission-critical environment *unplugged*

In the business war zone, you will find that there is a common theme to what turns a 'normal' work environment into a mission-critical environment. The speed at which projects must be accomplished, the frequency at which things change and the complexity of the world we work in affect the environment in which we work.

As you lead in the hot seat, where will you feel the greatest impact? Take a look at the snapshot below on where and how you might feel the impact on your projects:

Mission-critical environment		Impact
fast	➡	• turnaround times • decisions • delivery
changing	➡	• priorities • business plans • teams or leaders • customers
complex	➡	• global business • remote team players • cross-functional teams • shared team resources

Three key elements that are common to the mission-critical business environment are:

- Fast – how quickly do things need to happen?
- Changing – what's changing around you?
- Complex – what's the structure of the world you're currently working in?

Take a minute to review the chart and think about some of the situations you face today in your business. If any of this applies to your world, chances are your leadership seat is probably feeling a little hot!

THE HEAT IS ON

When I stepped back into my new role at Nortel on the M&A integration team, we had 90 days to integrate the new companies and their products into our supply chain. That meant all new products had to be available in our sales and order management system for all global customers. I was tasked to organize a cross-functional team of project managers (you know, one of those matrixed teams I've been referring to) from different internal departments, plus a couple of key individuals from companies we had acquired. And in a week, I had to present a 30-60-90-day plan, a mini action plan (you'll hear me refer to this frequently), to our M&A executives.

▶▶ **Fast forward** *to Chapter 06: "Spark Creativity" for more on the 30-60-90-day plan.*

Some of the actions in my 30-60-90-day plan included:

- Brainstorming and documenting short and medium-term actions with new team members
- Assigning ownership of the tasks and actions
- Documenting the gaps and missing resources
- Meeting our new partners or customers via several teleconference calls
- Understanding and documenting how orders would be processed and delivered around the world as we brought each of these new companies into the fold

We were a brand new team with new leaders, a new mandate and different corporate cultures coming together as one. The fun was just starting. We still had to execute our plan.

NO TRIBE HAS IMMUNITY

Robert Milton became the young CEO of Canada's major international airline in 1999 – something he had dreamed about since he was a kid.[3] As he stepped into his dream job, he faced what might be considered one of the most turbulent times in aviation history.[4] But in 2003, Milton led the way to save Canada's national airline and position it for success in the global marketplace. By the time 9/11 hit, Air Canada was well into its

spe

cost-reduction model. A year later, new jets had been added to the fleet[5] and load capacity had increased. Last year, Air Canada floated its frequent-flier program on a stock exchange, with a listing valued at more than $2 billion.[6] Here's the fascinating part – despite the enormous challenges and heavy media criticism, Milton didn't jump ship. He stayed at the helm and continued to lead the company. The lesson here: even if you do attain your dream job, you still won't have immunity from the challenges caused by today's fast pace – and there will be days where it might cause you some real grief. When you're having one of those days – just remember, you're not alone and no one is immune. In fact, at one of my recent leadership workshops, we reviewed the leadership hot seat caused by the mission-critical environment, and how each of the workshop participants have been impacted by it. Although this was a very diverse group of leaders from very different businesses, there wasn't one individual in the room who had not experienced the hot seat in one way or another. Here's just a sampling of some of these leaders and the businesses they represent:

- Owner/manufacturer for a lingerie and ladies apparel
- Administration team for a nuns' convent
- Federal government manager
- Senior project manager for a global IT company
- Chief financial officer for a legal firm

So what does that tell you? Not even nuns are immune from the hot seat!

▶▶ **Fast forward** *to Chapters 08 to 10, which focus on three powerful principles and actions to help you succeed in this environment – integrate, communicate and execute.*

> "In my years as CEO we have had to deal with a hostile takeover attempt, the high-tech meltdown, September 11, the Iraq War, SARS, and most recently, oil prices approaching $50 a barrel. When I was growing up, I used to dream of running an airline one day. I had no idea that my dream might become a nightmare.[7]"
>
> *– Robert A. Milton, former president and CEO, Air Canada*

In the HOT SEAT

WHAT'S SO HOT?

These are hot and fast times. Gone are the days of calling your team into a meeting room. These days you'll be setting up conference calls across time zones and leading people you may never meet. The workplace has been redefined and so too has leadership. Here's why:

1. The speed

Information overload: There's e-mail, voice mail, Internet, text messaging…instant access to almost anyone or anything anywhere. More information has been produced in the last 30 years than during the previous 5,000 years. The information supply available to us doubles every five years.[8]

Wired up and wireless: Technology has delivered hand-sized wireless devices, with 24/7 e-mail coverage – even if you're sitting on the beaches of Thailand.

2. The new face of business

Products, people and their knowledge are changing rapidly: That means changes in several areas, including business priorities, plans and leadership.

People power the knowledge economy: Knowledge is becoming one of the world's most important products. Canada is committed to becoming "the most connected nation in the world" through the development of its knowledge-based economy.[9] An estimated two-thirds of U.S. employees work in the services sector, where knowledge is an important 'product.'[10]

Downsizing and disappearing: In *Fortune* magazine's first list of America's 500 biggest companies known as the Fortune 500 (published in 1956), only 29 out of the 100 firms topping it could still be found in the top 100 by 1992. During the 1980s, a total of 230 companies (46 percent) disappeared from the Fortune 500.[11]

3. The complexity

Doing more with less: After years of downsizing, a turbulent economy and world crises like 9/11, SARS and bird flu outbreaks, lean teams are working with fewer resources in less-than-ideal environments.

The new face of leadership

"You're my new boss. How old are you?" demands the former head of ad sales.

"I'm 26 years old," replies the new boss. "How old are you?"

"I'm 51."

"Wow!" the new boss says." That's like a year older than my dad! So, that's weird!"[12]

Consider this scenario: an established, 50-something head of advertising sales has just been advised by his brand new boss that he is no longer head of ad sales because of the company's recent merger, but the good news is he'll still have a job. Only minutes earlier, the new boss confesses to a young woman as he was taking the elevator up to his new office that he "doesn't have a clue what he's doing" in his new role as a leader.

The scene is from the movie *In Good Company*. It certainly portrays a relevant and accurate depiction of what has been happening with some current leadership trends that affect big business today.

Younger generations are moving up quickly through the ranks or skipping right over the ranks and into some serious leadership positions, while older generations are moving on or being replaced. That means older leaders are now reporting to younger bosses. It also means a shift in values, principles and attitudes as younger generations are taking on leadership roles with an entirely different mindset than their predecessors.

If you're one of these up-and-comers taking over the leadership of established or older teams, or if you're the young owner of a new company working with more experienced partners, you and your team will face some challenges.

Back in the '80s, I led my first very large team at 22 years old, yet the majority of my team members were in their forties. The impact of having little experience and taking over a team was that I quickly needed to establish credibility and respect while learning the job.

In this decade, with the baby boomers entering retirement, and the shift to a knowledge-based economy, young skilled workers are moving up quickly, with little or no leadership experience. In earning credibility and respect from their teams, new leaders can expect to face older team players who will question their ability and a younger generation with a 'what's in it for me' attitude.

If you don't deliver, team members won't stick around.

> "Managers will need to find new ways of influencing their young workers as they will vote with their feet if they are not treated well…"[13]
>
> *– Barbara Moses, career guru*

DUDE, YOU'RE NOT MY BOSS

On one of the first days I was working for Research In Motion (RIM), a global innovator of wireless devices, I was introduced to a senior manager who in actual fact was not so senior. He was just 26 years old. He was assigned to my team for a project to launch RIM's BlackBerry in Australia. He happened to overhear a discussion I was having with our administrative assistant about the new organization chart we were creating to keep track of which teams were working on what projects around the world. After hearing that he would report to me, he said, "Dude, I don't work for you yet. I still work for the vice president of Business Integration. I'm just checking things out." By 'things' he meant checking me out – as his boss! If I didn't pass the test, he had no intention of coming over to my team. This was my first experience with this mindset, and I wasn't sure who the leader was in this case.

Funny thing was that that very morning I had heard almost the exact same words from my then-six-year-old son, Daniel, as we went through our usual 'eat breakfast and get dressed' frenzy before school. "You're not the boss of me, Mommy," he declared as I made a futile effort to get him to change his shoes! It's an interesting comment from both a six-year-old and a 26-year-old, and it's an accurate reflection of the sentiment of today's employees. They believe that "you're not my boss; I'm my own boss." It's a very powerful mindset and it's what will be leading businesses in the future.

spe

TOUGH CROWD

Today, the new generation has been described as "smart, diverse, autonomous, interactive, edgy and optimistic." The X and Y generations (born between 1965-1994) will make up a very large group of the employees you'll be leading (or could be led by) – more than 60 million generation Ys in the U.S. alone.[14] Here are some of these generations' attitudes and principles:

- Has come to expect everything immediately, including challenging career opportunities
- Tends to be unimpressed with authority and respect those who demonstrate competence and advanced skills
- 'What's in it for me' and 'work to live' attitudes are prevalent
- Understand technology better than any other generation
- Are skeptical of everything, from authority to brand names
- Will face conflict and challenge rules
- Work independently with a focus on technology[15]

So it doesn't matter how young or not so young you are as a leader today. You must understand the shift in workplace principles and attitudes of today's employees. No longer is there a great need for workplace security and long-term careers. Employees are more independent and self-driven, ultimately developing a varied career path.

Readiness

So how can you prepare for this new face and pace of leadership – this mission-critical environment? How do you make sure that you are leading properly and not just flying by the seat of your pants?

By being ready – being prepared as best as you can for what you don't know. Because the one thing you do know, the one thing that is constant, is change.

That's where the military model and other fast-paced leadership models are very powerful. One thing that was drilled into me throughout my years as a military leader was the need for readiness. Preparation and contingency planning for upcoming missions, challenges, events. Section 2 of this book reviews 13 principles that will help you develop that readiness and provide you with the tools for better preparation and planning – and a game plan.

> "It's not hard to understand why speed counts when it comes to national defence...On a few of my projects, we have found ways to cut the yearlong [project] process down to as little as three or four weeks. How can we accomplish that?...For the vast majority of projects, speed really does count...The key is this: When you have a single-minded focus on something like speed, it encourages creative, innovative thinking.[16]"
>
> *– Terry Little, former head of U.S. Air Force's Center for Acquisition Excellence*

THE GAME PLAN TO SEIZE YOUR LEADERSHIP POTENTIAL

Coming up ahead, you'll find a collection of powerful leadership principles that you can use to establish your readiness for the fast-paced business environment. You can incorporate these principles as part of your leadership game plan since they come from the experience, attitudes and insights of very different leaders, leading incredible things.

Each of the upcoming chapters will provide you with important pieces for your game plan:

1. Great principles to get started – Principles that will help you focus on empowerment, delegation, quick decision-making, planning, synchronizing the team, expanding your potential, etc. With that focus comes backbone and the ability to be flexible and plan for the inevitable changes you'll experience at the current leadership pace.

Focus = forward. Having focus moves you forward

2. An action plan – As in this section, the end of each chapter will contain simple tools and templates to help you lead effectively in today's world.

Action = momentum, direction, progress, results

3. Accountability – To move things forward and make things happen fast, you must have an environment of ownership and responsibility at all levels. There is little time for ambiguity, or worse, a lack of willingness to step up to the plate from team members. As a leader, the principles you apply and action you take will help you create the most important requirement for accountability and ownership. You must start at the top and lead by example. It's up to you.

Accountability = ownership. Lead by example

Having a solid game plan will provide you with the right approach. Putting your game plan into action creates the right leadership attitude. And to seize your potential and lead the world you want, you'll need the right attitude!

> "Ability is what you are capable of doing.
> Motivation determines what you do.
> Attitude determines how well you do it."
>
> *– Lou Holtz, legendary university and NFL football coach*

What's next?

Feel the need for speed. No matter what you want to lead, the mission-critical world will be a part of your leadership reality – a reality that will involve tough missions with faster-than-ever turnaround times and where priorities are continually changing to keep up with the demands of customers. It's a reality with tough-to-please teams who are demanding credible and accountable leaders – leaders who must focus on empowerment, growth and well-being…or else.

But the pace of leadership today and the things that make it more challenging are also the very things you'll likely be seeking for yourself; after all, there are many who think the greatest challenge delivers the best opportunity. Leadership will take you on a path that is exciting, invigorating, reenergizing, and full of adventure. Get ready for an incredible opportunity.

> "In the Consumer Products business, being first to the market or hitting a defined marketing window with a quality product requires us to always look for ways to improve or reduce our execution schedules. As such, we're often called 'speed merchants.'"[17]
>
> *– W. Scott Cameron, speed merchant, Procter & Gamble*

spe

ACTION PLAN

Feel the need for speed

1 GET READY FOR THE HOT SEAT.

- Prepare for the mission-critical environment – a fast, changing, complex world
- No tribe has immunity – it doesn't matter what business you're in

2 AIM FOR ACCOUNTABILITY.

- Ownership at every level is key to success in a fast-paced environment
- Think accountability versus authority
- Remember the tough crowd – the current demographic of employees and leaders is unimpressed by authority and demands "what's in it for me?"
- Lead by example – step up to the plate, demonstrate ownership and be accountable

3 READINESS.

- Put some thought into your game plan: preparation and planning will help you manage the pace
- Strap yourself in and enjoy the ride

ed

PART TWO

13 PRINCIPLES TO LEAD INCREDIBLE THINGS!

THE BUCK STOPS WITH YOU

Turning the tide, you are on the incoming wave
Turning the tide, you know you are nobody's slave
Find your sisters and brothers
Who can hear all the truth in what you say

Shaking the Tree, Peter Gabriel

ACCOUNTABILITY

Make a difference

Clear sense of purpose

Guts to be 'the owner'

Selflessness

Don't pass the buck

Step up to the plate

Stepping up to the plate

Imagine trying to become a leader in one of the most corrupt third-world countries on the globe. Where bribes and payoffs are such a way of life that politicians have made anti-graft policies (the gain of illicit monies and valuables) a key campaign platform for a recent national election. A place where the average citizen still has to pay bribes to almost all levels of government to get simple documents, such as vehicle licenses or birth certificates.[1] Added to these political problems is AIDS, a continental disaster of such epidemic proportions that approximately 12 million children are now AIDS orphans in sub-Saharan Africa alone. That number is expected to rise to more than 18 million by 2010.[2]

Now imagine that, like many of the country's citizens, you have limited education, little money, and to make matters worse, you're a woman. A woman in a very male-dominated, corrupt society. But a woman on a mission.

What do you think are your chances of succeeding when all the odds are against you? Not great, right? Well, you'll be inspired to hear the story of one remarkable woman in Kenya, Africa, who stepped up to the plate with nothing more than a commitment to make a difference. With very little education, resources or leadership ability, she impacted the lives of many, even as an underdog.

My family first heard of Mama Zipporah a few years ago – she has attracted small amounts of media attention – when my mother caught a documentary featuring her story on TV. After learning about Mama Zipporah, it came as no surprise to me when my mother, somewhat of a 'bleeding heart' when it comes to children, announced she was flying to Nairobi, the capital city of Kenya. Besides visiting a niece who lived there, my mother wanted to visit Mama's orphanage. She was planning to bring clothing and toys to the orphanage, but later returned with a new mission in life – to do what she could here in Canada in her own small way to bring a greater awareness to these AIDS orphans on the other side of the world. What I didn't realize was the impact this would have on our family.

> "The increased spiral of adult deaths in so many countries means that the number of children orphaned each day is expanding exponentially. Africa is staggering under the load.[3]"
>
> *– Stephen Lewis, UN Secretary General's special envoy for HIV/AIDS in Africa*

SMALL LEADER. BIG IMPACT

Mama Zipporah's efforts to create a better Kenya began in the '80s when she started a feeding program for the orphans in the slums of Nairobi. In her words, these children are victims of physical and sexual abuse, as well as neglect and abandonment, and were being routinely 'thrown out' by parents who either no longer wanted them or couldn't care for them because they had AIDS. Unable to continue being a mere observer to their misery, Mama Zipporah stepped in to help these children in her own small way. For some time, her efforts were supported by a large global fundraising organization. But the program's financial support was eventually pulled because she was not educated and was not a man. After years of feeding these orphaned children with some support from the local government, she was approached by seven of the orphans who had big plans – they wanted to get an education. Appreciating Mama's efforts, the Nairobi government asked her to consider starting an orphanage with its support.

She adopted all seven of the children into her small home while caring for her own three children and began what is now the Huruma Children's Home, on the edge of the beautiful Great Rift Valley. Moving to their small parcel of land in the Ngong Hills outside of Nairobi, Mama Zipporah and her husband built a shack of a home to make room for more children in need. I guess there's some truth in the saying "if you build it, they will come." Word of Mama's kindness and her small project spread throughout the community every day. She now provides shelter, food and clothing for hundreds of children in her expanding 'shack' and loving home, now a government-certified educational center.

accoun

> **AIDS ORPHANS INTELLIGENCE**
>
> **A children's issue around the world**
>
> Consider these statistics:
>
> • Every minute of every day, on average, a child dies of HIV/AIDS.
>
> • Every 14 seconds, a child loses a parent to AIDS-related causes.
>
> • By 2010, an estimated 18 million children are expected to have lost one or both parents to AIDS.[4]
>
> This is not just an African problem; this is the world's problem. If you don't start saving one child at a time, where do you start?

AGAINST ALL ODDS

Today, Mama Zipporah continues to drive change. Despite the challenges she faces, she continues to take personal responsibility for many of the abandoned children in her homeland. Her accountability and inner drive to make a difference, combined with passion and sense of purpose, are helping her beat the odds day by day as a leader in her community, a leader impacting a global issue.

How did she become accountable? Mama Zipporah made a choice to make a difference. While she started small, she had a noble and powerful purpose – to assume responsibility for the vulnerable children of her country, or as she sees them, the leaders of tomorrow. Who would have thought two decades later she would be running a large orphanage and a recognized educational center for her orphans and the community?

That's not to say things are rosy – being an accountable leader is not easy. In fact, things continue to be very difficult for the orphanage. Money is a scarce resource. So is food. Mama Zipporah, her family and small team of employees work together on a daily mission to get enough funding to buy food, clothing and supplies for the growing number of children, from a day old to 18 years of age, who continually come to her. The children also receive an education and life skills to help them succeed as adults in life.

> "It's my prayer I can raise a big team of children and teach them leadership qualities. My mission is to empower children in need to become productive members of society through rehabilitation, education and self-reliance skills."
>
> *– Mama Zipporah, leader and founder of Huruma Children's Home*

Perhaps we might consider Mama Zipporah lucky, because for the past decade she has had a clear sense of purpose – something some of us may never achieve in a lifetime.

Through sheer determination, courage, risk and selflessness, Mama Zipporah has managed to bring her small local African mission out into the world. Media interest has resulted in international volunteers and donations, and local fundraising has delivered thousands of dollars. Every penny of it is poured right back into the hands of these children. The funds have provided a well with clean drinking water for the orphanage, and a source of income, selling clean water to the local community. She is building a school, dormitories and even a business conference center for company meetings and local events to drive funds back into the orphanage.

I recently had the opportunity to ask Mama Zipporah what she believes are the most important reasons she has been able to overcome some insurmountable odds to succeed on her mission. Call it a higher power, unified consciousness, God, or whatever you want, Mama Zipporah believes that when you are living out what you're destined to do, some higher power steps in to make sure you get what you need. She sums up her success in three ways: (1) faithful partnerships – which will provide financial, spiritual, business or emotional support; (2) her conviction that we are each accountable for the world we live in and need to give back to those who are less fortunate; and (3) the ability to empower and educate the Kenyan children of today so that they can realize their potential in life.

tability

Be accountable. Give back. Take action. For many of us, leading a mission that faces such incredible odds would make us throw in the towel. But Mama Zipporah dreams of doing more – much more. With her passion and accountability to the growing number of orphans in Kenya, she is well on her way to bringing those bigger dreams for a better orphanage to reality.

I don't think leadership can get any better than this – making the world a better place. Nobody's passing the buck here.

The principle: Be accountable. The buck stops with you

The principle we're talking about in this chapter is accountability – your ability *and* willingness to step up to the plate and make a difference. Your willingness to take the good with the bad and own it.

> "The price of greatness is responsibility."
> – *Sir Winston Churchill*

Leadership books and business magazines are full of spectacular 'big gun' stories – amazing corporate leaders making zillions, hard-driving rock stars and visionaries who turn their inventions and dreams into gold. They dream big. They get rich. And they inspire. But there is a different kind of inspirational leadership out there that has nothing to do with money, celebrity or glory. It has everything to do with making a difference through accountability, impact and a belief in yourself as a leader.

While accountability is often defined with negative connotations like "liability," "answerability" or with a nasty business stigma like "you're going to be held responsible," accountability can take leaders to new heights. Accountability is one of the true differentiators between a *real* leader and a *figurehead.*

Accountability *unplugged*

Accountability = ownership. Taking a leadership role is to accept ownership of the task at hand, the team you're leading, and the mission you've taken on – for better or worse.

Like the other principles in this book, I view accountability as a powerful positive force and principle to lead with. An accountable leader who is willing to 'step up to the plate' will breed loyalty, respect and a team of willing players who will go the extra mile – where they themselves become accountable. Accountability has a certain sense of 'stickiness' to it. As a leader, if you hold yourself up to be accountable, it will encourage others to do the same. And the more you do it, the easier it becomes.

Accountability is a driving force. Just as Mama Zipporah created significant and positive change by assuming responsibility for Kenyan orphans, your own personal willingness to 'own' a project versus 'supporting' it will get you better results. Perhaps you've made the choice as a talented interior designer to start your own company and deliver a quality service – to 'own' what you create. Your service to create beautiful, functional spaces will improve your clients' lives and well-being. How you run your business will affect the small team supporting your company, your administrative staff, your right-hand man. And the results – your bottom line – will definitely impact you. Whether you achieve success or failure, no one else owns what you're creating. Entrepreneurialism is accountability. This is very different accountability, however, than the situation you've just read about in Africa. Regardless, being accountable ties into everything you do as a leader: how you run your business, the quality of service you offer, your attention to clients' needs, and ultimately, your results.

Accountability in business can be a real axis point – a central point upon which your leadership can be based. Being accountable should be one of the first decisions you make as a leader, and one of the first principles you add to your game plan. By introducing accountability into your plan, you create a solid foundation on which to build other powerful leadership principles. The return on your personal investment – loyalty, respect, synergy, connection, execution, team integration – will make the initial and ongoing efforts worthwhile.

Without accountability at some level, it's difficult to move things forward. In fact, it's damned near impossible. It has to start somewhere. Why not with you?

"Leadership is an action, not a position." – *Donald H. McGannon, former CEO Westinghouse Broadcasting Corporation*

IT ALL STARTS WITH YOU

Let's get back to business now. How can accountability start with you? Being accountable, in a nutshell, is the essence of what a leader should always do and be. In business, it's hard not to get caught up in actions that lead to personal gain – gains like compensation, promotions, job offers, high-profile projects, business politics. But if you remove these factors, and all the energy tied up trying to secure them, what are you left with?

You're back to the basics of leadership. You're ready to step up to the plate (some consider this sticking your neck out) on behalf of a group of people and move them toward a common goal, regardless of the outcome.

So now leadership has moved beyond being about you – it's bigger than you and for a greater purpose. It's about others: the team, the volunteers, the kids, the company, the people, and the results you all need to achieve together.

It's easy to find examples of accountable leadership in the work of humanitarians like Mama Zipporah. Besides, humanitarianism is all about giving back. Her mission in a world of circumstance far from our reality might be hard to grasp, and her principles of selflessness and charity might seem very different from the corporate objectives many of us strive to meet. There are more examples we can point to. In the world of exploration, there is the story of Sir Ernest Shakleton, an Antarctic expedition leader who has been described as "the greatest leader that ever came on God's Earth, bar none." He spent almost two years saving the lives of his 27 men stranded with him on his 1914 Antarctic expedition.[5] Despite horrific climatic conditions, his profound sense of accountability to the well-being of his crew resulted in death-defying leadership.

So what about the business world? Unfortunately, right now in North America, examples of accountability have been sorely lacking. Think Enron and WorldCom, for example. And in some ways it's not surprising. It's pretty hard to cultivate accountable leadership in a business environment fraught with change and instability. The loyalty factor needs work. Many of you will be far too familiar with team leaders who are quick to lay blame and point fingers or who are in denial about why their team failed. These figureheads are sitting comfortably with their feet up on a desk, poised to head for the hills when the going gets tough.

But let's not forget the guys like Robert Milton, former CEO of Air Canada, who endured years of hardship and near bankruptcy, only to get kicked even harder with some unexpected circumstance, such as 9/11. But instead of 'jumping ship' when the going got tougher, Milton weathered the storm. In fact, despite intense media criticism, he stuck around to launch an aggressive restructuring program, renegotiated labor agreements, leased brand new cost-efficient aircraft, increased passenger payload and delivered a new and highly competitive product, Tango. Eighteen months later and named CEO of the Year in *Report on Business Magazine,* Milton has 'reinvented' the company and positioned Air Canada for a healthy profit.[6] Now that's accountability.

Reality Check: Accountability = responsiveness

Accountability starts with you – but it has to exist at every level. In *The OZ Principle: Getting Results Through Individual and Organizational Accountability,* authors Roger Conners and Tom Smith describe accountability as existing at many levels:

Personal

"A personal choice to rise above one's circumstances and demonstrate the ownership necessary for achieving desired results – to See It, Own It, Solve It, and Do It."

Organizational

"This new view of accountability can help revitalize the business character, strengthen the global competitiveness of corporations, heighten innovation, improve the quality of products and services produced by companies worldwide, and increase the responsiveness of organizations to the needs and wants of customers and constituents."[7]

tability

RED FLAG **Watch out for Teflon coating**

Accountability and willingness to own a project, and the risks and challenges that might go with it, is one of the first steps you can take to 'walk the leadership talk.' Be careful not to fake it or just pay lip service to your goals and objectives – demonstrate it. Get in there, roll up your sleeves, support your team members and fight hard when the going gets tough. Don't become a 'Teflon-coated leader,' a business expression that refers to leaders who avoid having anything 'stick' to them when the project is going awry, cleverly escaping any responsibility or accountability. If a team senses a leader is going to head for the hills when things go off the rails, it'll be much tougher for that leader to get the team's respect, focus and dedication to the project.

How to be accountable

> "Success on any major scale requires you to accept responsibility...In the final analysis, the one quality that all successful people have is the ability to take on responsibility."
>
> *– Michael Korda, editor-in-chief, Simon & Schuster*

So you've recently been handed a project and you are ready to execute. How can you incorporate accountability into your game plan? Here's how:

1 Clear sense of purpose

To successfully create an environment of accountability, you need to be clear about what you are accountable for. Lack of clarity, direction or knowledge of what is expected can get you into trouble. It's tough leading in a 'gray zone' or with wishy-washy goals and objectives. Next thing you know, the finger is being pointed at you!

If you know what's expected of you, you'll be better able to manage the progress you and your team are making. And you'll be able to better align the team with the right tasks to support the goals. Numbers, performance measures, goals, objectives – all of these things will help you establish clarity of purpose. If they don't exist yet, well, create them.

Get the answers to these questions:

- What is expected of you and the team?
- What is the specific end goal?
- What goals do you need to achieve? By when?
- Are there any performance benchmarks you are expected to meet?
- Where does your job start and end?
- What other key players or teams will you have to work with to succeed?

The way things are moving these days, with business in a constant state of transition, it's not often that you will jump into a role that is clearly defined. You might not have clarity on how your team fits into the overall goals of the company, and it might be up to you to figure it out so that it makes a big difference.

When I first got out of the military, I found myself in the entirely different world of business, so I was not only unclear about how the corporate world operated but also what my responsibilities were in my first business position. As the operations manager for a long-haul tractor-trailer company, an industry I really didn't know much about, I needed to figure out where I, with my small operations team and large group of truckers, could have the most impact on the company's overall objectives. And there was a ton of potential! Early on, I was being asked on a monthly basis to submit reports such as mileage/accident ratios, costs of fuel and maintenance, fleet usage and performance.

The monthly reports served an important purpose – they highlighted exactly where I needed to focus and created different levels of accountability. My team's performance, right down to the frontline drivers, greatly affected the safety of the fleet, which would drive down operational costs and deliver optimum performance from our resources. We developed clear goals and objectives for each team member – from drivers and dispatchers to operations coordinators. And the entire team, as a whole, became accountable.

accoun

Reality Check: Share the success, own the failure!

Back in my boot camp days, accountability was what I call an 'extreme' leadership principle. It was emphasized over and over again. One of my favorite drill sergeants put it something like this:

"Officer cadet, a couple things you need to know about leadership: You are accountable for the mission. That means you get to share the success with everyone on the team. But if the mission fails – you own it. Because if anyone on your team has failed, then you haven't been doing your job as the leader!"

No one ever said leadership was going to be easy, right?

2 Have the guts

One of the first commitments you can make to yourself and your team is to be personally responsible for the progress and overall results of your work. In other words, lead by example. When things go wrong, don't pass the buck. But do expect accountability from your team members.

I remember when I was a new second lieutenant stationed on my first air force base. Occasionally, we had to practice war games – military exercises that would last several days – to ensure our readiness, should the country's national security be under any threat (you'll read all about the trials and tribulations of this experience in Chapter 03). My role was as a platoon commander for the base defense force, a large team of soldiers responsible for guarding vulnerable locations on the base, including communications, command posts, headquarters, ventilation for the underground operations center, etc. On a particular exercise, we were conducting a 48-hour exercise, and I was responsible for establishing shifts and duties for dozens of soldiers around the clock. The problem was that it was the middle of winter in Northern Canada, about –25 degrees Celsius (–13 degrees Fahrenheit) with the wind chill factor, and I did not really have enough people to cover all the positions.

I quickly toured all the troop positions with my right-hand man, a warrant officer with 25 years' experience. After asking the troops if they were fine, we decided to leave the group in their current positions for one more hour, despite the cold, to allow the other shift to get some rest.

Wouldn't you know it, after we relieved this shift, one of the corporals made her way to the medical team because her feet were frozen – she had frostbite! How did my boss see it the next day when we debriefed the exercise? Despite taking precautions to check up on the troops, the frostbitten toes were my problem. The buck stopped right on my desk as the team leader.

RED FLAG Act like you're in charge

With barely a few months on the job as a second lieutenant, I was responsible for one of my troops getting frostbite (see "Have the Guts"). My colonel told me that I was off the hook for this "failure" because I had so little time under my belt. Instead, my experienced warrant officer was being held responsible for failing to keep a better eye on the troops. The colonel was teaching me a very important lesson. "But," (there's always a "but," isn't there?) he emphasized, "to be an effective leader you are responsible for the performance of your entire team – no matter who you've got working for you, no matter what your experience level. That's why you're an officer. Ultimately, you want to be in charge and you want your team to *believe* you are in charge. So you need to act like it."

He was right. I could pass the buck for the frozen toes due to my limited experience. But I knew deep down inside, to be taken seriously and move quickly from rookie to effective leader, I needed to accept where I needed to improve. I wanted to be accountable, not Teflon-coated.

3 Share accountability

The neat thing about accountability is that you're not in it entirely alone! Acting accountable creates accountability. Most people want ownership – your team players want something to call their own.

Be accountable – then share accountability. Let everyone on the team own a piece of the pie. Support team members so

tability

In the HOT SEAT

WANT YOUR TEAM TO STICK ITS NECK OUT?

It doesn't get much faster than the racing car business. So when your 'lean and mean' team is focused on delivering the crown jewel in the Champ Car World Series – Champ Car Grand Prix of Toronto – you need each and every player to step up to the plate.

Charlie Johnstone, the president and CEO of the Grand Prix Association of Toronto has to create an agile, decisive, make-it-happen team to deliver a world-class event. And big events come with big goals:

- 175,000 spectators
- $45 million of economic impact annually for the city of Toronto
- Raise hundreds of thousands of dollars annually to give to the Grand Prix Charitable Foundation, which has donated more than $5 million to children's charities

How does he do it? He creates that accountable environment with a team-based, solutions-based mindset.

"We have a problem, now what's the solution?" is Johnstone's mantra. Recently, one of his leaders made an overzealous commitment with a radio station for some public relations and marketing for this world-class event in return for 1,000 spectator seats. But the commitment would cost organizers the sale of 1,000 seats, something the event could not afford. Johnstone's response: "We don't have time to dwell on the mistakes that team members are inevitably going to make. The race date is not going to change."

Johnstone always expects the entire team to work together to examine the big picture and come up with a solution. As he puts it, no one can work as "an island" or in isolation. In this case, the team decided to move these spectator seats to another more affordable location and bundle the seats with some attractive giveaways for the winning spectators.

Your team needs to know that when they get into trouble, you are going to provide support. It's up to you as the leader to provide that safety net.

they don't fear failure. If they do, they'll be reluctant to do what's needed for success. When you lead a team with this principle, you can expect a team that will be willing to go the extra mile.

▶▶ **Fast forward** *to Chapter 08, "Link Your Team to the Mission." You'll read about some simple tools, such as the stoplight status report, to help you manage team accountability.*

What's in it for you... and your team?

Distinguish yourself! When you choose to be accountable, whether you're leading a team of three or 300, you can't help but have an impact on your work, team and the organization.

And that's a good thing. Would you rather be remembered as someone who stuck their neck out, or be forgotten as the Average Joe leader? You've made the right choice. Here's what being accountable can mean for both you and your team:

✓ **Accountability creates accountability**

Several years ago, I had a team of 25 or so export operations specialists who were responsible for coordinating shipments of telecommunications gear for Nortel Networks to more than 125 countries around the world. The work was intense and very exciting since each of these specialists dealt with customers in countries that most people had never even heard of.

All of the specialists reported directly to me, and it became a problem when I had people lined up at my door for a variety of different reasons. Needless to say, I wasn't getting much of my work done.

I decided to split this group into two regional teams – North and South American and Europe/Middle East/Africa, and Asia-South-Pacific teams. Each team was assigned a leader who was responsible for both her specialists and specific goals and objectives for those regions.

The result? A stronger team vision and clear team identity with a new regional focus. The teams and individual team players knew how and where they were impacting our overall goals.

accoun

The result: willing and shared accountability. And it had a big impact – on operations, productivity and morale.

✓ **Support down = loyalty up**

When you share accountability, a reciprocal effect occurs. Your team is willing to put their necks on the line for you, and in turn, create loyalty. There's something about working for a leader who you know will support you, behind the scenes, all the time, and is ready to step in if you ever need her.

✓ **Small teams. Big impact**

Accountable leaders create accountable team players. Here's where you can expect to have an impact on your team and the overall mission:

Teams & People (partners, team members, staff)	**Mission Impact** (project, department, company, charity)
• Personal development and growth	• Goals and objectives
• Sense of value at work	• Money, revenue, profits, stock
• Promotion	• New programs or processes
• Salary	• Improved current processes
• Rewards and recognition	• Team pride
• Career path	• Progress and momentum
• Employee satisfaction	• Customer satisfaction
• Professional training	• Success or failure

▶▶ **Fast forward** *to Chapter 06, "Spark Creativity" for more on the 30-60-90-day quick-hit plan and how to manage accountability as a leader.*

Hindsight is 20/20

Don't pass the buck

Unfortunately, today's business world is full of leaders who want the perks and privileges that come with rank and title, but they don't want to deal with the tough stuff. I call this *accountability avoidance behavior,* which ties right in with our earlier discussion on Teflon coating – slippery behavior where nothing really sticks. Some leaders have a way of sliding in and out of meetings or from project to project without owning any part of it.

I once had a product subject matter expert (also known as a SME) who would attend many of our product launch meetings when I worked in high tech. He always seemed to come to meetings and drop a 'bomb' on the conference table – things like "you can't do that, our team won't approve it" or "we're not ready to provide you with that program yet." Apparently, in his mind, his role on the team was simply to consult, which then translated in his mind into 'not required to take action.'

This would have been acceptable, if that had, in fact, been the agreed-to mandate. But it wasn't. What the team expected from this individual, and all other leaders at the meeting, was the solution. Mission-critical projects need action-oriented players, not bomb-droppers. Let's face it, with near impossible time lines and all of us working for the same team, everybody needs to jump in and help. We all work toward the same big goals and objectives – to help our company sell its products or services, with less time and resources in a highly competitive environment.

If you're going to deliver the bad news and you're accountable to the team, then help provide the solution to clean up the mess.

In time, this SME found some reason not to return to this project – too busy, other tasks were calling. I replaced him with someone who was willing to step up to the plate.

If you or others on the team shift responsibility or lack accountability, it reflects poorly on the leader. And there is a lot at stake:

- credibility
- respect
- trust that you mean what you say, you'll support the team and you'll do what is right for the people and organization
- a desire to follow you

Don't pass the buck. Honor what you sign up for. Be accountable and build a culture of accountability.

What's next?

As you step up to the plate and get ready to break new ground in your field, it helps to know that there are many people before you who have taken a successful leap of faith, probably even on a similar path, and can provide you with insight and support.

Leadership takes guts and it takes inner drive. Use that inner drive during your 'rookie phase' to your total advantage. Keep learning from the many success stories around you – because just like you, those leaders wanted leadership as much as you do. You've got to really want it!

accoun

ACTION PLAN

Share success, own failure

1 GET CLARITY OF PURPOSE.

- It's tough to step up to the plate if you're not sure what the batting order is or what inning you're in

2 LEAD FROM THE FRONT.

- Accountability creates accountability
- Demonstrate your accountability by sharing goals and progress – good or bad

3 HAVE THE GUTS.

- Prepare to take on the entire experience
- When things go wrong, don't pass the buck

4 PROVIDE A SAFETY NET.

- Expecting accountability means your team players should 'stick out their necks' – with your support
- Make sure you're available behind the scenes just in case your team players need you to help fight a small battle or solve an issue

tability

EARN YOUR STRIPES

I must believe
I'm a rocketman
I'm a superstar
I can be anyone
I can step beyond
All of my boundaries

Use the Force, Jamiroquai

INNER DRIVE

Breaking new ground

Balance drive with humility

School of hard knocks

New leaders are made from great followers

You gotta really want it

Right between the eyes

Wham! Some things just hit you right between the eyes. As you step into a leadership role, your 'rookie lessons' will be coming at you fast and furious. You might occasionally find yourself landing right on your butt. But don't despair because that's part of being a rookie – learning fast and earning your stripes. Pick yourself up, brush yourself off and get back at it. And don't forget those rookie lessons, because they will serve you very well for years to come.

Almost 20 years later, I still remember the lessons that knocked my colleagues and me right off our feet while we were leading in the early days. Today, I'm still using some of those same lessons as I continually break new personal ground and learn new things. The past years have also taught me how much you rely on those around you, your team – it always comes down to people.

Rewind. Boot camp 1986. Boot camp was where I started 'earning my stripes' as a leader. To this day, the 13 weeks of training has probably been the longest and most miserable time in my life. At the same time, it was also a period of great leadership insight.

Time: 0530 hours. The sun was barely up and the sergeants were already hollering while we were running at the break of dawn. "Let's go! Let's go! Let's go! Let's go." Some days we were out there, with 20- to 30-pound rucksacks, weapons slung over our shoulders, in combat boots, absolutely drenched in the pouring rain. We were training in the Rocky Mountains in the early winter and it was wet. Very wet.

Then there were the 'leadership assessments.' The entire experience of boot camp puts you on edge, but there's nothing like leadership task days. During these days, you're put in charge, you're 'in the hot seat' and assessed as a leader, possibly for the first time in your life. Cadets are called up one by one to lead different tasks for a short period of time. That was when your stomach dropped to your toes. All day long, you watch as other cadets execute their tasks and you believe you have this leadership task thing all figured out; that is, until your name is called. Then all hell breaks loose! It's always easier sitting on the sidelines and being a follower than it is being in the hot seat. Down deep, as I watched the other cadets screw up, I would get a false sense of confidence: When it's my turn, there's no way I'm going to mess up like that! I thought. That's what you think. Wait for it kiddo!

Now it's your turn. Panic sets in as you suddenly realize all eyes are on you, waiting, watching and silently critiquing every step you take. And you're thinking to yourself, "I have no clue where to start. I should have paid more attention to those leadership lectures…Can somebody please help me?"

> "Today's business leaders are coming to realize what the military has known for 150 years: simulation allows managers at all levels to practice converting informed choice into timely action. From such practice comes faster decisions, crisper execution and better integration." – Fast Company *magazine*

SIMULATING LEADERSHIP

One of the leadership tasks required during boot camp training was building a life raft for a simulated airplane crash – a favorite with our boot camp 'directing staff.' All of the tasks seemed to be about crashed airplanes, huge chemical spills or other impossible missions. Needless to say, most of us knew nothing about where to start with any of these unfamiliar tasks, but I guess that's what made it all that much more 'fun!' Here's what some of the 'fun' scenarios were like:

- There has been a terrible airplane crash and you've landed around water. You and your team of survivors need to build a life raft to reach a populated area. (You've got to be kidding!)
- Search and rescue helicopters are flying in for a medical evacuation in 30 minutes. Build a helicopter landing pad – now! (Won't this patch on the ground do?)
- We need shelter, a medical area, and a mess tent to feed hundreds of troops. Your task is to put together a 100-man tent. (I had a hard time putting up a two-man tent.)

inner

Reality Check: When you're up, you're up

It never ceases to amaze me how so many 'team players' on today's hot reality shows *(Survivor, The Apprentice)* fail to appreciate a very simple concept: How you support your team as a member will influence how much support you get from other teammates once it's your turn to lead. Keep that lesson in mind as you make progress up the corporate ladder. As we used to say in the military, "loyalty up equals loyalty down."

▶▶ **Fast forward** *to Chapter 05, "What Goes Around Comes Around," to get more insight on the subject of loyalty.*

GREAT LEADERS START SOMEWHERE

Boot camp was as much about being a strong team player as it was about building strong leaders – and the sergeants who conducted it made sure you got that point loud and clear. During one of the life raft tasks, one cadet was leading the task in the usual state of panic and confusion. I mean let's face it, most of us were in our late teens or early twenties and really had no idea how to lead anything. We all looked on as this particular cadet made notes furiously, trying in desperation to come up with a plan. One of our fellow cadets, Adams (we all called each other by our last names), kept yelling out loud that the cadet in charge wasn't leading us and no one really knew what to do – in an effort to sabotage the cadet in the lead. Most of us empathized with this poor cadet leader and tried to jump in, offering help, getting things organized for him – anything to make it look like we were occupied so the sergeants would believe things were under control. But Adams just kept criticizing loudly about the lack of direction and subsequent confusion.

Thankfully, one of the sergeants saw right through Adams' intentions. This was boot camp after all, and one of the most important lessons being taught was the value of teamwork and being the best team member possible when you're not in a leadership position – adopting a 'one die, all die' philosophy. The sergeants were on the lookout for guys like Adams, and anyone who wasn't acting in the best interests of the team or the overall mission – in this case, building a life raft. So they made a point of Adams making a point. "Adams, stop 'blading' your buddies! Why aren't you in there, providing support or making suggestions to help?! What kind of team player are you? Consider yourself in charge of the next task, we'll see how you make out!"

Life has a funny way of teaching us lessons. Adams was no better than the last leader – like him, he started out somewhat panic-stricken minutes after receiving his orders, then switched to running around for the next few minutes. Had the sergeant not pointed out the importance of being a team player moments earlier, I may have been just as happy to watch the little bugger die a slow leadership death. But we all got the sergeant's message about the importance of being a loyal and supportive team player and we all knew our turn would come up soon. Adams, on the other hand, never did get it. After several failed tasks and more undermining behavior, officer cadet Adams was deemed not fit for leadership and tossed out of boot camp.

RED FLAG

Don't 'blade' your buddies or your boss

It's easy to sit on the sidelines of the action and criticize poor leadership. Pitch in, use your initiative, offer support, make suggestions. Do something! One day you'll be in the hot seat, looking for that team player with energy, ideas and a willingness to make things happen.

SITUATION. MISSION. EXECUTION

My turn to lead a mission was still to come and if I thought the life raft exercise was bad, I hadn't seen anything yet. By the time I received my warning order (the initial details of my task), we had already had some exercise doozies – building a life raft, constructing an observation post to watch for enemy infiltrators, and some poor sucker had to figure out how to build his and hers latrines. My mission: to build a landing pad for the helicopters that were on their way to provide emergency casualty evacuation for an "airplane crash." Like the other cadets,

drive

I had 20 minutes and a team of seven cadets to get the job done. So I might have been a little gullible at the time, but for a brief minute or two, the sergeants had me convinced that these choppers were actually on their way. One never knew what to expect when playing war games.

There I stood, frozen in my combat boots. Then I remembered the platoon commander's aide-mémoire in my combat pant pocket – a small how-to guide on everything you needed to know about leadership, which had been handed out to all of us fledgling platoon commanders during the first week of boot camp. Unfortunately, as I flipped through it in my state of panic, looking for that chapter on how to build a helicopter landing pad, all I could find were pages and pages of unfamiliar military acronyms such as, "5. Regp (incl att sp units)" and "Sit, En Forces, Atts and Dets." – abbreviations for things like 'situation' and 'enemy forces' to remind the platoon commander of the many necessary items he or she had to plan for and communicate to the troops.

Time was flying by and reading this gobbledygook was getting me nowhere. As important as this guide was to missions, it wasn't going to help me this time.

PLANS INTO REALITY

I had to get over to my small team sitting in the rain and tell them what we needed to do. Then I got a sudden brain wave and thought to myself, who's your second-in-command? During the first two weeks of camp, we were continually drilled on appointing a second-in-command, otherwise known as a 2 i/c – your right-hand man to provide support. A gut feel led me to a guy named Zientek. Gut feel and the fact that I knew he had been a sergeant in the army reserves for years, so he was likely a boot camp veteran who knew a lot more about surviving these mini-missions than the rest of us. Within minutes, Zientek gave me a couple of great ideas and applied them to my task. We split up the team in two – one group was to find a suitable area to build the landing pad and the other would take inventory of the equipment we had to build it.

Reality Check: Leverage your team's wisdom and then execute

Pow! Two more powerful lessons that hit me right between the eyes as an officer cadet:

- Ask your followers for input. Their expertise can be critical to your success.
- Get good at executing your mission. Learn how to pull together a quick plan and then start turning those plans into reality.

Before I knew it, my time was up. After a serious debrief, I was advised that I had failed my mission. Ouch. I failed the mission because I had not executed the task. What did that mean? Basically, I had not turned plans into reality; I had not "made things happen." Although I had communicated effectively with my entire team and had assigned team players to specific tasks, my planning was weak and my execution was even weaker. Damn. Next time, I thought, I'll definitely pay better attention to those leadership lectures – lessons that included one very simple and powerful planning tool that could help any leader identify the overall situation, specify the team's mission and use a 'quick and dirty' framework to whip up an execution plan. Identifying the situation, mission and execution was what I needed to do in this case. I learned that weak planning meant poor execution.

My first failure was a devastating blow. But in the grand scheme of things, it was only a tiny glimpse of the bumps and hurdles I would experience in the real world, all with profound leadership lessons.

While leadership is an exciting journey, it sometimes comes with failure, and you need to be prepared to stay the course just the same. You've gotta really want leadership.

I'm not trying to scare you off the leadership path, but I want to emphasize that you must embrace the rookie phase and every lesson in it that crosses your path, including the tasks that knock you down on your derriere.

It's all about earning your stripes. Those are the lessons that will last a lifetime.

▶▶ **Fast forward** *to Chapter 07, "Combining Forces" and Chapter 10, "Executing Quick, Dirty and Sometimes Flawed" for more on leveraging your team and developing a simple execution plan.*

The principle: Earn your stripes

There's a process you'll likely follow during the rookie phase of leadership before you can earn your stripes. You will have to work hard, learn tough lessons and gain experience before you can receive those symbols of accomplishment – tangible things like position, title, rank, a diploma, a medal; plus, less tangible, but very important things, like respect and credibility. Each step of the way, one task at a time, you'll find yourself having to balance a ferocious inner drive with wise humility when making decisions to gain that much-needed respect as a leader.

Part of that process means that you'll also have to accept that you don't know everything – you don't know what you don't know yet – and you'll need to rely on others, above and below your rank, to accomplish certain jobs and succeed through this roller-coaster stage. Gain the support from people around you, such as team members, other leaders, mentors, family and friends, in the following ways:

- Partner with people who can provide support;
- Get direction and advice when you need it;
- Don't ever forget the help you had to get there!

Then you need to leverage that advice and your team so you can start earning your stripes. Know that you're going to screw up and recognize that you can maximize your learning from those inevitable hiccups. But most importantly, the phase is about having the guts and the desire to get you through the knowledge gaps and the hurdles that line your leadership path.

Once you earn your stripes, you can shoot for the stars.

"Good generals are made from great sergeants!"

– Major General (ret'd) Lewis MacKenzie

drive

RED FLAG **Once a rookie always a rookie?**

For those of us who tend to jump right into a challenge and continue to try new things, feeling like a rookie never really seems to go away. Here's how you might feel:

Apprehension: "This is a little scary."

Confusion: "Where do I start?"

Overwhelmed: "This is huge!"

Exhilaration: "I did it! I can't believe I made it! What's next?!"

Apprehension (here you go again): "How did I get myself into this now?"

"I have never been given a job that I felt qualified to handle." *– General Curtis LeMay, U.S. Air Force chief of staff, 1961-1965*

How to leverage your rookie phase

You will require a certain amount of humility as you proceed along your career path. Sure, you'll gain confidence, wisdom and years of experience that will remove a lot of the apprehension you naturally feel when moving into a new role. But I like General LeMay's philosophy (he's considered the father of the U.S. military Strategic Air Command). Chances are, when you're moving up the ladder, you'll be moving into a position that might feel bigger than you – not necessarily a bad thing, but it needs to be managed with a balance of confidence and humility.

So in a nutshell, here's my advice: Wise is the rookie leader who has the humility and self-assurance to accept advice and wisdom. Even wiser is the experienced leader who has the inner confidence and security to continue to do so!

Easier said than done; the tough part comes in the 'doing.' There is a certain inner conflict that comes with taking on a leadership role where confidence must be balanced with the humility required to accept direction.

Here's how you can leverage that rookie phase, even if you're in your 10th new position:

1 Get directions and be receptive

Anyone will do. The wisdom and inspiration you get during your leadership path doesn't have to come from people in big, sexy, high-profile positions. Look for the people who influence you, who energize you, and who demonstrate some key leadership qualities, regardless of their title, age or experience. You will get more impact from these people, no matter which industry or profession they come from.

Look around. You'll be amazed at the wealth of knowledge around you. I can think of so many different people I have received guidance from over the years:

• Colleagues and co-workers: While I was in a new exciting role, I remember complaining to one of my colleagues that I wasn't quite sure about the boundaries of my new job. I will never forget his matter-of-fact advice: just keep on grabbing whatever turf you want until someone "smacks you on the wrist," then you know you've gone too far!

• Wise followers: Wisdom does not always come with age or experience. I remember jumping into a global role at a new company and one of my very young team members who had joined the company only four years earlier was right out of university. He had great business savvy and insight on how to navigate around the inner workings of the company and the various personalities we'd be dealing with.

• Successful leaders: These days as a new entrepreneur, I'm learning a ton from any entrepreneur that crosses my path. It doesn't matter what line of business they are in – from valve manufacturers to camouflage suppliers to authors or software consultants, I get pumped when I hear their stories of courage, risk and accomplishment.

• Inspirational people I have never met: It doesn't necessarily take knowing someone or meeting someone to be inspired by them – and they don't have to be famous. But who isn't inspired by well-known personalities like Richard Branson, Oprah Winfrey, Heather Reismann, Bono, Madonna or Bill Gates? Then again, I'm just as inspired by some not-yet-famous personalities, such as Princess Superstar (you'll hear her story in Chapter 12). Go with what works for you.

Teammates. Army captains. Bosses. Chief operating officers. Junior team members. Depending on what you're looking for, they can all be valuable resources.

2 Free leadership lessons

What better way to gather wisdom than watching other leaders in action? I have learned a lot from being around the conference table over the years. And every team's conference table has its own culture and dynamics.

I remember as a very young second lieutenant going to wing commander 'O Groups,' which meant I was in a room full of military majors and colonels – senior leaders with a lot more gold bars on their epaulets than I had. As one of the leaders (albeit an extremely junior one), I was invited to attend the weekly meetings, along with all the other departments, to provide status reports on our organization and get briefed on what was going on – on the base, across the air force and with global military operations. Very intimidating. I learned very quickly how information flowed and the importance of being briefed on activities at every level of the organization. I also learned how each of these powerful men (yes, they were all men) had no problem 'blowing their own horn' – something women don't do quite so naturally.

Today, even as an executive, I often find myself in meetings with other leaders, watching and witnessing the impact of their actions or words, sometimes poor ones. Recently, I was present at yet another conference table with some of my employees. This was a high-tech director's meeting, also attended by many junior team members, most of whom worked for this director. During the meeting, she launched into a tirade about another executive in the company – actually a close colleague in the office next door – and accused him of being incompetent and not forward-thinking. I watched as her less-experienced team sat wide-eyed and speechless. She might have thought she appeared powerful to the team but she came across as untrustworthy and insecure, because as we heard in the earlier chapters, you never blade your buddies. My instinct was validated when my employees later mentioned to me how

inner

horrified they were to hear an executive harshly criticize a fellow colleague in front of the team.

So pay attention to the subtle (or not so subtle) dynamics at the conference table. The benefits can be big. Some things you might want to note: How is the senior executive keeping the global teleconference call on track with the many different personalities and personal agendas on the call? How is the community leader managing the disagreeable volunteer worker at the table? How is the project manager leading the team member who continually shows up to meetings without

Outside the corporate BOX

YOU'VE GOTTA REALLY WANT IT

I met ESPN football analyst Merril Hoge during the XXXVIII Super Bowl in 2004 in Houston. While chatting with this former professional running back in the jam-packed halls of the Hilton Hotel/NFL headquarters, I almost got knocked off my feet by a group of fans who rather aggressively asked for his photo and autograph. Hmmm, maybe I should be asking this guy for an autograph instead of giving him a hard time about not having a BlackBerry!

What these fans knew (and I didn't at the time) was that Merril was a bad-ass running back with the Pittsburgh Steelers and the Chicago Bears before he became an ESPN analyst. Of course, he didn't start out as a top running back. Like most rookies, he had more humble beginnings and made it to the top with the help of insight from teammates, veteran players/coaches and superstars.

Merril was inspired as a kid by an incredible professional football player, Walter Payton, an all-time NFL running back hero with the Chicago Bears. Known as Sweetness, Payton was recognized for his relentless training and preparation for the game as well as his speed, strength and drive.

During his rookie year, Hoge cleverly got the inside scoop on Payton when he participated in an arm-wrestling fundraising event in Vegas with one of Payton's teammates, then a rookie running back.

The rookie named Maurice told Merril that he had accepted the superstar's invite to train 'the hill' (a notoriously difficult and steep levee in Chicago). So he met up with Payton one Saturday morning, attacking the hill with a vengeance, proud of himself when he made it to the top. What he didn't realize was that this was just the warm-up; Payton told him they were going to run the hill 10 more times and then go do some interval training! Well, after attacking the hill three more times with his best effort, Maurice puked and decided it was time to pack it in.

According to Merril, Payton had an important message: *"If you want to be a superstar, you've gotta really want it!"* Merril knows exactly what that means. He was awarded the distinguished Steelers Iron Man of the Year for two consecutive years, battled physical conditions such as post-concussion syndrome and most recently survived non-Hodgkin's lymphoma cancer, and is now a successful sports celebrity, ESPN television and radio show host.

Principles Merril lives by:

- You've gotta really want it
- You can always *find a way*

Rookie lessons die hard.

completing her action items? Or, on a football team, how does the experienced quarterback encourage the team to finish a game with passion when they're losing miserably?

Free leadership insight is yours to take. All you have to do it sit back, relax and enjoy the experience as other leaders around you continually demonstrate the do's and don'ts.

LEADING WITH BALANCE

Leadership can pose many paradoxes, particularly as you take on a new team. Balancing the need to be confident and secure in your leadership abilities with the humility to accept wisdom from the team is one of them. It takes skill to keep that fine balance, but maintain the lead when required. Just remember humility in itself represents an innate inner strength.

> "Sometimes it's appropriate to take a step back and realize that you don't have to do it all by yourself. It can be difficult, though, for those who are too stubborn to take the risk of being humble enough to ask for help, or to take it when it is offered. Just remember that it's still your path, and you're unfolding, and accepting help now doesn't have to change that fact at all.[1]"
>
> *– Ma Deva Padma*

What's in it for you... and your team?

In a way, you're always following another leader – even when you've reached your pinnacle, someone or something will still be inspiring you. Understanding that you need support, knowledge and inspiration from all directions, either on or outside your team, will make you a stronger leader.

Merril Hoge's example is a good one. I think one of the best examples of this interlocking dynamic is in professional sports – an environment where the relationship of rookies and vets can impact a team's success. Think about it. The odds of reaching the professional level, such as the NFL, are huge. To get there, you already need to be a star, then you start all over again as a professional rookie. I bet that you won't meet an athlete out there whose success has not been profoundly and positively impacted by the guidance of other leaders – leaders who might have filled the role of coach, veteran team player or superstar athlete. As you keep climbing your way to the top, moving up into various leagues, building your experience, there is always someone else out there you can learn from. But don't get caught up in who you think is the 'right' person to be guiding you. Your boss may not be the coaching type, but someone else might have the wisdom you're looking for – an experienced team member, a colleague, another leader.

So what happens when you apply this principle, and really leverage your rookie phase to earn your stripes? Here's what's in it for you and your team:

✓ **School of hard knocks**

Leadership is a lifelong education where you move up that ladder with multiple lessons and experiences. Being open-minded to those leadership-defining lessons keeps you sharp. Sometimes the lessons might sting, but, hey, those are the ones you'll remember – for a long time.

✓ **Good leaders are made from great followers**

Remember: "Good generals are made from great sergeants." Being open to advice, guidance and support from those around you will help you get over the learning curve much more quickly. If you shut the door and stop the flow of good information, you'll limit the amount of insight you can get and prevent people from helping you in the future. And people can't help but respect a leader willing to take their advice.

✓ **Gain credibility and respect**

Avoid becoming the new hard-ass boss. If you take the high and humble road, your team will experience an open-minded, receptive leader willing to listen and learn from people at any level. The payback: trust, respect, a sense of value and an energized team.

inner

✓ Sharpen your leadership intuition

By tuning into those free leadership lessons, you will have a clear understanding of the leadership traits and principles that work – and you want to adopt. Nothing like witnessing others' failings to really start tuning into your own intuition. Nothing like witnessing other leaders' failings to help you target what areas you might want to pay attention to. Ask yourself this – if others are not performing well in a certain area, what do you feel is actually causing the issue? Dig deep, then start tuning into your own gut feel so you can develop your leadership intuition.

Hindsight is 20/20

Don't be a pompous ass

Congratulations, you're now a leader. That definitely deserves a pat on the back. Try to keep a couple of things in mind: Stay in touch with your followers, the very people who probably helped get you get where you are and will likely play a major part in your upcoming success. And remember – you don't know it all.

However, I've seen so many wannabe leaders forget this lesson – they strive to get promoted and then end up leading the very team they once worked with as a team member. This can be a pretty difficult position, but what do they do? The worst thing possible. Instead of gently transitioning from their role as team member to team leader, with a little grace and respect for those they are now leading, they blast into the new position, demanding an office and setting up the barricades.

My advice: Don't be a pompous ass, unless you've earned the right and the stripes. And even then, you don't really have the right, despite some brief moments of 'superstardom' in your career. No matter what, it's best not to forget HOW you got there and WHO helped get you there.

drive

What's next?

Ironically, after telling you that you need to balance inner drive and rookie intensity with humility and open-mindedness, I'm now going to suggest you get good at pissing people off! But not in a personal way, of course.

Sad but true, an important reality of good leadership is that you absolutely can't please everybody, nor should you try. I learned this lesson the hard way, but I learned it right at the beginning: During my rookie years, when you earn your stripes through hard work, lots of other people's wisdom and generally through 'school of hard knocks.' And those are the kind of lessons you never forget.

Lessons like, the sooner you focus on the mission at hand, and not who to please during a project, the better the chance you have for success.

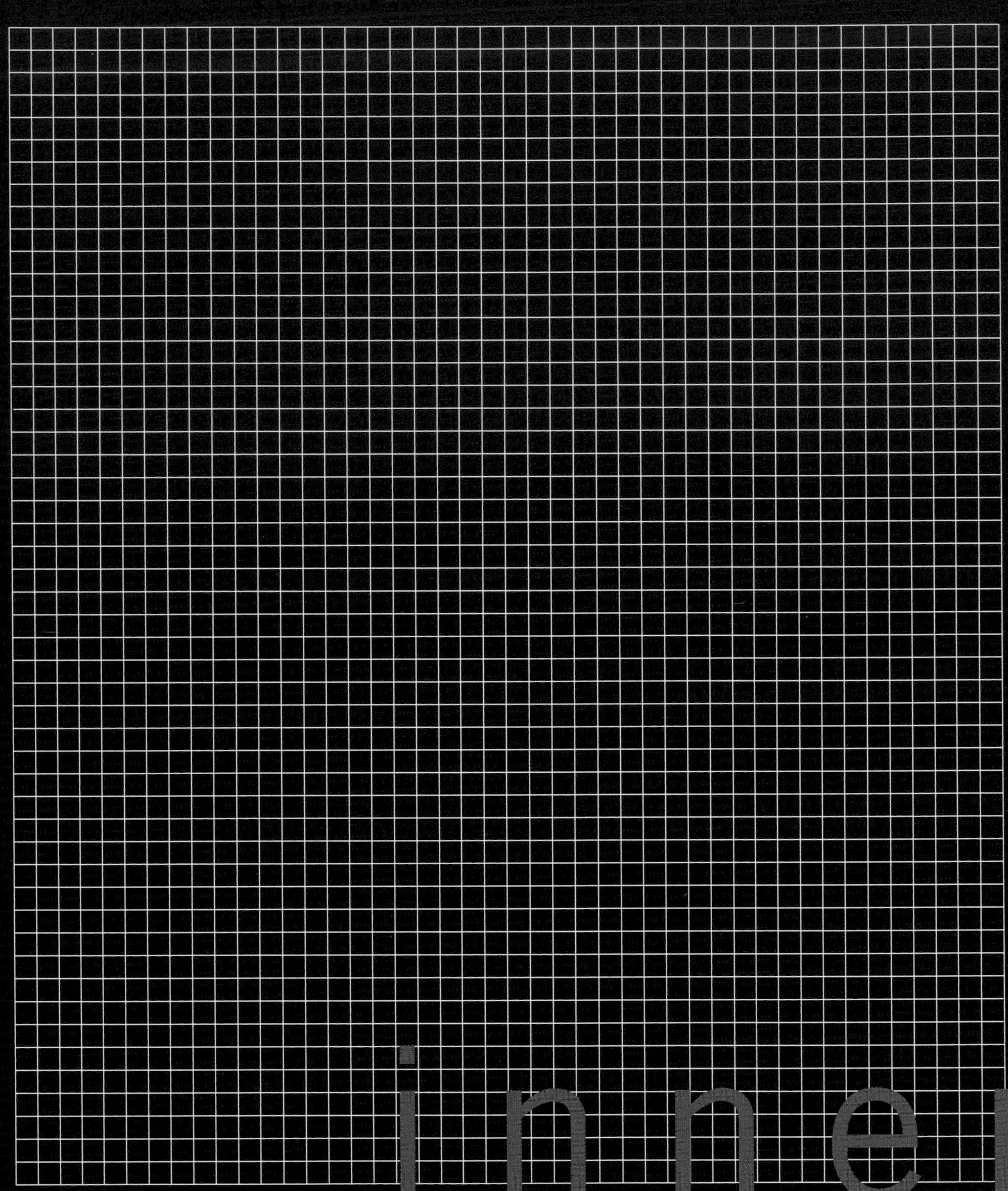

inner

ACTION PLAN

Adopt the rookie mindset

1 TAKE ADVANTAGE OF BEING A ROOKIE WHILE YOU CAN.

- You get some 'immunity' during the rookie phase but it won't last long
- Get a few of those inevitable mistakes under your belt

2 DON'T BE AFRAID TO ASK FOR DIRECTION.

- You're going to need support and guidance
- Be open to receiving guidance from all levels

3 OPEN YOUR EYES TO FREE LEADERSHIP LESSONS.

- Pay attention and listen closely to other leaders in their roles
- Don't forget: the boardroom is a great place for a leadership education

4 REMEMBER – "YOU'VE GOTTA REALLY WANT IT!"

- There's no denying it, leading yourself and a team at any level is not easy
- Accept that there will be challenges and then give it all you've got!

drive

YOU DON'T GET PAID TO BE LIKED

Close your eyes
listen closely
all that you've learnt
try to forget it
F*&% logic
Bravo to instincts

Sweet Intuition, Björk

CONVICTION

The new mindset

Perception perfection

Stand on your own two feet

Be prepared to piss people off

Going with the gut

Defending Canada

1986. I was posted to Canadian Forces North Bay for North American Aerospace Defence Command. The base was home to 414 Electronic Warfare Squadron, Fighter Group (FG) and 'the hole' – an underground three-story operations control center. As a second lieutenant, I was getting my first taste of one of the duties I would dislike the most but also learn the most from – war games. Even though I was a military officer, I was always in somewhat of a state of denial that I was, well, in the military. So upon reporting for duty and being advised that my secondary task was to defend the air force base, FG and the control center in times of heightened military readiness – let's just say I wasn't too thrilled. How exciting, I had an additional title as the base defence force (BDF) platoon commander. I could hardly wait to call home to my friends who were climbing their way up the corporate ladder at IBM. I just knew they would be impressed with my new fancy title.

The role of BDF platoon commander meant leading a large team of troops responsible for 'guarding' the base and any sensitive areas, such as communications towers, command centers, base headquarters (where the execs hung out) and ammunition compounds. Unfortunately, as I jumped into this role with less than enthusiasm, I did not start out on the right foot.

"You did what!?" Having a colonel yell at you is not the most comfortable experience. I had been summoned to base headquarters because the military police (read: very scary dudes) had written up a report in which I was the 'star.'

"Explain this to me again!" the colonel said to me after reading the report. "You thought it was a good idea to leave 150 weapons, unsecured, overnight, in a cafeteria because the troops were getting tired and needed to get home for some rest!? Lieutenant, do you realize this is a major security violation!?"

GOING AGAINST THE GUT

The only response that came to mind: "Well sir, putting it like that, I realize I've made an error in judgment, even though I knew in my gut it was not a smart decision at all."

When it came to these military war games, my leadership as platoon commander was just not shining through! After almost every exercise, I would end up in the colonel's office, explaining my actions for yet another bad decision. During a previous base exercise, which involved bitter winter weather (you've got to love those northern fighter bases), I had to account for a corporal's frostbitten toes. I hadn't followed an important military principle: Take care of your soldiers' welfare.

This time, the situation was a little different. My poor decision-making and our stash of unsecured weapons resulted in a serious breach of security. That breach could have impacted the entire air force base, which just happened to be sitting on top of a primary NORAD (North American Regional Air Defence) site. The site monitors air traffic over Canada and the rest of North America by the North Warning System, an extensive network of long- and short-range radars, which provide surveillance of potential attacks by aircraft, missiles or space vehicles.[1] In retrospect, I can see why the colonel and the military police had some concerns.

While filling out endless reports with the military police, I continued to explain my way out of this little mess. "Well, I talked to my warrant officers, and we decided that the weapons [50-plus FNC1 rifles], would be fine in the cafeteria unguarded until the next morning because we were all exhausted and needed sleep and…." As I was saying the words, I realized how ridiculous they sounded.

There were so many things to coordinate while leading this large team during base exercises – did I have enough resources to guard all the positions and do 24/7 rotation? Not usually! Had the troops been fed? What positions needed to be rotated at every new shift? Damn, we just lost 10 of our soldiers in a simulated attack at the base communications center! When can we get some sleep?!

But my explanations were really just poor excuses and the colonel wasn't buying them. I was in for an earful from the colonel. "I don't care what the warrant officer thought was a good idea. You're in charge and you made a bad decision," the colonel continued to reprimand. "You might just as well have handed over the weapons to the local criminal bike gang! What the hell were you thinking?"

Right about then I was thinking I was going to throttle one particular warrant officer who had persuaded me to make this dumb decision. All I could think about was how he could have led me astray like that. What I should have been asking myself was how did I let him lead me astray?

When I thought about it, the answer became obvious: I made the wrong decision because I did not want to be perceived as the 'bad guy' among my team. I didn't want to be the one that chose which team of soldiers guarded the premises for the next six to eight hours while the rest of us went home and slept. I didn't want to receive glaring sideway glances from the troops every time I stood up to make an announcement or walked through the platoon headquarters (HQ) because they were angry about a decision I made. You know the looks that tell you you're not respected, not liked, not supported. As a new leader, that can really shake your confidence.

RED FLAG

Perception perfection

I really disliked these war games at home, but they would only get worse when I was posted to Europe a couple of years later, just at the tail end of the cold war and the beginning of a whole new military era. In Europe, I would be 'bugged out' every month in the middle of the night – chemical warfare suits, gas masks, flak jackets and all – to practice more military 'readiness' (DEFense 'readiness' CONditions or DEFCONs as they were referred to) and logistics leadership in a simulated attack. Looking back, I realize these dreaded war games, which had a very real purpose, provided an interesting learning ground for some real and powerful leadership lessons.

So what led me to go against my better sense and intuition? Back in the platoon HQ, one of my warrant officers (I had two) managed to convince me that after a couple of days of this miserable and exhausting training, every soldier needed to get some rest. Lucky for us, the wing exercise commander, a more senior officer who plans the training, simulated attacks and scenarios for whatever we need to accomplish, had called a 'stand-down.' That meant "go home and get some much-needed rest or take a break from the subzero temperatures." Our platoon needed the stand-down possibly more than any other team. The troops were frozen, overworked and exhausted. My warrant officers – with 50 years of military experience between them – were pretty convincing. Send everyone home; we'll all come back in the morning, refreshed and ready to take on more tasks. After running on adrenaline and pretty bad military coffee for almost two days, why wouldn't I listen to them?

Except for one little thing. Gut feel.

My gut was telling me something else. We were a base defence force, which meant we all carried weapons that required special security procedures. Now if you know anything about weapons, you know that you don't just leave them out in the open without being locked up, right? In fact, you don't have to know anything about weapons at all to realize that. I knew that we should lock up our weapons – normal procedure was to take the weapons, breach blocks and all, to the 24/7 military police weapons lock-up. At the very least, our base defence force team needed to guard them. My gut, my intuition or perhaps just plain old common sense, was telling me that I should station four to six troops overnight to guard the weapons. Seems like a simple solution, but I gave in and let myself be convinced that no security measure – other than the cheap lock on the old door – would be required.

I made the popular decision and let everyone go home because the pressure to be a 'with-it' boss versus an 'unjust decision-maker' got the best of me. So, I did what lots of new leaders do – I did not listen closely to my own gut instinct.

I got what I deserved: a smack on the wrist and the personal humiliation of having to face my new colonel under these less-than-stellar circumstances. Next time, I thought, I would listen to my gut and do the right thing. That brief episode was enough to teach me a great lesson – leadership was not about 'perception perfection' or worrying so much about what others thought of me. It was about accomplishing the mission – reaching the end goal successfully. And having the conviction to do it.

The principle: You don't get paid to be liked

The sooner you face it, the better: You are not paid to be liked. This principle focuses on doing the right thing for your end goal and the big picture – whatever that picture may be. Maybe you're leading your own staff in a start-up company, or perhaps you're working with a large corporate group. Or maybe your team is a classroom of Grade 8 students. In each of these cases your end goal may be very different, but regardless, you will certainly have a tough time getting there if your primary focus is on 'being liked.'

Accept that not everyone is going to agree with how you do things, the decisions you reach, or some of the actions you take. Stepping away from the popularity contest to focus on your project's direction and progress will help you stay more objective and empower solid decision-making. Ultimately, you'll be a much stronger leader who will gain greater respect. So in the end, you'll still accomplish your goal and earn the team support – the same support you would have needed to win the popularity contest!

> "Failure is necessary to achieve success and maintain it. Otherwise, there is a danger of becoming arrogant or becoming afraid of losing.[2]"
> *– Billi Lim, failure guru*

I made some mistakes as a new leader and a second lieutenant, but if ever there was a 'right' time to mess up, it was then, early on in my career. Learning through mistakes at the beginning of any leadership experience will help you examine and leverage those important lessons so you can apply them again and again to future leadership challenges in any situation. As the saying goes 'fail first.'

Making the right decision instead of the popular one will require that you do the following:

- Be less concerned with what everyone thinks, something I call 'perception perfection.'
- Take the more difficult road instead of the line of least resistance.
- Develop your self-confidence and stand firm even among experienced teammates.
- Learn to trust your gut feel or that little voice that is inside you – your intuition.

I consider myself lucky to have made some pretty bad decisions early on. It didn't take me long to realize that I wasn't getting paid to be liked – I was getting paid to do the right thing. And this lesson has served me well over the years.

GET READY FOR IT

With the business world moving at a whole new pace, leaders don't have much time to get into the groove. Even if you're a new leader, chances are you won't have much of a grace period to get comfortable and confident. You'll be faced with making a tough decision before you know it. And it might be a very tough decision, or a decision that you have to make on the spot without time to get more information. It might even stop you in your tracks, causing you to second-guess yourself. In any case, if you focus first on the end goal and then the people or emotion side of things, you will maintain better clarity on the right thing to do.

The high-tech industry has been very volatile, and as a leader I have been faced several times in my career with the unfortunate task of having to lay off or fire someone. Getting rid of people – no matter what the reason – is a tough job and requires some tough decisions. For example, you need to get rid of 15 percent of your team – management doesn't care who. Who do you choose? The poor performer who happens to be filling a critical role? The single parent who is raising small children? Three or four other wonderful team players who are talented, hard workers but not in mission-critical roles?

There's no question: Making a decision that impacts people, outcomes, business and maybe even some success is difficult. As my master warrant officer used to say to me, being able to stand on your own two feet and make a decision "is what separates the boys from the men [or the girls from the women] and the men from the leaders." Adding this principle to your game plan mix is an essential ingredient for your success as a leader.

This type of decision-making will require a combination of:

- One part gut instinct;
- One part bouncing ideas off others;
- One part 'standing tall' and believing in yourself; and
- One part knowing you've done your absolute best, regardless of the outcome.

How to do the right thing, not the popular thing

You're going to face all sorts of hurdles, and some days you may wonder how you're going to get through it all. But that's what makes being a leader and sitting in the hot seat such a thrill.

Among your possible challenges you could be facing:

- Team players not pulling their weight
- Dysfunctional behavior such as bullying
- Layoffs due to poor business performance
- The majority of your team disagreeing with an important decision you've made

How do you set yourself up to do the right thing? Keep in mind the following points to help you deal with the pressure and manage perception perfection!

1 Business is business. Remove the emotion

At the end of the day, most of the challenge in making decisions or taking action has to do with the 'people factor.' We are social beings – we want and need to be accepted and supported. But in order to make decisions objectively, we need to step back and focus on what is logical in terms of the project, not necessarily what feels good in our heart.

Laying off one of your well-liked team players will not feel good. You'll be concerned about what he or she thinks of you as you're delivering the bad news. It's tough not to think about how much impact you have over someone's life. And you'll be concerned about what everybody else thinks too.

2 Remember the end goal

Always keep the end goal front and center. For example, in the short term you might need to develop some new customers; in the long term you may need to grow the business by 10 percent. Or maybe you need to cut operating costs by 20 percent.

That will keep you objective when faced with a tough challenge. What is the end goal? What are the key objectives that you and your team members are trying to attain? How is this challenge impacting that final goal? What final decision is far more likely to help you reach that goal?

▶▶ **Fast forward** *to Chapter 09, "Connect the Front Lines and the Big Picture" for more on how to keep your operations and tactics tied closely to your vision.*

3 Stand firm and stand UP!

People will challenge you, particularly if you've recently been promoted to a new leadership position. Consider it a rite of

Reality Check: Free speech

Leadership is often a balancing act. On the one hand, you want to empower people to speak up and challenge you on occasion to keep you sharp and thinking. On the other hand, you need to temper empowerment and the 'open forum, freedom of speech' environment since this can sometimes lead to 'cocky' or potentially disrespectful interactions, which can undermine your authority in the eyes of your team.

In this case, you will have to stand firm. Pull back on the reins, get things back on a respectful track and have a one-on-one meeting with the team player who is taking the empowered environment one step too far. A quick reminder behind closed doors of who's in charge might be necessary to reset the freedom that is being taken for granted.

"Making people mad was part of being a leader. As I learned long ago…an individual's hurt feelings run a distant second to the good of the service.[3]"

– Colin Powell, former chairman of the Joint Chiefs of Staff and 65th Secretary of State

passage as you enter a new role, 'earning your stripes' and surviving the 'tests' that are thrown your way to see how you handle them.

Over the years, I've had to deal with different team members throwing 'boss-challenging bombs' my way. Some of your 'bombs' may be packed with disrespect and undermine your credibility. This is when you'll need to believe in yourself, stand up for your decisions and have confidence in what you're doing.

4 Think success. Not popularity

If you think you're doing a good job as a leader based on the fact that everybody likes you and the decisions you make, you might be missing the mark. Think about whether your focus is on pleasing people rather than producing profit.

Take a step back and review your decisions and actions. Are you making decisions solely on the target without taking into consideration any team concerns? Or perhaps you're at

Outside the corporate BOX

DON'T TAKE IT PERSONALLY

How do you produce a live national television show five days a week and meet the corporate goals of increasing viewers, delivering high-quality programming and newsworthy information – all with a team of volunteers?

The last thing Karen McLaughlin is concerned about while 'leading in the moment' is her popularity. She has a one-hour mission. And everyone is watching. Karen is the producer of "*daytime*", a community-focused television talk show that delivers local information and entertainment. In fact, it's the people in the community that create the show: Karen's team is made up mainly of volunteers.

This national cable television station, and others like it, trains thousands of volunteers to work beside professional producers like Karen to deliver programming to millions of customers. It's no wonder Karen is sometimes affectionately called 'the crazy lady' when things get hot.

To succeed in a dynamic environment with a changing team of volunteers, Karen always sticks to these principles:

- Always think ahead: What could go wrong? What's the backup plan? You always need a backup plan – in live television you can always plan for the unexpected and something usually goes wrong.
- Instill a sense of urgency: make sure everyone is clear about roles, positions and show times; a 'timing watchdog' equipped with a stopwatch is critical to keep the right pace.
- Don't let anyone take anything personally! When you're accountable, you've got to do what you've got to do.

"You've got to ride the adrenaline rush – you've really got to love what you're doing. You can't worry about what people are thinking of you. I always tell my team before a show not to take anything that happens while we're filming live personally. This is live television and when the clock is ticking in that control room and you're the one that is accountable, you're going to have to yell once in a while!"
– Karen McLaughlin, daytime *television producer*

convi

the other end of the spectrum, taking great care of your team's 'wish list' – allowing team members time off for 'nice-to-have-but-not-mission-critical' training, or letting others move to a flex-time schedule to suit their family needs. How much longer is it taking you to reach your goal and are you still able to deliver on time?

The idea is to strike a balance. You can't lose sight of your team but you need their support and motivation while you concentrate on the mission. And as long as you generally balance the interests of the team with the goals of the organization, most people will understand radical mission-focused decisions when reaching the target is at stake.

Sometimes the organizational goals outweigh the people factor; sometimes the people factor is paramount. Nevertheless, as long as the team realizes that they are a valued part of the overall process, you, as boss, will create an environment of:

- Respect
- Trust
- Credibility
- Loyalty

RED FLAG **Taking the end goal too far**

We've established the need to maintain a crystal clear focus on the end goal so you don't get too sidetracked with emotion, popularity, etc. That said, it's critical to remember that leadership is always a balancing act. Beware of taking the mission too far and being so tied to the bottom line that you tromp all over your team. That just isn't cool. And it won't work for you for very long either – unless you offer some other powerful incentives – big compensation packages, heavy-duty stock options – to keep that team on board. Your team's motivation to support you and the mission are critical to your overall success.

Yes, you need to stay focused on results – targets like launching a new product by a certain date, increasing revenue by 15 percent, expanding your sponsorship program, increasing your school's grade point average. But you absolutely must keep top of mind how you're going to achieve success. And achieve it with your team.

What's in it for you... and your team?

Once you accept that it's important to be respected for your leadership ability rather than your 'likeability,' then you open the door to more freedom and success. Here's what you can expect when you add the principle 'you are not paid to be liked' to your game plan:

✓ **More freedom**

Even if you're a truly amazing boss, there will always be someone who doesn't like your style of management or decision-making. So you might as well take away the 'pressure to please,' because you only have a 50-50 chance of doing so anyway. And when you remove that pressure and accept that some grumbling is inevitable, your hands are no longer tied behind your back. Expecting criticism releases you and allows you to stand on your own two feet.

✓ **Better decisions**

Being concerned with pleasing everyone will only cloud your judgment, options, actions and decisions. To be effective, remove the mental clutter and focus on staying objective. Give yourself permission to focus on what's really important to get the job done. Your objectives may require a focus on people – you might have to add new skill sets, cross-train current team members or change people's roles. If you're worried about disrupting the team's current dynamics, you might not be able to make the changes necessary to reach your target just yet. You may have to focus on people, but that doesn't necessarily mean you have to please them.

✓ **Less wavering, more respect**

Wishy-washy leadership is very frustrating, to say the least. And being wishy-washy is a direct result of indecisiveness, which can tie right into being too concerned with what the team will think. Working for an objective and decisive leader supports project momentum and can result in better overall action. And that means you'll also have a motivated team that respects you for making the right choices instead of just the popular ones.

Hindsight is 20/20

Beware of butt kissing

As a very young entrepreneur, John Ferraro started selling meat from the back of a minivan. A decade later, Retail Ready Foods has reached upwards of $85 million in annual sales and continues to grow exponentially. His latest venture, a risk management company that derives 'forward contracts' for cuts of beef from the live cattle futures market, is just one more example of his visionary leadership. In Ferraro's world, CEO seems to stand more for 'chief entrepreneur and opportunist.' It certainly seems to be what he does best.

Ferraro always run his own show (I would be remiss if I didn't mention that he has a fabulous right-hand woman to assist him). But he has had his setbacks – and some of them have come from trying to be his employees' friend.

"I spent years trying to be friends with the people on my team. As a young manager, I wanted to be liked. I socialized and hung out with the people who I hired, who worked for me, and were responsible in helping me drive my business forward. Although there is a lot to be said for empowerment and a fun working atmosphere, if you don't manage it well, this can be a very dangerous scenario. The end result for me, in some cases, has been employees whose energy has been focused on what I want to hear instead of what I need to hear and what's right for the business."

If you focus on being liked instead of respected, you can expect the following:

- Sanctioning a 'kiss the boss's butt' atmosphere or a team of 'yes men,' which results in people focusing on pleasing you instead of telling you what's really going on. Very dangerous!
- Becoming completely equal with your team, making it difficult to take the lead when things get tough
- Inaccurate information from the front lines
- Missed opportunities – if you don't have accurate information, how will you know what's really going on?

"Creating a team of people that wants to please you instead of doing the right thing stagnates your business. If your priority is making friends or getting your butt kissed you are missing out on a lot of lost opportunity!"

– John Ferraro, chief entrepreneur and opportunist, Retail Ready Foods, Mississauga, Canada

What's next?

Sometimes you have to take the emotion out of leadership. Once you have the inner strength to hold your ground on tough decisions and establish yourself as a credible leader, you're good to go. Respect and credibility are important 'power tools' for your leadership toolbox.

Leadership is a balancing act – you'll read that a lot in this book. Once you've figured out the importance of standing firm on decisions, you'll also need to connect with your team players to achieve success.

Sound a little contradictory? Perhaps. But that's all part of the fun and challenge.

Being able to connect at a real grass roots level with your team, while at the same time able to pull back objectively, is a powerful leadership balance. Sure, you don't get paid to be liked, but that does not mean you should create barriers between yourself and the very people who are going to help you make it happen! Once you've developed your own leadership balance and have solid footing based on confidence, strong common sense and good 'gut feel,' you can filter back in some of those leadership qualities that you do get paid for. Really getting to know your people will increase everyone's potential.

Make the connection.

convi

ACTION PLAN

Think end goal – not popularity

1 SOUND AND TIMELY DECISIONS ARE A PART OF YOUR REALITY!

- This might be easier said than done but it's very real
- You'll be required to make fast decisions without the complete or big picture
- You might lose sleep over some of the decisions you need to make

2 POPULARITY IS NOT A REALISTIC GOAL. RESULTS ARE.

- Don't get caught trying to be liked – it's a no-win situation
- Beware the need for approval – you'll stray from the end goal
- You can't do it alone. Surround yourself with people whose opinions you respect and trust, so that when you do need team insight, input or 'buy-in' for decisions, you know your talent and who you can trust

3 THINK THE 3 Cs: CONVICTION, COMMITMENT AND CONFIDENCE.

- Conviction, commitment and confidence will help you stay focused on results and keep a balanced approach

ction

KNOW YOUR PEOPLE

People they come together
People they fall apart
No one can stop us now
'Cause we are all made of stars

We Are All Made Of Stars, Moby

CONNECT

Step out of the ivory tower

Get 'people intelligence'

Coffee and donuts strategy

Lighten up

Break down barriers

Square pegs in square holes

If you can't beat 'em...

Try to imagine your worst job – a position you have absolutely no desire for, managing a team you inherited and have nothing in common with. To top it off, it's located in a remote area accessible only by airplane and so cold that winters last 10 months of the year and temperatures average around –30 degrees Celsius (–20-something Fahrenheit) – it's cold, darned cold!

Welcome to Goose Bay, Labrador (I can already hear you saying, where?), the place where I held my least favorite job of my entire career as the mobile support equipment officer (MSEO) for the base transportation organization. In other words, a fancy title for 'mother trucker' in charge of many truckers and heavy equipment operators – a girl's dream come true. Just kidding, of course.

I had survived a war zone in the former Yugoslavia and returned to Germany for my next posting. When my military career manager (responsible for moving me around the world) explained to me that she had good news and bad news, I knew I was in for a doozy. The good news was that she had the absolute best, most-exciting career move for a logistics officer ever. I had been requested by the United States Air Force joint movements control officer to join an exciting 'joint' military team who coordinated international military deployments. After working in the excitement of central Europe for three years, this was another wonder job: a very cool high-profile position working with different militaries in National Defence headquarters in our nation's capital, Ottawa.

The bad news? If I wanted to be posted to the same location as my fighter-pilot-then-husband (he was going to the other side of the country, to the remote northern location of Goose Bay, Labrador), I'd have to accept the only not-so-high-profile and lateral position available. Unfortunately, I'd have to take a position that I would never have desired in my wildest dreams, or should I say, in my worst nightmares. I basically had a choice: follow my own exciting career path, or follow my husband's. It was the ongoing struggle of the 'double-income no-kids' era. I took the position as MSEO.

I went from globe-trotting, Paris shopping, wine tasting, Chamonix skiing and occasional war-zone experience to a completely other extreme – hunting, fishing, blackflies and a team of unionized employees – an entirely new leadership and living experience. I could not have landed anything less sexy if I tried.

I had another choice: I could either wallow in my misery, which seemed pretty darned appropriate under the circumstances, or make the best of this really crappy posting in the middle of northern nowhere. (Apologies to all of you hunting and fishing lovers out there – it's just not my thing!)

...JOIN 'EM

So I bought a spiffy Yamaha snowmobile and decided it was time to start a family. And I embraced this job and the new team I would be leading to the best of my abilities.

I had a new office space located in an aircraft hangar at the end of a NATO fighter base – a hangar that smelled like diesel and JP-4 (jet fuel) and housed all of the equipment to keep the runways clear of snow and the jets de-iced and refuelled. My new team included 45-plus unionized heavy-equipment operators and truckers who operated dozers, graders, runway ploughs, de-icers, backhoes, spreaders and flatbeds. Military bases often employ civilians from local communities, and in this particular role, almost three-quarters of my team was from the community. The team had never worked for a woman before, and it was the first time they'd be led by someone who knew almost nothing about what they did for a living!

So how do you successfully take over a team and gain credibility *and* respect as a leader when you don't even fully understand each member's job? I had a lot of time to figure that out as I sat in that hangar on a NATO forces flying base, in my office overlooking the runway.

MIGHT AS WELL HAVE SOME FUN

I wasn't ready to start learning how to drive airplane de-icers, refuellers or plows. But I had to get to know both the team

con

members and our objectives – to keep this 10,000-foot runway operational 24/7 while handling all of the other things that came with the job. I had to manage planning and operations, including the lack of resources during heavy winter shifts, overhead costs and overtime, and equipment maintenance. I also had to get to know the team, their job skills, employees' strengths, weaknesses and performance capabilities. Another ball I had to juggle was understanding the new culture I now worked and lived in. I might have been in Canada, but there are very strong cultural influences that came with working in the country's remote provinces, as well as in the East Coast, which is an entirely different ball game than working in, say, Ottawa. Some of the workforce was used to 'leveraging' a good government social system, which, when applied the right way, can somehow legally allow workers 10 weeks off work for every 10 weeks of work completed. Quite an interesting challenge as a leader to have to balance normal resource issues on top of a virtually unwritten law of 10 weeks on and 10 weeks off!

Yes, to do this new job, I had some challenges ahead. But first things first: I had to get to know my team so that I could know what I was really working with.

Get to know your team. Sounds simple, doesn't it? Perhaps, but it takes a concerted effort on a leader's part to do this, particularly when you don't know anything (and I mean anything) about your team's field of expertise. Throughout my career, I've walked into an office or hangar or garage to meet my new team members and without a word exchanged, I could 'feel' them evaluating me with their stares – usually because I was a woman working in a very male-dominated business. (In the 1990s, around 10 percent of the military population were women, and only approximately one percent of them were officers.) So, I suspected this was no exception in Goose Bay. You don't have to be a clairvoyant to read the message behind the stares: "How is this chick going to lead us? She hasn't got a clue what we do."

Well, this time, the team had it right. I didn't know how to do what they did, but that didn't really matter. Sure, you gain more immediate credibility if you have the same skills and areas of expertise as the team, but to be an effective leader, you don't have to know what all of your experts know.

LET THE EXPERTS BE THE EXPERTS

One path to becoming a leader is by 'moving up through the ranks,' starting on the shop floor or in the mail room, as they say, and working your way up. But in the military, and in many companies, you move from one position to the next, or to completely different companies, and take on entirely new responsibilities. The most important skill you can bring to the table is your ability to quickly take a team to a new level or in a new direction, more so than understanding each team member's area of expertise. Case in point: What did I know about leading a multinational team in a war zone? My skill was – and is – developing plans and then making those plans a reality, not necessarily having the same experience as my team members.

The higher up you go, the bigger the team or organization you'll likely lead. It won't be realistic to know everything that everyone does, at least not immediately. However, you should definitely take the time to appreciate the objectives of your team, longer-term goals, and underlying issues your team might be facing, such as resources, training, equipment or general direction. This will provide you with an immediate understanding of where your team will need your leadership support most and where your priorities should be. One last thing, you must understand the skills of your team, who are your strong players and how you can leverage the skill sets they offer. That takes getting to know your team.

So that's exactly what I did. I climbed into the passenger seat of a runway plow to see what it was like at 0300 hours (read 'very early in the morning') to blast down a 10,000-foot runway with snow spraying 100 feet high and wide. It was a rather eye-opening experience! Needless to say, that was just the beginning of my education – the 'fun' had just begun. That was only one operator and one piece of equipment. Lucky for me, I would experience all of it, from graders to backhoes to runway plows to de-icing machines.

> We believe that a person is a person through other persons, that my humanity is caught up, bound up and inextricably in yours.
>
> *– Archbishop Desmond Tutu, Nobel Peace Prize winner*

Reality Check: Rolling up the sleeves

Taking on a leadership position where you don't have the specific skills and expertise of your team members may seem a little daunting at first. You will have to make a real effort to gain respect through your ability to take the team collectively to a new level rather than 'wow' team members with your knowledge of the work they do. Here's a very simple trick: People respond positively to a leader who respects what they do for a living. So show some respect by rolling up your sleeves and spending time actually *experiencing* your team's day-to-day world. In turn, their respect will come right back at you. You will also have the added advantage of better understanding your front lines.

CHATTING. GRUMBLING. CONNECTING

Besides 'rolling up' my sleeves to understand what my team members faced on a daily basis, I had another tried-and-true 'get to know your team' strategy that I had used many times before. It was the perfect time to use it.

I was lucky to have a people-oriented second-in-command – my warrant officer. He had two things going for him: he had worked his way up through the ranks as a trucker so he understood more about the equipment and skills of the team we were leading than I did. And he had been working with this team for about a year – that's one more year of experience than I had. So he had a good knowledge of how some of these team players ticked – who the talented and hard-working team members were, the 'problem children' or more difficult individuals, and the challenges I might face going forward. Together, we decided to set up a Friday morning 'coffee and donuts' session in the cafeteria – not a meeting per se, but a more informal 'chat session.' This would provide everyone with a general update of what was going on in our transportation unit and on the base – information that would pertain directly to their jobs, like fighter squadron deployments, NATO exercises, new defence initiatives or equipment, resource updates and even budget cuts. The coffee, donuts and informal setting kept the gathering casual, which is the best way to get your team to open up.

These types of sessions have the potential to become 'grumbling sessions.' People will tend to tell you more about their issues than what is working well for them – it's only human nature. So do what you have to do: Allow some of the griping, as long as it's constructive. It can open your eyes to aspects of the organization that need work. But remember to keep these free-flowing sessions on a positive track to encourage tangible feedback on operations and any other areas you need information on. The important thing is to end on a positive note – what can we focus on as a team to keep morale up and make this a fun place to work? Here's what my Goose Bay team came back with: one Friday a month, a pre-assigned 'shift' would be responsible for organizing a 'cook-up.' That's what they wanted! I would never have guessed that cooking would have motivated this bunch of men, but it did. And cook-up they did. Jigs dinner, flipper pie (yes, seal flippers) and a variety of other local 'delicacies' that they had caught hunting or fishing at their cabins.

The flow of these sessions went something like this: update the team, open up the floor, listen to the inevitable grumbling, respond to the grumbling, change the direction to focus on positive discussion, request constructive feedback or input on new initiatives, and end on a good note. There you have it. A simple coffee and donuts session.

> Never tell people how to do things. Tell them what to do and they will surprise you with their ingenuity.
>
> *– General George S. Patton, American military leader*

Just like that, everyone was updated and everyone had a say. Some team players even had some influence on initiatives. Good connection had by all. I got to know them better, they got to know me, and we all had a forum to communicate.

Reality Check: Sometimes size doesn't matter

Developing good 'people intelligence' should not just happen with a small, manageable team in place. The size of your team shouldn't be an issue.

I've worked with leaders who can chat with hundreds or even thousands of employees – on a first-name basis. When a leader can connect with someone in their organization and have a conversation about their family, outside interests as well as work issues, the impact is usually pretty remarkable. There is something powerful about feeling like your leader actually knows you as a person and not just an employee.

CONNECT IN COMFORT

After a few months, my team seemed to be much more comfortable with their 'new boss lady' even if I wasn't a trucker. These men started realizing that whether I knew, or didn't know, how to do their jobs, it didn't seem to matter so much. I could still support them, understand their work needs and provide the necessary leadership to make sure our team supported this NATO air force base. And at the same time, have a little fun.

Somewhere along the way we definitely connected. Four months after my arrival, I found out I was pregnant. Now how do you announce that to a bunch of truckers? My men took it in stride. One day when I showed up at my office, the guys were hanging around the lunchroom and all had grins on their faces. I knew something was up. Much to my surprise, when I walked into my office I discovered that it had been redecorated and dimly lit. Some of my bookshelves had been removed and replaced with a big comfy couch. When I asked the men what all this was about, they smiled and said, "Well, we've been thinking you look awfully tired in the afternoons, ma'am, and so we thought you might like a little rest every once in a while." You've got to love a bunch of men thinking about your well-being while you are pregnant!

This was not my dream job; far from it. This was not even my dream team. Looking back, this position was about making the best of a situation, and rising to the challenges of leading in an area I knew nothing about. It was every bit about focusing on the people and the mission.

And what a bonus when your team puts some of that focus back on you. Although I still can't imagine what my colonel would have thought of the afternoon naps!

The principle: Know your people

Leadership is all about the people. Everything in business comes down to them. This principle is about connecting at a genuine level with the people who are going to help you succeed as a leader. Through this connection with your team, you'll be far more likely to help them succeed and grow in their roles, and their careers. It doesn't matter if you're leading a team of truckers or a team of high-tech project managers, it all comes down to the people. No doubt about it, your success or failure will be based upon your team.

Chances are that you won't have to experience my worst case – a job you don't want and a team you have nothing in common with. But you never really know where you'll land, and the worst-case scenario may lead to incredible things for you. My job did.

Hopefully your current circumstances with your team are entirely different. Maybe you've just landed the job of your dreams and get to pull your own team together. Congratulations! Or you may have inherited a team that has been together for some time. Or maybe it's a combination of circumstances – you're moving into an exciting new role, a team already exists, but you're also going to be creating some new positions.

No matter the situation, one thing is plain and simple: As a leader, your job will be a lot easier if you enjoy the people you work with because you'll be spending a lot of time with them. Getting to know your people will ultimately help you make better decisions, align individuals effectively with the mission, spark creativity and execute successfully – all the things a leader needs to do with their team to succeed.

Being a good leader isn't necessarily about being an expert in your company's industry or business or the team's skills and knowledge; rather, it's about your ability to manage people and goals in the most effective way.

I call it 'people intelligence.' And knowing your team is the first step in being able to effectively lead your team.

> "Good leaders make people feel that they're at the very heart of things, not at the periphery. Everyone feels that he or she makes a difference to the success of the organization. When that happens, people feel centered, and that gives their work meaning." *– Warren Bennis, adviser to John F. Kennedy and leadership guru*

HUMAN NATURE

It's human nature to respond better to someone you know and connect with. You'll gain a tremendous amount of insight by getting to know your team players – insight that is critical to you doing a better job. Information like:

- their training, experience and special skills;
- how their skills fit into the role they are now filling;
- their career aspirations;
- who they are as a person: family, cultural background, etc.;
- personal information that might impact their work and your goals, such as a family illness.

Reality Check: Think like a coach

The world of sports relies on this principle. Know each of your players' strengths and weaknesses, how every player works with each other, what motivates them to give their utmost, and what's happening in their lives that can impact their game. The coach doesn't need to be a star quarterback or goalie before becoming head of the team, but he needs to know how to bring out the best in his players to win the game. People intelligence is a must for any coach or leader.

When do you give your best to a team? Is it when you have a leader who understands what makes you tick, your goals and aspirations, and who genuinely looks out for you, or is it when you have a leader who is focused on his own goals, career and aspirations?

When you look at it in that light, it almost seems like a no-brainer, doesn't it?

How to really get to know your people

So there you are, a brand new boss with a new team. I recommend you start team-building by getting out of your office and the comfort zone of those four walls and maybe even rolling up your sleeves a little! Here's how you can start building that connection with your team:

1 Take your time. Then make your move

You're pretty excited about your new position. It's natural to want to get in there and make some changes to get things moving fairly quickly in a certain direction. But don't rush to establish credibility by immediately changing your team's world. Sit back for a bit and get to know the lay of the land. Take a few weeks or even a month or two to walk around, talk to people, establish team meetings to encourage input and feedback and, generally, get an understanding of the new world you've just entered. Who are the people on your team? What are they all about? Where does your team need support? Where are things working well? What areas need fixing? Take your time to get smart.

RED FLAG **Make your mark**

It's human nature to want to put your own unique mark on things – after all, that's why you're a leader. Make sure the mark you're making adds value, and don't create change just for the sake of changing things. Action without good cause can result in inertia.

con

Streamline operations

When I stepped into the high-tech industry as a manager of export operations, I was taking over a team of 25 people who reported directly into the manager – I had 25 direct reports! I couldn't help but recall a philosophy we had in the military – frontline leaders should never have more than seven 'directs.' Seven seems to be a number that is considered to be the maximum amount of people one can effectively manage. I knew within a week that 25 team members lining up at my office door every day with a question or a problem was not going to work. The reporting structure was definitely going to change.

And change it I did. But I took some time to do it. I 'surveyed the land' and got to know each member on my team. Not just on a first-name basis but *who* they really were as employees and people – their roles, strengths, skills and experience. I could use all of this knowledge to develop a new team structure that would be more efficient to manage but not create too many barriers or a heavy hierarchy. Within a few months, I established a cross-training program between different functions to minimize the 'pigeonholes' that had occurred – team members stuck forever in certain positions. I reorganized the team by market regions, which created an opportunity to promote a couple of team members to market region leaders. Each would have more than 10 employees reporting directly to them. It wasn't necessarily the frontline leadership of the military, but it sure was more effective than 25 direct reports!

"Never mistake motion for action." – *Ernest Hemingway, author*

2 Get the lowdown firsthand

Leverage whatever information you can gather from the workplace and the people working in it to learn more about your own team members. Chat with departing team leaders or current bosses, review employee files (if they exist) or organize one-on-one sessions with your team members. Obviously, the past team leader can provide you with some good background on who's who. Spending some time with your new boss to get her viewpoint is also valuable. Perhaps she can provide additional insight on strengths, resource gaps, people successes or issues you should know about. What's on employees' minds? Raises, changes, promotions, career moves. Are there personal concerns you should understand? I have had employees with drug addictions, financial problems and family health issues and all of these issues impacted the work and required my attention in one way or another.

Be proactive so you can hit the ground running and ensure that you don't get blind-sided by any surprises. Then park all that great information and validate it by getting to know your people – yourself.

I always take information passed on to me with a certain grain of salt. As a new leader, you might see people and things in an entirely different way.

CASE STUDY **You're fired!**

The high-tech world certainly creates a lot of movement for people within the industry. I have had many opportunities to lead many different teams and take over teams from other leaders. On a couple of occasions, I have had outgoing leaders tell me to get rid of certain people – employees who didn't pull their weight or did not work well with the team. On one occasion, I was told by one of our company's vice presidents (who had actually hired two of my team members) that one of the first things I needed to do was to fire a couple of my people. He felt they were liabilities. Apparently, one of them didn't have the right depth of technical knowledge and the other often made inappropriate comments in front of some of our biggest U.S. customers. My question: Why hadn't he fired these employees instead of passing on what he felt was a serious problem to another leader? I didn't fire either of these employees. Instead, I chose to make my own judgment call. And I validated what is normally the case – this VP was 50 percent right. There were some issues that needed to be addressed but not to the extent of removing the employees permanently. In fact, both of these individuals became top-notch team contributors once we did some digging and got to the bottom of some key problems.

3 Coffee and donuts in the front lines

I'll be the first one to admit that getting out of your comfort zone and connecting with your team is not always that easy to do. But it's worth the effort – it's one of the best ways to connect to your front lines.

If you're willing to commit to this less formal but important gathering, you will reap some great benefits. Make a point of listening to your team on a regular basis, weekly if possible, share news, provide updates and don't forget to celebrate even small successes.

Back when I was an inexperienced second lieutenant, my captain had me spend a week of 'on-the-job training' with each of my units (I had a 75-member team divided into several different teams). They were located in different facilities and had very different functions. Regardless of the team I was with, each Friday morning usually began with a 'coffee and donut' chat to keep the communication lines open between all parties.

Over the years, I have experienced and created a number of different versions of these 'coffee and donut' chats, from 'lunch and learns' to really informal 'TGIF' get-togethers with more of a 'beer and wings' theme. The key is this: Providing a less-formal meeting environment encourages people to open up, giving you the opportunity to get their input and simply connect with people in a different way.

RED FLAG Fraternization

Fraternizing which refers to socializing outside of work hours with 'other ranks' or your team members was really frowned upon when I first joined the military. In some cases, one might even be reprimanded for it. The reason was simple: If you have friends on the team, it's very tough as a leader to be objective and make the right 'people decisions.' And the optics are bad. Socializing or lunching with a select few can cause animosity among the team members who don't get to hang out with you, although this should not be confused with working together. Socializing can be a great way to connect, but consider the impact of your actions on all team members.

"You must love soldiers in order to understand them, and understand them in order to lead them."

– Henri Turenne, French military leader

Outside the corporate BOX

GOING OVER THE EDGE – TO CONNECT

How do you connect with your team when your company has a workforce of 39,000? Some teams go to extremes to get connected.

Seagate Technology, the world's largest manufacturer of disk drives, used to be known for a 'back-stabbing' culture and firing its people in the middle of meetings. But Bill Watkins, an aggressive team-builder and chief executive officer since 2004, has been steadily working on changing that corporate environment.

An avid mountain biker, Watkins has created Eco Seagate, an annual team-building event for his worldwide team sparked by his own interest in extreme sports (think cliff-climbing). The weeklong event attempts to break down barriers between groups of employees in an environment where job titles aren't used. By placing employees into 40 teams of five, giving them tough challenges like repelling down the face of a 300-foot cliff or fire-walking, they are forced to pull together, push through intense physical challenges and accomplish goals as a team. Talk about rapid bonding!

The result? People in that corporate culture connecting at a global level. "You need to have this attitude: it's a team, we stick together," Watkins says. One goal, he says is to enable everyone to see each other as human beings, instead of the nameless "marketing guy," or the "engineering guy" to help eliminate "functional silos" that exist within companies.[1]

con

What's in it for you... and your team?

Investing time and effort in people creates great returns. Focusing on your team will definitely help you bring out their best! Here's what's in it for you.

✓ **Everyone wants to be a star**

Getting to know your people will help you align the right people to the right job. It will help you fit the square pegs in the square holes, instead of trying to force people with certain skills into roles that require something completely different.

Everyone's a star in their own right, and everyone fits well in some position somewhere. If you find that you have people on your team who are not thriving, it doesn't necessarily mean they don't belong there. Perhaps they're just poorly suited to their current roles at the time.

When you understand your team's strengths and skill gaps, you'll be able to make better 'people decisions,' including who can do what job, who is best suited to help you co-lead or support you as a 'second-in-command' (see Chapter 07, "Combining Forces," for more on the '2 i/c'), and whose job needs to be re-aligned so their skills are being used effectively.

Bring out the stars. If you take the time to understand your team, they will feel a lot more valued and definitely more understood. And with a sense of increased value comes a greater desire to perform.

RED FLAG

Too many square pegs

When you don't have the luxury of creating your team from scratch, but instead are inheriting a group of people, you might just have to live with what you've got. You may not have all the skill sets or personalities you're looking for. You might even have too many 'square pegs' for the 'round holes' you need to fill. Sometimes 'making do' is the order of the day. But by getting to know your team in a more in-depth way, you will certainly have a clear understanding of what you do have and where you may be able to effectively realign the inherited team.

nect

✓ **Create a two-way information flow**

Creating a team environment with a good flow of information is a two-way process that starts with you. Being accessible to your team will encourage people to take advantage of your open-door environment and not just walk right past it.

✓ **Start building your credibility**

Making an effort to connect with the team demonstrates the value you place with them. That, in turn, will help you gain some of that much-needed credibility.

Hindsight is 20/20

Open the doors, not the floodgates

So you've opened up the doors, started the chat sessions and you're now far more connected to your people.

Even if you're highly people oriented and the consummate extrovert, it's just a lot easier to stay in the office than to step out of it. Leading a team demands a lot of energy to keep your team engaged, motivated and working together. You have to deal with problems on the front lines, customer complaints, clashing personalities, etc. So when you're getting to know your people and encouraging a more 'open' communication environment, you may end up opening the floodgates, allowing other 'issues' to really rise to the surface.

Mixed in with all of that good two-way communication and team building can come the finger-pointing, for many different reasons, such as disgruntled employees who feel you don't deserve the boss's job or those who feel they should have received that promotion. But, you don't want to create a negative or 'boss-bashing' session. That needs to be dealt with behind closed doors. Keep people focused on providing input, feedback and constructive suggestions. Allowing a 'grudge-match' will only bring the team down. It takes a confident leader to open the doors. But it takes a smart leader to manage it!

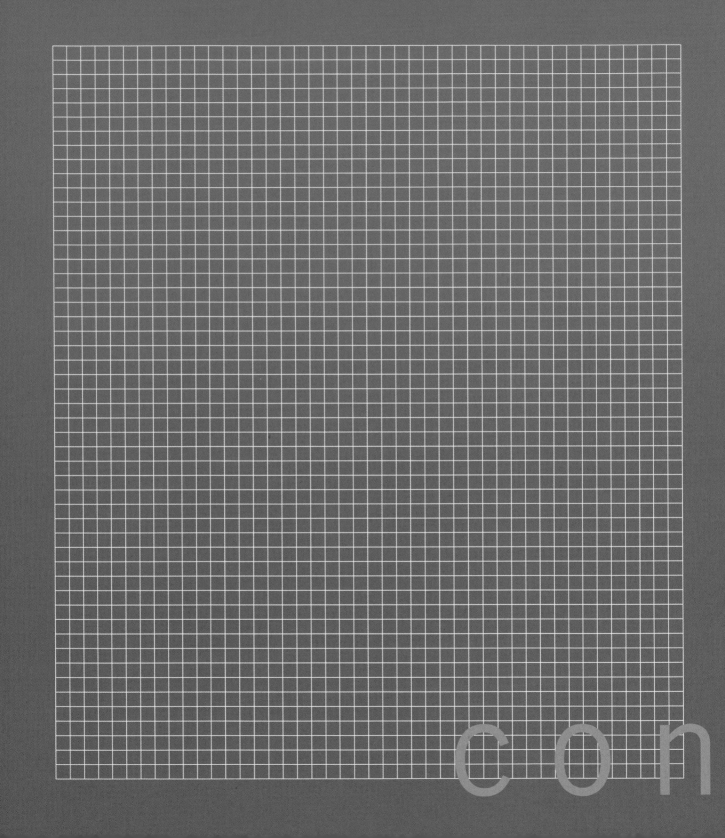

con

ACTION PLAN

Step out of the ivory tower

1 CLOSE THE HANGAR DOORS.

- Create opportunities for 'non-work' discussions in a 'non-work' environment
- Get to know people outside the workplace and leverage that different connection back at the office

2 GET PEOPLE INTELLIGENT.

- Establish a personal connection. Know your employees instead of getting acquainted with them
- Hobbies, kids, family, travel, sports, passion, goals. The more you know your team, the better you can lead them

3 USE THAT INTELLIGENCE WHEN TIMES ARE TOUGH.

- Knowing your people better will help you align the right resources and skills with the right job
- When things are mission critical, you'll be better prepared to make effective resource decisions

nect

WHAT GOES AROUND COMES AROUND

Don't give up
You've got a reason to live
Can't forget we only get what we give

You Get What You Give, New Radicals

RESPECT

You get what you give

Loyalty down = loyalty up

Everyone is significant

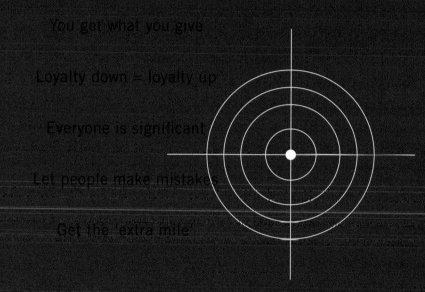

Let people make mistakes

Get the 'extra mile'

He had it coming

I promise this is not another war story. Well, not yet anyway. But it does take place in a war zone. And it happened to be here that I received a strong, but entertaining, reminder about the power of treating people with respect – or not.

You might recall reading in Chapter i, "Seize the Decade," that in March 1992, I was tasked with leading some of the planning and organizing for the deployment of one of the largest moves in United Nations' history at the time. And since Canada was going to be the first country to deploy into war-torn former Yugoslavia, it was critical our troops and supporting equipment were 'on the ground' and 'on time.'

THE MOVE DUDES

So there we were on site in Daruvar, north of Bosnia and west of a town called Pacrac – or somewhere between 'no-man's-land' and 'snipers' alley' – however you prefer to look at it. My logistics team was increasing in size by the day. I had gone from a one-woman show to a team of two with the addition of my Croatian translator, who quickly became my 'jack of all trades.' Some Norwegian and Swedish soldiers and their captain soon joined us. Our team was a mish-mash of many things – an interesting mixture of language, culture and experience. I had my work cut out for me. Coordinating this multinational team and keeping everyone well connected to our logistics mission in a continually changing environment was no easy feat.

What seemed like many weeks later, but was really only days, our final two team members arrived from Germany. These movement control specialists, otherwise known on this mission as 'move dudes,' would quickly become my right-hand men.

Unlike the rest of my new team, Corporal Henderson and Master Corporal Jodoin were familiar faces. Back in Germany, the pair was part of my movement control team, trained to support the movement of any military regiment, battalion or squadron, from tanks to fighters to helicopters, anywhere in the world. Within the military, these trained specialists were a close-knit bunch with a powerful network of colleagues around the world, because that was where they worked – everywhere. Their work often involved hanging out in the back of military transport aircraft to move equipment around the world, set up logistics sites in weird and wonderful places, or, in some cases, drop equipment off the back of aircraft with parachutes at extremely low altitudes – otherwise known in the good old days as 'low altitude parachute extraction' but now considered too dangerous a role.

15 MINUTES OF FAME

Upon their arrival, the move dudes quickly noticed and remarked on the number of press on location with us. The reconnaissance team and newly arrived peacekeepers were getting a lot of press, especially yours truly. Not only was I the only female in a uniform among thousands of soldiers for the first few weeks, but I was also in a leadership role. So I often had microphones shoved in front of me, cameras flashing around me and, at one point, specific requests from major news agencies like Reuters, for example, to do some close-up shots with UN flags waving behind me. The media seemed to eat up the G.I. Jane image and it was almost embarrassing. My picture was showing up in international papers and local dailies, where I was quickly becoming known as 'Kapetan Andela.'

My 15 minutes of fame extended over a week or two, and I thought I was doing a great job representing my country. I became particularly good at dodging tricky questions from the BBC and other media organizations, such as, "How does it feel to be a woman working in such a macho-oriented culture *and* a war zone?" What I really wanted to respond with was, "Geez, one woman, 2,000 men, every girl's dream!" But instead the professional in me took over.

As the mission got underway and became more complicated, more and more troops hit the ground and Canadian headquarters decided it was time to send in some public relations (PR) pros to continue fielding media queries. So, fresh in from Canada arrives one of these PR experts, ready to jump in and start managing some of the media requests.

resp

And what a pompous ass he was! Let's just say that he didn't get off to a good start with my team. In the midst of extremely long days, while flying by the seat of our pants to handle one challenge after another, 'Captain PR' began to throw his rank and march around our location like he owned it. At one point, I walked past him as he was having an intense discussion with the move dudes. Actually, he was yelling at the two corporals to place top priority on tracking his gear or 'kit,' which had not yet arrived from Canada. Like they didn't have enough to do that was not of *international* importance!

Oh boy, had Captain PR made a fatal error in judgment! Movement control specialists are a particularly proud breed of military. Not only are they a tight-knit group who take care of each other, but also they possess the cocky attitude that goes with special units – a 'don't mess with us buster' sort of attitude.

So here's this officer (who really had no authority over these guys even though he outranked them) telling key players on my small team that they needed to give his gear priority. Meanwhile, these men were already working 18-plus-hour days, trying to manage other aspects of this operation, such as organizing small details like the arrival of millions of pounds of equipment. Well, I couldn't stand on the sidelines while this happened, so I headed over to intervene and knock some sense into this knucklehead.

I must have had a look on my face as I approached the group, because Jodoin responded with a smirk before I could say anything: "Don't worry ma'am, we'll handle this one." What he politely meant was that I should keep out of it.

With that, my master corporal (MCpl) turned to the angry captain and said, "Yes, sir, we will see what we can do, sir. We'll get right on that!"

I knew my MCpl all too well – he was no fool and a confident character, and would not accept being treated with any lack of respect. In fact, I have seen this particular fellow challenge his leaders in the past, me included. I knew that it was very likely that this captain was being told one thing and something else was going on behind the scenes. What I actually thought would happen was that one of the move dudes would tell this PR guy what he could do with his gear. But instead, they surprised me with their diplomacy and tact. Something must be up, I thought.

I was right. I caught the two corporals snickering some time later as they were doing some paperwork to send back to our logistics team (the bulk of my team had remained in Germany). I got one of those "What you don't know ma'am won't hurt you!" responses when I asked them what was going on. After pushing them for a few minutes, more out of concern that I might end up in jail if I didn't get to the bottom of this, the truth came out. They had, in fact, dropped all their priority tasks for the day to comply with this captain's demands.

Oh yes, they were taking care of his stuff, alright. His personal effects – consisting of things like boots, extra clothes, books, CDs, family photos and other items you would need to stay sane and a little more comfortable while deployed in this war zone – were being tracked by the move dudes' entire worldwide network of colleagues.

But they weren't just being tracked, they were being rerouted away from our location. Henderson and Jodoin had located the gear on its way to Germany. Had everything gone smoothly, Captain PR's belongings should have arrived within a week or so to our location in Daruvar, Croatia. Instead, because of Captain PR's unpleasant demeanor and lack of respect in dealing with these troops, they were going to have influence on him in ways he would never have known. His favorite things, upon arrival in Germany, were going to get 'priority tagged' in a completely different direction – to Norway in a remote place called Bardufoss NATO Air Station, 69 degrees north (that's very north). I could almost imagine the response the pair would come up with when Captain PR was desperate for some answers on his stuff. "Oh, why don't we check on that for you, sir. It should have been here weeks ago!"

I decided to leave the moving of the gear to my specialists. I figured that after a few more weeks of yelling orders at my corporals, this fellow would probably shift from throwing his weight around to begging for their help. Or he might turn to me for help in resolving his growing problem. If the PR Captain was lucky, he might get his gear in another month or two. Maybe next time he'll think twice before he disrespects those he considers to be the 'little guys.' What goes around definitely does come around. And in this particular case, it was going to take a whole lot longer to go around!

The principle: Respect goes around and comes around

This principle is about getting back what you give. Some things will come right back at you like a boomerang. When talking about respect, that's a good thing. If you give respect, you get respect, and you create an environment that encourages it all around. Without respect, you can't put other principles to work for you.

Respect can take you a long way with your team and help you to get steps closer to accomplishing your goals. Why? Because respect is one of those fundamental things that most people need – people want to be respected because it indicates a sense of value or worth or significance to the team. While it's somewhat of an intangible reward for hard work, respect can be highly motivating and can be your number-one leadership power tool.

Respect does not come with being the 'boss,' having a title or a big office. It comes from good solid leadership and it's one of the first things you need to earn from your team. Some leaders just have what it takes to earn such high regard. They have a tremendous presence that people seem naturally drawn to, and can pull a cohesive team together with seemingly little effort. You know a leader is admired and respected when people talk about her behind her back and the things that are being said are actually all good.

How is it that some people seem to be more respected than others? How do they earn it? A leader can earn respect for a myriad of different reasons – excelling at whatever the business is, 'leading from the front' or leading the way, making great decisions or driving the business to an enormous level of success. And, of course, they can earn more respect if they respect those who support them. The leader who is respected can have an entirely different influence because of that respect factor – respect drives people and motivates them in a powerful way.

If you have already created an environment of respect, it's much easier to get what you need out of people – especially when times are tough or your team is under tremendous stress to deliver. This is where morale and loyalty are tested.

What's the flip side? I'm sure you're familiar with what it can be like, working for a boss who waffles and has difficulty making decisions. It's hard to admire this kind of leader. It's frustrating and it can put you and your team members in difficult positions.

So what's the alternative? Effective and efficient decision-making comes with strong leadership. Perhaps you've witnessed this entirely different leadership style in action. You're in a meeting and an issue comes up that will impact a timeline, and people don't know what to do. Bam! Your boss makes a decision: switch to the other supplier, find another source. You can't help but think this leader can really grab the bull by the horns and make decisions when they're needed.

Making decisions effectively can lead to respect. So can leading by example. In fact, all of the leadership principles we cover in this book can lead to respect. And that's what makes respect a leadership power tool: it is interconnected with almost every principle and action a leader needs to take.

YOUR POWER TOOL WHEN TIMES ARE TOUGH

If you want to succeed in a mission-critical environment, respect is a fundamental cornerstone for success. How are you going to be able to get people motivated and moving in the right direction, sometimes doing things they might never do or want to do – where they might be required to work long hours, or work in tough conditions?

Respect is especially vital while leading mission-critical projects that can take your smooth operation and highly efficient team to utter chaos in a hurry. While you may normally allow for plenty of team input, certain times or projects may demand

resp

more of an authoritative approach. Think of a hospital emergency room or a paramedic team – lots of fast direction, lots of orders, lots of action. If you've been together as a team for a while, it's likely you've faced these situations together before and your team will feel comfortable with your quick decisions and immediate direction.

If you haven't been working together long, well, let's face it, in a mission-critical environment there isn't much room for consensus management. People might get yelled at, or even removed from positions if need be. This is about accomplishing the mission, not worrying about people's feelings. But when things settle down, it's a great time to reflect on the mission and the things that had to happen to make it happen, because the mission-critical environment can get ugly. A debrief of what worked and what didn't is a very powerful method to get your new team gelling again.

So consider respect as an underlying 'must have,' something you need to figure out and earn right from the start. Because without it, it will be tough to get other principles working for you. And it will be tough to have your team working for you and sticking around when times get tough.

A very familiar example for me is sailing with my father. We can be sailing along on a gorgeous day in his 32-foot sailboat, with three to four other guests. But if the wind picks up, all hell breaks loose. He starts yelling orders at me and another crew member (usually my mother) to start pulling on sheets, watch out for the boom, get the gib down or grab the wheel. Sailing can be like that, going from calm to mission critical very quickly, and you have to get used to the captain yelling orders at you. But we all know better. My dad is typically an easy-going guy who has a wonderful way with people, except when eight-knot winds kick up and the mainsail needs to be hauled in and the gib taken up. Then look out! You can't take it personally.

If you want your team to help you move mountains, volunteer those countless hours, work long days for your small company or go that extra mile, they need to respect you and you'll want to foster a respectful environment.

The best way to get it is to give it.

RED FLAG **Rank ≠ respect**

Respect is earned. It does not come with gold bars, titles or positions. It is not something you can acquire. People need to believe in you, they have to want to follow you. And you have got to work for it.

How to get respect

In the mission-critical environment, where things are moving at warp speed and timelines are aggressive, your people are the difference between success and failure. Your team can stand in the way, or right there beside you, in reaching your goals or achieving your dreams.

To make things happen, you are going to need people on your team to get onside and stay onside. You will need them to really pull their weight because you'll be asking a lot from them, things like:

- Sticking with you even when the going gets tough
- Doing mundane, sometimes even tedious tasks, to get the job done
- Working all hours of the day or night
- Rolling up their shirt sleeves to do things they might not even be trained to do

Here are some simple things you can do to give respect and ultimately earn respect.

1 Make everyone count

Respect is simple. It starts with taking a sincere interest in people. If you're genuinely interested in someone, where they come from, what their skills are and how to best incorporate them into your mission, you will already be at a huge advantage. You already realize that everyone is significant, no matter who they are, what they do, or who they work for (even if it isn't you). Everyone can make a difference.

There may be times when you think you have nothing in common with the person you're working with or for. But it doesn't mean you can't respect what they do. Talk to people, pay attention to various roles and understand where they add value.

Simply put, get nosy! Take a look around you, ask the administrative clerk about her children or your taxi driver where he's from. Everyone comes with a story and everyone has value. You could be amazed to discover that the taxi driver was once a national soccer star in his native country.

CASE STUDY **Who would have thought?**

In a fast-paced industry where your team members might change every six months and leaders come and go, one doesn't necessarily pay attention to their anniversary start date with a big company, unless of course, you're one of those lucky individuals who might have some stock options 'vesting' or some other bonuses attached to your company start date. But even then, things like that can fly right past you. So when someone does, it's a big deal. I was riding in an elevator one morning with Terry, one of the facilities/maintenance workers at Research In Motion. I got to know him quite well during my three years with the company. Whenever I called the facilities and maintenance department with some need – a lamp for my office, a new white board or an air conditioner that needed repairing – this fellow was always there promptly. My colleagues used to comment on why they had to wait a week for a white board when I got same-day service. On this particular morning in the elevator, Terry said, "Good morning, Angela. Hey, congratulations by the way! It's your third-year anniversary today at our company."

Well, wouldn't you know it! I hadn't even realized that it was *exactly* three years since I started as one of the company's product launch directors. On my first day at the company, Terry and another fellow had come to help me set up some of my computer equipment. I asked them about their jobs, experience, years employed by the company, and made other general conversation. I would like to think that the reason behind the prompt attention to my facilities and maintenance needs over the past few years was probably a direct result from the first day we met. Respect and a genuine interest in people can go a long way.

Believe that everyone is significant. From the custodian to the CEO, people at any level can have great influence on your day and in your career, making your life either easy or difficult.

Reality Check: People can sense respect

It doesn't matter whether you have lots in common with someone you're working with or absolutely nothing. (And you will often find yourself working alongside people who have a profession or trade you know nothing about.) What's important is that you understand and respect the value different personalities and skill sets add to a team. People can sense respect *or* disrespect a mile away.

> "Take care of the team equipment manager and they will take care of you!" – *Merril Hoge, ex-NFL running back*

2 Recognize the team behind the scenes

Everyone counts. Now take that thought one step further by turning it into action. That might mean providing a small nod of recognition for a job well done or a pat on the back. The important thing is the acknowledgement.

I had this discussion one day with ESPN sports analyst Merril Hoge – a great supporter of Research In Motion's BlackBerry in the NFL as a result of marketing programs we developed with the league. In turn, he was getting a tremendous amount of technical support for his BlackBerry – VIP treatment, in fact – from my technical team, while he was on the road with ESPN in his current capacity as a football analyst.

Merril practiced what he preached. He took down the names of the technical team who supported him so that he could 'repay' them for their extra assistance. (I have to tell you, the Pittsburgh Steelers jackets, ball caps and autographed action shots went a long way!) I'm long gone from that team now, but I have a hunch that Merril is still getting privileged support!

By taking care of the equipment managers, as Merril calls them (or the guys behind the scenes and not the football heroes who get all the attention), you're acknowledging a group that helps the team work effectively.

We had a similar position in the air force called the supply technicians. Though not necessarily high in rank, these technicians were the gatekeepers of all the cool military supplies – everything from light mesh jungle boots to Ray-Ban

resp

flying glasses. Because these guys always had something you needed, they had a lot of influence. Treat them with respect and you got the awesome pair of U.S. aviator kid-leather flying gloves. Treat them poorly and chances are they wouldn't have combat boots in your size. (They might be able to find you some old Second World War stock instead.) I did a lot of flying back then, and a flying suit in men's size extra small was nearly impossible to get. Thankfully, I had learned the respect lesson early on in my career, so I always managed to get good flying gear that fit.

Recognizing the behind-the-scenes players, those who are not so front-and-center is important. Show respect, take care of those team members and share some of the glory to create a more cohesive, valued team. Then highlight their value to the rest of the team.

And that really comes down to knowing your people – something we looked at in Chapter 04. So let's take that one step further. Demonstrate respect and value for what your team is doing by understanding their day as best you can. That might mean participating in sales calls and getting on an airplane to visit sales reps or partners in different cities, walking the pavement with them and listening to clients' feedback. It might mean spending a day on the phone with your customer service managers and facing the stress of handling angry people for hours. Or it might mean coming in one weekend with your volunteer committee to decorate the hall for the charity event.

3 Do unto others...

Simply put, you shouldn't treat people in a way you wouldn't want to be treated, or expect them to do things you wouldn't do. This approach ties right in with 'leading by example' – another important principle that can deliver respect.

What sort of hours do you keep at the office? What about your team? What about sick days, is it easy for you to miss work? Does your team have the same flexibility? Put yourself in your team's shoes, especially if you have similar roles. Doing so will go a long way to create a positive working relationship and environment.

ect

Sure rank has its privileges, and when you've worked hard to earn those extra stripes, you deserve the rewards. People understand that, within reason. But people are also astute. If they sense that you're sending them off in a direction that you yourself would not go, they'll be a lot less motivated to perform and they certainly won't respect you for it. Be aware of situations or tasks that you really would not want to do yourself. Then think twice before expecting your team to take them on.

Ask yourself this: Would you like working for you? Would you put up with the conditions, hours or environment your team has to put up with? Every once in awhile ask yourself those questions. You might be surprised by your answer.

CASE STUDY **Could you work for you?**

I walked into the ladies' room one day, while working at Nortel Networks as the manager of export operations, and found a young girl, probably around seven or eight years old curled up on the couch. When I asked her who she was and what she was doing there, I found out that she was the daughter of one of the women on my team. She was sick and couldn't go to school. Her mother later explained to me that she had to get an order out to one of her international customers overseas, and that no one else on the team could do it. So she had brought her sick little girl in that day because she felt obligated to get the order out. Wow! The first thing I thought to myself was, 'could I put up with a job like that?' There's so much pressure on you that you have to get your sick child involved? On the other hand, I was lucky to have such a dedicated team member.

But as the leader, I needed to do something about it. I sent my employee and her little girl home that morning, and I made sure it never happened again. I implemented a team 'backup and expansion' program, where every export operations coordinator trained someone who wanted to learn about their market region, country and customers. Net result: everyone had a backup plan in case they needed time off, and at the same time, everyone learned about a country or customer that interested them. I, in turn, was able to look at myself in the mirror. Respect for my team meant my team respected me as a leader.

> It is more important to have somebody who is a good motivator of people rather than just a good businessman, so we look for people with good personalities, people who will put people who are working for them first, rather than themselves.
>
> *– Sir Richard Branson, founder of the Virgin Group*

4 Let people make mistakes *and* go to bat for them

Sad but true, this action is sorely lacking in so many leaders today. After years of downsizing, right-sizing, merging and acquiring, and chapter 11 declarations of bankruptcy, the workforce has become a place of insecurity and instability. As a result, 'to each his own' has become the prevailing attitude. That means bosses are far less likely to stick their neck out for team players, less likely to buffer them from the sometimes nasty blows of tempestuous customers, internal swipes of other departments who might be competing for projects or resources, or from the day-to-day challenges of our complex business environment. Going to bat and providing 'air cover' (air force lingo for people looking out for you) is your job as a leader.

Reality Check: Going to bat

Going to bat for your deserving team members is a sign of a true leader. Taking on a high-profile position where you stand up for your team and put yourself on the line simply takes guts. It also takes passion and a real belief in your team members. And that's where you will derive respect.

During this high-pressure time of big objectives, fewer resources, money and people, you'll need your team to 'step up to the plate' and take on more responsibility. That means you are going to need people who are comfortable taking risks and making decisions. You're going to have to respect what they do and empower them to do it. Without empowered team members you will have a tough time getting what you need done.

◄◄ **Rewind** *to Chapter 01, "The Buck Stops With You," for more on leadership accountability.*

CASE STUDY **Who says politicians don't mean what they say?**

Years ago, as my career was getting underway, I had a brief stint in politics. While studying for university, I got a part-time position in a very influential office – the office of Marcel Roy, a then-senior member of parliament (MP) in the Canadian government.

There I sat in Canada's beautiful parliament buildings in my very own office overlooking the eternal flame – with not a lick of experience to show for it! One evening, I volunteered to stay late until Mr. Roy returned from his many meetings, while his executive assistant and right-hand lady tended to other business. I was not usually left on my own because of my lack of experience dealing with the challenges of an MP's office, which could include anything from responding to questions from senior government officials to phone calls from angry constituents.

As luck would have it, I got a call from a senior government official who was angry. As soon as I answered the phone, he started barking at me. I was working for a member of parliament from Quebec, and should have been answering the phone in both official languages, French and English. Apparently I had not done so. The fellow at the other end of the phone became extremely belligerent at my faux pas and began to yell at me in both official languages. I could, in fact, speak French very well. But the more he yelled at me, the more I could not pull myself together to say a single word in French. This only made him yell more. By the time he hung up the phone, I was in tears, humiliated and worried about how my boss would react and whether I would have a job the next day.

My boss walked in as I sat there sniffling, and asked me with great concern (in French) what was wrong. When I told him, he immediately picked up the phone, contacted this individual, and with me sitting there wiping away the tears, reprimanded him for the way he had treated me and dealt with his staff. I can't remember if this individual was a minister or a senator, but I do remember the discussion the next day. The team was very impressed that Mr. Roy took this apparently 'very senior' individual to task for how he had treated me.

This was not at all the reaction I expected – I really did think I

resp

OFF THE SET AND INTO THE FIRE

How do you talk a renowned pop star out of wearing her clothes? Ask Philip Kates, the award-winning director of Sarah McLachlan's hit video, "Into the Fire." Kates managed to convince McLachlan to disrobe, cover herself in mud, and then shoot under a waterfall as the mud washed off – in mesmerizing slow motion. And it won him top music video honors as Best Music Video of the Year in 1991 at the Canadian Juno Awards. Luckily, I got to work with this director the one time I was a TV star. (Okay, I had one small line in a TV commercial, and I kept all my clothes on. But I did experience the opportunity of working with one of the best!)

Kates has been directing international television commercials and music videos for the past 15 years. A creative mastermind, Kates worked his way up through the ranks, spending years editing music videos and television commercials before making it as a top-notch international director.

As usual, I was fascinated with the leadership behind the scenes. I was in a world I knew nothing about – film directing – so I spent some time chatting with him about his rise to success.

Well, he's persistent for one thing. As a cocky young film student at Toronto's Ryerson University, he managed to land a tremendous opportunity – he was invited by Don McLean, owner of Partners Film Company, a top production company in Canada, to a shoot on a set, only to get thrown off the set by a director who didn't know he had permission to be there. Kates phoned Mr. McLean to get back on the set, only to get thrown off the set yet again. due to some other misunderstanding. Years later, McLean would be thanking Kates for the great job he was doing as an award-winning director with Radke, one of his company's subsidiaries.

This initial 'blip' at the front-end of Kates's career ties right in with a saying he believes in: "Remember the people on the way up. They're the same people you meet on the way down!" Or as he put it, "Thank goodness I wasn't an asshole before, because I'm being hired by people I hired years ago."

Working in the film industry as a freelance director, Kates is often leading teams that have been preassigned by the production company, and they are often people he has worked with many times before. Kates values the work of the people who pull a successful shoot together, even if he's only working with each team for a short time. After all, what goes around comes around. They could all end up working together again in one way or another.

"There are all sorts of ways of letting people know you appreciate them. But even spending time talking to an underling, treating them like a person, asking them about themselves, showing them some kind of sincere interest in them as something other than their (perhaps menial) role shows that you see them as a person, not just their job. And while that's not exactly a thank you it's a sign that you respect them."

Philip Kates, music video and TV commercial film director

was done. But it had a huge impact on how I felt toward my boss and my job after this incident. I had a newfound respect for him and was willing to work harder and longer hours for this man and his team. He could throw almost anything at me after that. I felt valued. And I decided that it would be the first and last time I would ever cry in an office. I made another commitment: one day when I had people working for me, I would stand up for my deserving team members much like that MP stood up for me.

Taking a stance on behalf of your team players is a sign of a true leader – a sign of someone who believes in themselves and their team. That's how you get the 'extra mile' and respect.

What's in it for you... and your team?

Believe it or not, some of the less-assuming positions in a company or organization can have a lot of influence. And they can literally make the world go around – or make your stuff go all around the world, as my move dudes did!

It doesn't matter if you're on an elevator with a maintenance worker, or in a war zone with soldiers, never underestimate how far a little respect can go. And never underestimate how far you can go as a leader when you cultivate an environment of respect with your team.

What kind of return on investment can you expect from using this leadership power tool?

✓ **First, the cost is cheap**

It costs you nothing to dole out respect where it's warranted, at all levels. The investment is low, the return is high. You just never know how treating different people with respect will come back to you in some wonderful ways.

✓ **Employees will stick around**

Success in today's challenging, fast-paced business environment requires endurance, durability and even longevity, and that longevity means staying power for the people on your team. Imagine yourself as an entrepreneur – you're putting every minute of your waking hours, energy and brainpower into this start-up. This is definitely not a case where you can afford to lose the good people you have cultivated. You want good people to come, grow and stay for awhile.

People want to feel respected and valued for what they bring to the table. Treating your team members with respect creates more of a harmonious team atmosphere. This doesn't mean that when the going gets tough, you can't yell, point fingers or dictate to get things done. I've had the opportunity to team up with various television producers. In a high-pressure environment like live television, you often have to resort to a 'dictator' style of leadership. And that might mean getting loud. But in the words of an ESPN producer, whose set I got to sit in on during a Super Bowl pre-game show, you should "never flip out!" Even when the s%#t hits the fan.

✓ **Get the extra mile**

As I learned many years ago, people will go the extra mile for a leader they respect, especially for a leader they know will go to bat for them when necessary. Why? It all boils down to security. If you know you have some 'air cover,' you'll be far more willing to take a few more chances. An individual is far more likely to be motivated to work harder and take on additional responsibilities beyond their initial job description when they're taken care of and treated in the right manner. Respect can increase team flexibility and the mileage you get out of your team.

✓ **Access to a whole new network**

Everyone has a 'network' or a group of people they can connect with to get things done. But you won't be able to access that network if you don't treat the person who owns it with respect. I'm sure if the move dudes felt some respect from the 'Captain PR,' they would have put the word out across their global network and expedited the arrival of his gear. Instead, his precious items took the long way there.

✓ **Loyalty down = loyalty up**

I have had people stick by me through thick and thin, and actually fight to stay on my team despite the temptation of promotions to other teams. And I have done the same with bosses I respected and wanted to keep working for. Respect isn't always that easy to get but it's certainly easier to give. And believe it or not, it can carry more clout than dollars.

The same two move dudes you heard about earlier told me weeks after we returned from the war zone that they took turns 'standing guard' outside my bedroom door at night. They felt I needed a little extra protection from the all-male troops outside. Now I'm not actually sure how much 'standing guard' they did, perhaps more of a 'keeping an occasional eye out' for me, or something like that. Regardless, that was loyalty! I gave them respect and loyalty, and I got it back...in ways I could never have imagined.

Give respect. Get respect.

resp

RED FLAG **Empower, sink or swim?**

Over the years I've seen some interesting 'empowerment' strategies – a favorite seems to be 'sink or swim.' In other words, kick the employee off the proverbial dock to see how they do – if they make it, great; if they don't, well, maybe they weren't cut out for the business anyway. I prefer another approach, where at least if employees start sinking (due to lack of experience or resources or whatever), then someone is standing on deck ready to throw out a life ring. A little more encouraging for the team member taking that leap off the dock, don't you think?

Reality Check: Everyone is significant

As you move into leadership positions, make a commitment to yourself and your team that you will never become one of those leaders who underestimates or minimizes the value of the lower profile roles on the team or in the organization as a whole.

> "We must build a new world, a far better world – one in which the eternal dignity of man is respected."
> *– Harry S. Truman, 33rd President of the United States*

Hindsight is 20/20

Demanding respect or creating fear?

"As your leader, I encourage you from time to time and always in a respectful manner to question my logic. If you are convinced that a particular plan of action I've decided on is not the wisest, tell me so. But allow me to convince you and I promise you right here and now no subject will ever be taboo…except of course the subject that was just under discussion. The price you pay for bringing up my Chinese American origin…I collect your f#@%ing head! If any of you sons of bitches have anything else to say now is the time!... I didn't think so."[1]

– Lucy Liu in the movie Kill Bill, *after decapitating one of her team players' heads gives her team a quick lecture on respect and questioning the leader*

It never ceases to amaze me how many leaders I have worked with who suffer from the notion that fear equates to respect. They believe that hollering, yelling or bullying their team – generally creating a topsy-turvy environment where people are on their toes – garners respect. It seems some leaders start overvaluing their own importance, due to their new title, role, office or whatever, and lose sight of the value of all of the roles on a team or in an organization. These same leaders started off in a cubicle themselves, only to get promoted, get an office and then close the door. Team members who were very recently colleagues are made to feel like they are approaching the 'lion's den' whenever they need to speak to the boss.

Don't lose respect for the very people who are helping you get to the top and don't lose sight of the fact that you were once where they are now. Be careful you don't become too nearsighted, only seeing those things you want to see or hearing what you want to hear. Because that's exactly what you'll get. People will tell what you want to hear if that's how you like it…or sometimes nothing at all if you're leading a reign of terror.

So, as you rise up through the ranks, do enjoy the perks and the privileges. You deserve it. Leadership is big responsibility. But remember: don't get too lost in the position. Stay focused on the team and respect the contribution of all team members, regardless of rank. Chances are you will end up needing every single one of them someday, probably soon. Smart leaders understand the value of everybody on the team or in the company!

ect

What's next?

Respect will help you get the most out of your team, especially when you really need it. Respect breeds respect. When you value and respect people, chances are you will get their support and respect right back. These days, with fewer resources and time available, you'll need every inch you can get and you'll need a team that's there for the long haul.

So that's respect. But what about passion? How do you fuel the fire to keep your team energized?

You need to spark passion and creativity in the front lines, even if the front lines are at the 10-yard line. Your next challenge!

ACTION PLAN

You get what you give

1 EVERYONE IS SIGNIFICANT.

- Treat people at every level with respect – all jobs are important
- Make a connection, even when you think there isn't one
- Everyone has a network – people at any level can have a tremendous amount of power and influence

2 LEAD FROM THE FRONT.

- Respect what your team does – get out there with them and understand how they do their job
- Don't expect people to put up with a work environment that you wouldn't work in

3 WHAT YOU GIVE IS WHAT YOU GET.

- Loyalty down = loyalty up
- If you give respect you get respect

ect

SPARK CREATIVITY

The future's in our present hands
let's reach right in, let's understand
If you want it, you've got to believe

Believe, Lenny Kravitz

ENERGIZE

The energized environment

Passion = potential

Release the creative

Believe

Dreams into reality

The 30-60-90 quick-hit plan

The petri dish

HOUSTON. 2004. I looked down over a sea of tens of thousands of spectators from the 'cheap seats' section of the Reliant Stadium and couldn't get over the intense level of energy. Wow! It was the Super Bowl XXXVIII pre-game show, and Aerosmith just had us rocking in our seats to "Dude Looks Like a Lady." Out of nowhere, five parachutists with yellow parachutes and big Aerosmith logos jumped from the low stadium rafters onto the football field (well, low if you're jumping with a parachute) – from a height of about 1,000 feet. Then, from a giant screen, the spectators were directed in synchronized fashion to do a giant wave around the stadium, holding red, white or blue one-foot squares of cardboard that had been placed under our seats, all while the American national anthem was playing. The impact – all 70,000 of us turned the stadium into a huge moving American flag. The guy behind me was yelling in his cell phone with tears streaming down his face. "I can't believe I'm here – it's so beautiful!" Something about football games and national anthems bring out a whole new sensitive side in men! God bless America.

Amidst this frenzy, I realized that I was probably the least deserving spectator at this game. I didn't know much about football, let alone important details like which two teams had won a spot in the coveted Super Bowl game or who were their quarterbacks. Luckily, a few days before the big game, while seeking refuge in the Hilton Hotel spa, (the Hilton was the headquarters for the NFL and possibly the last quiet corner of this buzzing fan-jammed city), I was able to fill in my football knowledge gap.

While picking my nail color, I happened to mention to the aesthetician that I knew little about the game and even less about the teams. I was there because of my marketing savvy, certainly not because of my football savvy! I told her I was a little concerned about a couple of upcoming meetings I had with the CEO of the Super Bowl Host Committee and a radio show interview with the 2 Live Stews – a hot sports radio duo with a hip-hop style who has since been featured in *Sports Illustrated* and voted Best Air Talent of the Year in 2005 by ESPN.

"Girl, how can you not know it's the 'Pats' and the 'Cats' playin' this Sunday? You better brush up; you just can't go to all those meetings without knowing somethin' about who's playin'," she said as she filed away. "If I were you, I would go have a chat with that nice guy sittin' right over there getting a pedicure – he looks like he's gotta know something about football!" Well, she couldn't have pointed me in a better direction.

This gentleman knew a lot about the Super Bowl and the NFL. In fact, it was his business. I ended up getting a pedicure next to this very nice TV football commentator and analyst who just happened to be an ex-NFL 'bad-ass running back' with the Pittsburgh Steelers and later with the Chicago Bears – Merril Hoge. Of course, I had no idea at the time what a bad-ass running back was, but I have since been thoroughly educated. What better way to get prepped for any meeting with the Super Bowl Host Committee executives than by an ESPN football analyst and ex-NFL star running back? After chatting with Merril Hoge briefly, I came across in my meetings like a marketing director who knew at least something about the event where I was marketing my product!

So what was I doing at Super Bowl XXXVIII? There's only one reason why I was 'working' and participating in some of the most prestigious nightclub parties, awe-inspiring fireworks shows and incredible weeklong celebrations around one of the most important events on the continent.

SEE THE POTENTIAL

I had seen the potential in an idea by one of my team members, Vince, while working with a leading-edge technology firm. His own personal passion in football led to the idea that sparked some great creativity for a marketing program. It was the beginning of my involvement with the NFL, and here's how it started.

Vince, a technical integration manager with a quiet demeanour worked on my team with Research In Motion (RIM), the creator of the BlackBerry. As the marketing and business integration director, I had a team of managers who worked closely with our U.S. business customer base – big companies all in big

> "When I approached my boss about my BlackBerry and NFL idea I was very nervous. My ideas were vague and unstructured. I knew where I wanted to go, but knew very little on how to get to the end goal. Adding to my fear and doubts was the fact that my ideas were beyond the responsibilities of my current position and training. Nevertheless, I approached Angela for her leadership and counsel. She listened to me and truly put thought and action into my ideas. After helping me define the scope, setting goals, milestones, and measures to gauge success, Angela empowered me to turn my ideas into reality."
>
> *– Vince Washington, BlackBerry technical integration manager, RIM*

cities. This team was responsible for supporting these customers by integrating our BlackBerry technology with the customers' infrastructure. This team's strength was in technology.

Vince was not a sales manager nor was he involved in business development. So when he came to see me with an idea that would involve both of those skill sets, the easiest answer I could have given him was very simply, "No, Vince, it's not your job. That's not our turf. We don't have the budget." Or "This will create work." Or, an all-time favorite response, "We're not in the business of giving away our product!" I think you get the picture. But, what kind of fun is an attitude like that? I'm always open to new ideas because I believe that when you follow a little adventure, you will definitely find creativity.

This was no exception. I listened to Vince and decided to support his idea.

Vince had a passion for football. Passion, by the way, is a key to realizing your potential. Back in college, he was a wide receiver for the University of Michigan Wolverines, one of the big football schools in the U.S. He had an amazing network of players, coaches and some celebrities now playing or working in the NFL – people he had played with during his college days who had later moved on to the big league. His big idea? He wanted to explore the potential of bringing together his powerful NFL network (and sports savvy about the industry) with RIM's product – the BlackBerry. At the time, the BlackBerry was a leading-edge e-mail device primarily adopted by big business, such as the legal and financial industries.

Vince saw great potential for the BlackBerry to be used as a powerful communication platform within the NFL – the NFL league itself, the 32 teams in it and their IT directors, the coaches who are on the field, in the office or on the road, and the players. But Vince had no idea how to test his idea or where to get started. He needed help to turn his idea into action.

My marketing mind started spinning its wheels. This could be a HUGE opportunity. The largest and possibly most powerful sports organization in the United States, maybe the world, could be using, or relying, on our technology. Influential NFL players who could pack influential product testimonials. Potential access to a great network of other partners that the NFL organization might introduce our team and company to. Hmmm. Let me think about this for a minute. Vince brought us a slam dunk…or should I say, a touchdown.

Well, I thought it was a slam dunk. Others weren't so sure. Some of my colleagues had other words to describe our idea – a 'petri dish' – which I suppose meant an experiment of some sort. They were concerned the petri dish might create more work to already overburdened resources, cost us money with no guarantee of return on investment and, worst of all, impose on other departments' turf and create the dreaded 'turf war' within the company. Despite the resistance, I still believed that Vince's idea had some great potential, not to mention real merit. Besides, I didn't see it as trespassing on someone else's turf so much as expanding our own particular box.

Sure, we didn't have a clear idea of what the outcome would be…but when you're breaking new ground, do you ever? I decided to keep this petri dish growing.

RED FLAG

Creating a new space means bending old paradigms

If you're ever accused of creating a petri dish, your leadership approach is probably on the right track. Seeing potential in an idea and inviting creativity will require some out-of-the-box thinking and possibly a little rule bending; you might even end up pissing some people off! When you're confronted by colleagues who don't support you or you get blocked by other obstacles, take a step back, adjust your path to navigate around the obstacles, and keep believing that you're heading in the right direction.

THOUGHT INTO ACTION

At least now I had an understanding of what the obstacles in our path would be – concerns about job turf and workload. We had to find another tack to get the wind in our sails.

To move Vince's idea forward, we required some internal damage control. Nothing that a little planning and some documented goals and objectives couldn't fix. And maybe a little creative marketing to go along with them.

The first thing we did was draft a 30-60-90-day mini action plan to clarify goals and minimize our obstacles. This 'quick-hit' plan enabled us to get the cooperation we needed from the company, at least for the short term. Vince had some preliminary discussions with his NFL contacts, so we documented which NFL teams were showing a medium-to-strong interest in our product versus some of the other products they had already adopted. We estimated the potential increase in sales over three, six and nine months that we might expect from these teams. We helped Vince prioritize his immediate and short-term actions, such as educating the NFL IT leaders on the power of BlackBerry and getting the product adopted where there was strong interest. And most importantly, we clarified potential turf issues inside our company so that my colleagues wouldn't see this project as threatening in any way.

▶▶ **Fast forward** *to Chapter 08, "Link Your Team to the Mission," which provides some great insight on integrating your team with the task at hand.*

Getting a quick plan in place was important, and Vince walked away after our planning session with a couple of immediate to-dos to get this petri dish started. There was another advantage to this session: we needed to create some 'hype' so people would be excited about this new client. Never hurts to grease the path a little, so I tasked Vince to come back with some autographs from NFL players. He showed up with exactly what we were looking for in just a few weeks – signed helmets from Pittsburgh Steelers Tony Maddox, the NFL chief himself, Commissioner Tagliabue, and from the Oakland Raiders' Jerry Rice, considered the game's greatest receiver.

"Oh," I exclaimed when Vince proudly presented me with his major coup. "This is fantastic! Who's Jerry Rice?"

> "Like many ideas, there are always concerns and risks to be evaluated. It's also a reality that everyone may not like your ideas. Having strong leadership allows you to navigate those obstacles." *– Vince Washington, BlackBerry technical integration manager, RIM*

The principle: Spark creativity

Encouraging creativity and generating ideas are not reserved only for people in strategic positions. The job belongs to everyone, right down to the team players on the front lines.

Leading with this principle is about finding new ways of thinking and doing business. To keep an open mind for generating creativity you need to have an energized environment, where team members feel safe, confident and motivated to bring ideas forward no matter how crazy. As a leader you should understand how to bring out the best in your team – and that includes creativity. When do you come up with the best ideas and are the most inspired? What might help your team keep the great ideas flowing? Put yourself in your team's shoes to stay connected with what keeps people generating ideas.

> You can paralyze an organization by having consensual management, and you can debilitate an organization and the best people in it, if you are autocratic and dictatorial. The entrepreneurial quality that a lot of trail blazers in the media businesses have, and the personal passion to take creative risks and to think outside the box, are as important as they ever were.[1]
>
> *– Christie Hefner, CEO, Playboy Enterprises*

Maybe your mind really flows with crazy ideas and big dreams first thing in the morning after you've grabbed that cup of java (my mind really gets buzzing with my latte-to-go in hand and my favorite tunes blaring). Back in my marketing days, by the time I pulled into the parking lot of some of my corporate giant employers, I would be so energized I would run right into my office, grab my colored markers and map out crazy ideas all over my white board. Some would turn into reality, others would get wiped away.

Energizing creativity and ideas requires your ability, as a leader, to believe – to see the potential and release the creativity of people on your team. Rather than 'boxing' people in with preconceived skill sets, allow some flexibility to line up passion and skills with the mission at hand and the sky is the limit! Maybe someone on your team works in an administrative capacity but has dreamed of getting into sales – can they provide support to the sales reps? Or another team player wants to get into public speaking – can they deliver a 10-minute talk on an inspirational topic at the next quarterly planning session?

Once you blend a little open-mindedness with leadership support, you'll witness more thought turn into action. You'll also earn the respect of team members, boost confidence in their ideas and encourage more effort and action behind the idea.

Need more evidence to lead with this principle? How about that fact that we're now working and leading at a pace in today's business where timelines and goals are more aggressive than five years ago or even five months ago and technology, processes and attitudes are changing at greater speed. A little creativity and ideas from the team will help to keep you on your toes and do things better, smarter, faster, different. If you don't foster that environment, someone else might beat you to it.

Looking for new ideas, new ways of doing and growing business or new products, services, customers or clients?

Energize. Empower. Believe. And spark a creative explosion.

> You are empowered to inspire by having been inspired, so think big, let your dreams be grand.[2]
>
> *– Ma Deva Padma*

How to spark creativity in your world

> I'm doing a lot of work on what causes creativity. It's living in the moment and that happens when we're under two years of age, drunk, on drugs or having an orgasm…The trick is to recreate those conditions at work and get people to leave their issues at home.[3]
>
> *– Chip Wilson, Lululemon Athletica mastermind*

Chip Wilson of Lululemon Athletica, a hip yoga wear and gear company, believes in an 'In-the-moment' mindset to set up the right environment for creativity. The company's own manifesto highlights 'in-the-moment' thinking: "Do it now. The world is changing AT SUCH A RAPID rate that waiting to implement changes will leave you two steps behind.[4] With 30-something retail outlets from Toronto to Tokyo, and hundreds more on the way, when Wilson "does it now" he seems to be doing it right.

So what helps create that spark? In Wilson's company, out-of-the-box thinking creates an environment for creativity. Simple things like changing a person's title from 'salesperson' to 'educator' can set the tone for a more freethinking team.

And from such freethinking can come some very powerful, maybe even radical, ideas that can create some great publicity. For a recent Lululemon store grand opening, the company announced that the first 100 customers who showed up and "got naked" were given free Lululemon clothes. The alternative Lululemon leader goes one step further when it comes to energizing his teamwork environment to bring out the best. When asked in an interview why he expanded his stores when he did, Wilson claimed that he needed to create the right environment for employees. The environment you create can release or block creativity.

> I ended up with some really fantastic people working for me...They want more than we could offer them out of one store. So it was about making the best situation for the people working for me, having them reach their goals.[5]
>
> *– Chip Wilson, Lululemon Athletica mastermind*

CREATE OUT-OF-THE-BOX THINKING

To foster this thinking you need to energize the environment and believe in ideas to bring them to reality. Here's how.

➤ ENERGIZE THE ENVIRONMENT

To energize and empower your team, be a freethinker and support freethinking and you'll bring 'good' ideas, the ones with great potential, forward.

A safe open-minded environment comes from open lines of communication. That's what brainstorming is all about, and it's also a key element to creating the freethinking environment you're looking for. So, any simple brainstorming activity might incorporate these familiar requirements:

- No idea is a bad idea.
- Everyone must put forth an idea no matter how silly it is.
- All ideas must be written on the white board for the team's consideration.

I'm suggesting you go a few steps further in your next brainstorming session. I'm not saying that you try to uncover the next design guru, but encourage a more open team so that you allow for different ways of thinking and doing.

1 Off-the-wall ideas

Team meetings are a great place to create a freethinking environment. Allocate time at weekly team meetings for new idea discussion or 'weird and wonderful' research from entirely different industries. Set up some time after your regular business discussion to add 'new thinking space' to the agenda. As leader you might want to start the ball rolling, but get team players to pitch in each week. A team who sees a big-picture, out-of-the-box leader at work should have no problem adopting the same philosophy.

2 Fun or fear factor sessions

Off-site sessions that incorporate business with brainstorming or team-building exercises that might even incorporate a little 'fear factor' (we did some indoor rock-climbing for confidence-building once) are a great way to energize and connect team players who don't normally work together, as well as increase the team connection.

3 An open-door policy

Let people know they can approach you with ideas – one on one – if they feel less confident around the conference table.

CASE STUDY **Take it to the sky, part I**

I'm a huge believer in off-site sessions. Not long ago, I was trying to get my key customer, a T-Mobile marketing and branding team to buy into a sales incentive and rewards program. We wanted some financial support from this U.S. team for my program proposal that would reward the best sales team and sales representatives for achieving or exceeding, shall we say, aggressive sales targets for that quarter. The reward: flights in real fighter combat aircraft. A couple of ex-air force pilots I knew had set up an exciting air-to-air combat business so the general public could experience what it was like to be a top gun for a day. My team and I set up an off-site session we called Take It To The Sky to get everyone hyped. To maximize the people connection, we organized mixed teams, which included members of my team, our sales team and our U.S. partner's group, and invited our internal research and development team to come out for some competitive team-building fun. Our Take It To The Sky challenge included rock climbing, themed T-shirts, and some socializing, snacks and signature martinis (my favorite) afterward. We didn't get the financial support we were looking for, but we did create a newly bonded 'end-to-end' product launch team that went right across our company, from the people who designed our products and developed the software, to product managers, to sales and marketing staff, to our customer and largest partner and its team responsible for launching our latest and greatest device. The result – a more connected cross-functional team who felt comfortable to put ideas out on the table.

RED FLAG **The funnel**

Not all ideas will be good ideas. And not all ideas should be supported. But in order for the best ideas to surface, you've got to invite the good, the bad and the ugly ideas, and then put them through a funnel to weed out the winners from the rejects. You've got nothing to lose by inviting all ideas – as long as you don't set up false expectations that every free-wheeling idea will become reality.

➤ EXPAND IN-YOUR-BOX THINKING

Want to get the best out of your team players and maximize their potential? In addition to creating the right environment, you need to allow job flexibility through an 'expand-in-your-box' approach.

Everyone on the team has an important skill or function to support the team mission, but the 'box' in which we've been hired should have room to 'flex'…to expand responsibility, take on new projects or increase scope. Customers' needs are dynamic, organizations change continually, and to keep up with that pace, a team player's job or role needs to change shape from time to time as well.

Allowing for some expand-in-your-box movement can bring out the best in people. It increases morale and motivation, necessary for generating great ideas on the front lines. And it's a lot smarter than losing someone on the team because they have outgrown their box.

Empower individuals

Encouraging your team to think about how to better their current roles and even expand in them creates a very healthy team and organization. For example, you might see team members looking to grow in one of these ways:

- You lead a customer service team and one of your reps wants to expand the number of products they support;
- You're a vice-principal of a school and one of your teachers wants to learn new skills to get into guidance counselling;
- Or you run your own company and your faithful administrative assistant wants to help you get into business development and expand your market.

It doesn't matter what you're leading – a team of customer support specialists, an editorial staff, a group of school teachers or a team of volunteers for a cable TV show, here are some simple ideas to help your team expand its potential:

1 Creative titles

Do you have the flexibility to allow team members to design their own job titles? Being proud of your title and position is extremely empowering.

2 Big-picture work

Can team members support a new team goal or company initiative? Is there something they can do to be a part of the big picture? Can one of your team members represent the entire team on your behalf for the planning of the next departmental meeting?

3 The wingman

Does anyone on your team have mentoring, coaching or leadership aspirations? Can they mentor or coach an intern, student or new employee? This is a win-win situation – they get the experience and you now have more time on your hands as the intern's role grows. You might think about developing a cross-training program to develop people's skills.

4 Alternative duties

What makes your team members tick? What are they personally passionate about that might be tied into their job? Is there a secondary task they could take on that supports the goals of the team and allows them to incorporate their passion? Let your team members participate in training or professional development that ties into their passion and team goals.

CASE STUDY **Take it to the sky, part II**

When I was leading my team at RIM, I had an administrative assistant who wanted to expand her skills and learn more about marketing and coordinating corporate events. She had absolutely no background or training in marketing. She was committed to learning a new project without letting it interfere with her day job (read: take wonderful care of me and our other execs). In other words, she would take on this added role in her 'spare time.' So, I coached her to set up a large three-day event with our key client and our support teams. This required more than just planning and coordination for three days of meetings, meals and entertainment for more than 30 people: our goal was to get our partner very hyped about our product so they would focus on it as one of their new key offerings.

The result: the off-site session was a tremendous success and we were going to get the focus we wanted from our partner. But more importantly, our administrative assistant's confidence, passion and creativity got a huge boost. Guess what she's doing today? Coordinating corporate marketing events full-time.

By encouraging expansion among your team, you'll not only add passion and creativity to the mix but you'll likely get more hours from your team members, who are eager to perform and please. Leaders who don't invite this type of growth could find themselves looking for new crew members because their team could be looking for new opportunities elsewhere.

Outside the corporate BOX

A ROCK STAR ON EXPANDING 'THE BOX'

Lenny Kravitz doesn't appear to get boxed in by any limits as a leading-edge guitar player, musician and lyricist who was retro before retro was cool. His creativity is evident in his eclectic music style and powerful guitar riffs. But true to his out-of-the-box mindset, he has not put any limits on his creativity — his latest accomplishments range from moving music to delivering design:

- In 2002, Kravitz received the Microsoft Windows Media Innovation award for his pioneering use of digital media to distribute music securely and freely over the Internet.
- After 15 years as an ultra cool rocker (okay, so I'm a little biased) Lenny has created Kravitz Design and added interior design, architecture and, most recently, a fashion house and home line to his already distinguished list of credentials. How's that for expanding the box?

"You know, creativity is creativity, and it doesn't matter if it's with a paintbrush or with a piano or with a film script or with a photograph. I love that because I guess some people tend to do one thing – and they can be amazing at it – but the kind of person that I am, I need to keep moving forward...today people want to put you in a box and say 'Gordon is a photographer.' But then you start whipping out the symphonies and poetry and movies. You put us all up in a place where there are no limits."[6]

– Lenny Kravitz in an interview with Gordon Parks, legendary artist and photographer

"I spend a lot of time trying to encourage my team to do that – to stretch their minds. One way is through a program called Inspire Me Day. A creative team has to take the rest of the department out to do something inspiring unrelated to advertising...One team took us to a Mexican wrestling match and they showed up in costumes and masks, like some of the more ardent fans. One idea that came out of that was a new slogan for a sports network.[7]" *– Judy John, chief creative officer, Leo Burnett*

BELIEVE. THEN ACT LIKE YOU BELIEVE

Talk is cheap! Once you've established the right environment and encourage job flexibility to get the good ideas flowing, help bring them to reality.

We all need someone out there to believe in us, to realize our dreams. And it's important we help others realize their dreams by believing in them. Make sure you're extending that same support to people on your team who are just like you!

Here's how you can believe, then act like you believe.

1 Clear the path for new ideas

If you support someone's idea, remember that it will take effort to turn that creativity into reality. Good ideas can only gain momentum through individual, team and leadership support – that means you, other team members, other leaders, executives or partners. So, you'll need to evaluate how implementing a new idea will shift the current world in a positive direction or impact someone else's team or organization and then gain buy-in from all the parties. You need to clear the path and maybe take some heat. Remember the petri dish.

2 Find the wind for your sails

To get off the ground, all ideas need some 'wind.' The greater the impact or change an idea may cause, the greater wind you will need to drive it. If we go back to the petri dish example for a moment, Vince's idea required a couple of key things to come to reality – one of which was my support and guidance to create the necessary momentum for the project. But because this idea was also going to impact other teams and introduce a potentially new distribution channel or customer, we required some executive support to make sure we could navigate internally without too much friction. I knew exactly where to go – the company's chief operating officer happened to be a freethinking, open-minded leader who has a reputation in the industry for being the 'wind' in many up-and-coming executives' sails. He gave us the 'wind' we needed by approving a 90-day period to get the idea off the ground.

Reality Check: Getting your second wind

If you still don't have the support you are looking for to get key stakeholders on board, you may need to broaden your horizons and go for the second wind! Don't give up, but instead look for external or executive sponsorship from a different level in the company. Having an external go-ahead, even if only for a few months to give the idea some traction, could be all you need.

3 Take baby steps and show quick hits

This is the best way to get a creative idea up and running, especially if it's going to impact other teams. All you need is a little momentum and some speedy results to help that idea become reality. Your best bet is to pitch the creative idea as a 'temporary' endeavor, project or plan – with a three-to six-month duration. That should be enough time for you to start putting the plan into action. Nothing like results, even short term, to create momentum. (See next page, In the HOT SEAT box for details on gaining the necessary buy-in from colleagues or execs, with at least enough time to get your team's creativity up and running, and creating a 30-60-90-day game plan.)

TALK IS CHEAP:

SHOW ACCOUNTABILITY WITH A QUICK-HIT PLAN

1. Create clarity and confidence with rules of engagement

Mitigate any you're-stepping-on-my-toes risk by developing rules of engagement between your team and others that might be affected by changes. If your new idea is going to impact another team, you'll need to establish an understanding of how team players will work together.

2. Show accountability

The quick-hit plan will show commitment by putting the plan down on paper. The plan should detail a simple list of goals, objectives and actions to be taken by individual team members for the next 30 days, 60 days and 90 days. This documented plan ensures the focus is on meeting pre-established objectives that are aligned with the team and the organization. Keep track of progress on a monthly basis and share the results with other team members, leaders and key sponsors.

3. Get (at least) temporary buy-in

People are more likely to support new initiatives if they don't feel like they have to make a huge commitment. Introduce an idea and its impact as a temporary initiative that must prove itself before you require greater commitment from your team, other departments or other external parties. Then start delivering on the 'win-win' results you laid out above. Set up progress status meetings or updates to review the actual progress that is being made based on your 30-60-90-day plan. The results then become more tangible and real for your sponsors and colleagues.

We used these same steps to get Vince's idea and the petri dish to start growing. Vince's idea would be affecting his workload to some degree, as well as impacting our sales and marketing team and, therefore, our own team players. So, we needed agreement with the other team members to mitigate task overlap and get executive support.

At the end of our NFL project, my team witnessed firsthand how a small creative idea really ignited. And we got an extra pat on the back for our efforts. Don Morrison, RIM's chief operating officer (COO) (who provided the initial thumbs-up), later told me that he thought Vince and I had helped change some of the RIM culture – with the NFL behind BlackBerry we were bringing the device to the mainstream before BlackBerry had been successfully introduced into retail channels. I would like to think he was right. "The NFL idea came out of the blue. It was different, fresh and completely unexpected. And in the end it was a great success," says Morrison. "However, not all ideas and decisions have the same happy ending, but that is typical of innovation. One good idea can more than offset the downside of others that fail. The point is, if you want to run a customer-focused team today, you need to open yourself and listen closely when good ideas surface from the team members that are interacting with the marketplace every day. In fact, it is a sign of maturity that a leader encourages and creates that kind of open, receptive environment. It takes courage, but it pays dividends."

What's in it for you...and your team?

> "A sense of adventure is really about waking up every day not with a sense of dread but with a sense of possibility." – *Unknown*

What happens when you create an empowered environment and believe in your team members? What's the result of sparking creativity from the front lines? Even with a small team, the results can be far-reaching.

> **CREATIVE INTELLIGENCE**
> C = E + 2D
> **Creative = empower + delegate + disappear**
>
> Once you've sparked creativity on your front lines and paved the way with the right environment and support, think empowerment. A good military motto suggests that once leaders do their job, it's time to sit back, delegate and disappear.

The NFL project took some months before it really got off the ground. Vince and I had to keep close tabs on its progress, as his newly expanded role meant that he would be working longer days supporting the additional workload and making up for the time new work encroached on his original responsibilities. Initially, Vince's focus was to introduce the product to his network of NFL contacts, and later to set up face-to-face meetings with the league's coaches, IT managers or administrators who showed a real interest. It was going to take time and effort to cultivate this new sports partner, which had not yet been drinking the 'BlackBerry Kool-Aid' like some other industries.

Within months, however, Vince was reporting incredible progress. Several NFL teams and their IT departments had taken BlackBerry on board as a trial and, in some cases, permanently as part of their overall IT solution. Being able to show this type of result to our team and leaders was critical to keeping this project alive.

The project grew in leaps and bounds – the BlackBerry device has a reason for being nick-named "Crackberry." Within two years, the BlackBerry had been adopted by football players and coaches, high-powered NFL execs and team owners, sports TV celebs and radio station hosts, and the 32 teams of the NFL and the league's administration office.

> "Creativity implies risk…Climates that support the task aspects of creativity provide the freedom to do things differently, empower people to act on their ideas, encourage active participation, and provide support to the people involved in creative tasks.[8]" *– Daniel Levi, Group Dynamics for Teams*

Scouts also use it to report in real time to their personnel directors on how sought-after players are doing on the field. Behind the scenes, the Super Bowl Host Committees use it for planning and on-site execution. Special applications have even been built for gamers who want to use their BlackBerry beyond e-mail and phone capabilities to play fantasy football. And now, two years later, there is no stopping the petri dish as headlines in U.S. newspapers like "High-tech Ideas Drive NFL's New Plan" describe it "fitting that a BlackBerry played a critical role in the NFL's new labor deal."

> "This leadership was extremely important to me. Having a leader who believes in you is empowering! It energizes you to give everything you have to the project. It gives you confidence in taking calculated risks. A mistake is not seen as a failure but as an opportunity to learn and actions are maximized for the benefit of the company." *– Vince Washington, BlackBerry technical integration manager, RIM*

The next time someone on your team comes to you with an out-of-box idea that might not fit into their role, my advice is to give it a second thought. See the potential. Release the creative. Baby steps or big leaps. It's all good!

Here's what could be in it for you…and your team.

✓ **Passion**

Allowing team members some influence and flexibility on how they might achieve business results creates a vested interest in their job. Tapping into the right skills means increased passion for what they are doing. Why wouldn't it? They came up with the idea.

✓ **People growth**

Encouraging an expand-in-your-box mindset will motivate team members to look at things differently, come up with unique ways to do things better and even take on more responsibility.

"Because its very nature is the lack of a fixed form, the enormous energy of The Creative is indefinable.[9]"

– *Ma Deva Padma*

✓ **Performance and results**

A motivated team member who is given the opportunity to expand becomes an energized player. Energy drives results!

✓ **More creativity**

What goes around comes around. Creativity feeds on creativity just like great energy can create more good energy. Putting creative ideas into reality will inspire team members to continue to think creatively.

✓ **They grow. You get to go**

As your empowered team takes on more responsibilities, you are creating your own growth strategy. By growing others into bigger roles you get to look up and out for your future.

RED FLAG

Remember. You don't get paid to be liked!

Sometimes saying "no" is necessary. When? If you've released all this potential and creativity and all you get back are bad ideas. Or when a team member wants to expand in her role, but she hasn't been performing well in her current duties or proven herself in other ways. Sometimes a suggestion is not a win-win for the team or organization but more self-serving. A good leader will have to say "no" from time to time. You'll need to determine if the needs of the mission, individual and the team are being met. And you'll have to judge whether the "potential" you are releasing will provide a valuable return on investment for the team and the overall mission.

"Individual and group creativity can survive only in organizational environments that support it. Although organizations often say they want to encourage creativity, their actions might not support creativity. Organizations want both stability and change, and this contradiction creates problems.[10]"

– *Daniel Levi,* Group Dynamics for Teams

Hindsight is 20/20

Saying no is easy. Saying yes is smart

Change in today's business world is inevitable. Creativity is necessary for change and change is paramount to growth. Don't just get used to change. Create it!

Unfortunately, a common reaction of leaders when they're challenged to think a little differently is, "No, that can't be done." Or, "No, that's not within our mandate, or our goals or objectives. Sorry."

Don't be a naysayer. Don't be afraid of a little work and a little risk – that's where you get most of your results. It's a proven fact that creativity is what drives teams, organizations and companies forward. What better way to keep people motivated than to allow some expansion within the box. Creativity does not come from the word "no." Go ahead, live a little!

What's next?

You've seen the potential, you've empowered and delegated responsibilities and you now have a small team of high-performing players, ready for the next challenge. The great thing about growing people around you is that the more you bring people 'up,' the higher up you can go.

How can you get to the next level? How can you keep adding to your success?

One winning strategy to continue growing your team and provide personal expansion is to combine forces and develop co-leaders. Leaders need co-leaders.

Having a second-in-command, a '2 i/c', a right-hand woman, a 'go-to' person or a co-creator – however you want to do it, whether it's identifying someone on your team who has complementary skills, or someone who can back you up in tough times, or an individual who can help you get to an entirely new level – is your key to your success. And your succession plan.

After all, the sum is greater than the parts!

ACTION PLAN

Take a calculated risk

1 ENERGIZE YOUR ENVIRONMENT.

- Be a freethinker and make freethinkers
- Let people expand in their box; it will expand yours

2 BELIEVE. THEN ACT LIKE YOU BELIEVE.

- Pave the way
- Find the wind
- Show quick hits

3 C = E + 2D

- (Creativity through empowerment, delegation and disappearing)

4 GET 'BUY-IN' WITH A QUICK-HIT PLAN.

- Remember talk is cheap, action is everything

gize

COMBINING FORCES

> If you want to kiss the sky
> 'better learn how to kneel
>
> *Mysterious Ways*, U2

SYNERGY

The sum is greater than the parts

Pursuit of greater goals

Expand your strength

Fill in the gaps

Share the spotlight

"What the f@&!"

"Sorry Ange, I just don't see it. This talk show and its audience really have nothing to do with our target market – the audience is a bunch of housewives, not the business customer we cater to. I'm not really interested in supporting this program."

What the hell?! I couldn't believe it. Was I hearing this guy right? He couldn't really have said "NO," could he? I put my phone on mute and looked at my marketing manager who was shrugging her shoulders and shaking her head.

The reality was that the guy on the other end of the phone happened to represent Research In Motion's then-largest U.S. partner, responsible for distributing our product all over the United States, for the lion's share of our company's revenue at that time. Whether I liked it or not, this director from T-Mobile and I were joined at the hip when it came to deciding what programs we would create to launch RIM product. He had veto rights, particularly since I was looking to him to fund three months of free airtime and service for the more than 350 leading-edge 7230 BlackBerry devices we were proposing to give away at approximately $69 per month for service per $399 device.

Okay. So I admit, he didn't think we were as important to him as he was to us. Our products certainly weren't his hottest-selling devices or biggest revenue generators. He distributed products for many other companies and we were only just getting into the retail market, where T-Mobile had tremendous strength. At this point, BlackBerry sales accounted for only about 0.05 percent of the revenue for this huge U.S. carrier ('carrier' being, in this case, a company that sells and distributes wireless products). But part of the RIM culture and employee mindset, which is probably where some of the company's immense success comes from, is that the company was destined to be huge even though it was still small in comparison to other device manufacturers. We didn't feel small, and we sure didn't act it.

But our client didn't see it that way back then. And he did not feel that the audience of supposed 'housewives and stay-at-home moms' would provide the return on investment we would want from one of our joint marketing programs.

So what was this huge opportunity that was getting vetoed by this very experienced professional in the world of mobile devices and personal digital assistants? Here's a clue. What TV talk show host has 30-something million viewers a week, a net worth of more than a billion dollars, and has been known to give away thousands of dollars worth of gifts, such as UGG boots, video iPods, Burberry coats, diamond-studded watches and, more recently, houses, on her TV show? You've got it. None other than Oprah, the reigning leader of TV talk shows and one of the most powerful brands and testimonials in the world.

Which led me to ask myself at that very moment, what kind of nut bar says "no" to Oprah?

NOTHING BIG COMES EASY

Oprah's team was shopping around for high-tech giveaways for its upcoming "Oprah's Favorite Things" show, airing in November 2003. During the annual 'top-secret' special event, audience members had no idea they had landed a seat on the episode until Oprah announced it when she greeted them while the cameras were rolling. It remains the hottest ticket in town. Why? Because after Oprah introduces the products she loves, she hands one out to each and every audience member to take home. These products (sometimes worth thousands of dollars) have included designer clothing, accessories, foods, high-tech gadgets, cars and more.

Anyone involved with the show behind the scenes is sworn to absolute secrecy, and that included us. What's so unique about the show, from a marketing perspective, is that it goes well beyond the usual formula of a celebrity endorsing a product. Millions tune in to the show as Oprah gives a mini-review of how she uses the product and a testimonial of how much she enjoys it or the added value it's brought to her life. Oprah's stamp of approval has turned previously unheard of products into overnight successes. So having your product featured on this show is, indeed, a major marketing coup. Lucky (and hysterical) audience members go home with carloads of wonderful goodies while Oprah keeps her ratings up and gives back, sharing some of her fortunes with the world. It's a win-win for all.

What could RIM offer? Oprah was already familiar with an older version of the BlackBerry, the 6710 model with a larger black and white screen, which she had apparently enjoyed tremendously. But her team was looking for the latest and greatest in handheld devices, and there were several 'smart phones' and wireless digital devices in the running.

So there was our challenge. We knew we had exactly what she needed – the BlackBerry 7230. This was RIM's latest device, and our team had only just launched it with T-Mobile as our new entrant into the retail market. It was small, had a color screen and appealed to a wide audience. If only we could convince T-Mobile to throw in the three months of free service we were looking for, we would have an absolute winner. Oprah's team was choosing the final products over the next few weeks, so I had a very short amount of time to come up with a compelling package to beat out any other competitive product and convince the naysayers that this was the right time and focus for this type of marketing program. Just as importantly, we had to plan for a lot of fine details, such as logistics to get the devices to Chicago and up and running with service, not to mention technical support and some sort of tracking process for the devices so that we could manage who received the giveaway devices and follow up after the show.

I suppose I could have taken this high-profile gem of a project and run with it when I was first assigned the opportunity. Just as we were taking the 7230 to market, I received an e-mail from RIM's CEO late one night with a short note that gave me some brief details about the Oprah show opportunity and said something along the lines of "Ange, this one's for you," which basically meant go figure this out. It's not every day that you get a high-profile opportunity such as this one – definitely the type of project that can put you out there, front and center. As I saw it, it was the type of project that any marketing leader would die for. And I suppose I could have had my team do all of the behind-the-scenes work and kept all of the good stuff to myself, especially the spotlight. Yes, it's sad but true – some leaders do actually keep all the glory. But I knew better.

Nothing comes easy. And any kind of high-profile project is going to end up requiring lots of support, from people at all levels. I was going to require 'buy-in' inside and outside the company to support this somewhat *avant-garde* program. (There was a power struggle within our company with regard to which teams should be leading the project.) I was definitely going to require some tactical support, someone to help execute all of the details to make sure this very high-profile program got off the ground without a hitch.

So how do you get key decision-makers on board, acquire internal resources to support an immediate project, guarantee that Oprah's team chooses your product and have a mission-critical marketing program launched in a few weeks or less?

Not by yourself! You need to combine forces, unify support and fill in your gaps with additional skills. In a short amount of time, there was a lot of work to be done. I needed:

- Buy-in from our partner to support the program
- Agreement from internal stakeholders on the cost of the giveaways
- Support from our internal branding team on special packaging for this giveaway
- Tactical planning for the logistics, technical support and tracking of the devices for post-program support

And that was only just the beginning. Giving stuff away was easy. Planning to make sure the program was a success and that we could measure its impact took teamwork. In this case, I definitely needed a right-hand man or woman to handle some of the pieces of this project and make sure we were ready on time. Leaders need co-leaders. And like many other programs I've led, this program required synergy between all players – inside and outside the company.

THE RIGHT-HAND MAN

This is where Lindsay, the-soon-to-become-right-hand, came in. She was my not-so-experienced but extremely enthusiastic marketing manager, who was ready for a challenge. This would be a project where strategy and execution would happen at the same time. We only had a few weeks to bring it together, yet we certainly had a few obstacles to overcome. If we didn't start working on the details and get everyone's buy-in within a week, we wouldn't be successful.

So I took a risk and set forth with a two-pronged attack: I had Lindsay get working on the many details to deliver BlackBerrys to the "Oprah's Favorite Things" show audience members while I worked on getting 'agreement in principle' for the program by all parties. Basically, we had to act like it was going to happen before we had agreement, or we wouldn't have the time to make it happen once we got agreement.

Lindsay was responsible for pulling together a 'tactical plan' of every detail that would be required to get this program off the ground, such as packaging for the BlackBerry that would appear on TV in front of millions of viewers, plus the behind-the-scenes logistics of shipping, customs, air time, device tracking, technical support, etc. In the meantime, I headed up some of the more strategic issues, such as gaining buy-in from internal departments to support everything from product branding to finance, as well as influencing our friends at T-Mobile to support the program. And, most importantly, I was keeping the Oprah team engaged and convinced that our 'package' was ready to go *and* should be its product of choice.

So we combined forces and created seamless synergy. We worked together, cooperating, supporting each other to fill in all of the gaps, covering off for each other when necessary – doing whatever needed to be done to make sure the project was a success. And that meant rolling up our sleeves and doing tasks we might not normally do. This is the kind of synergy you can create by having a great sidekick.

Here was Lindsay's perspective on how we worked together:

> "I remember going to visit my mom in Mexico just a few weeks before we needed to be at the Oprah show – it was a trip I could not cancel. I stood in your office and made a to-do list on the white board of some of the details that needed to be managed while I was gone. You laughed and said that I did a great job of 'delegating upwards.' By the time I returned, the to-do list was all checked off – you had taken care of my tasks for me, along with the many other meetings and negotiations you were involved in to make this opportunity real for our team. Very few employees would take the risk of delegating upwards to their boss but I felt empowered enough. Very few bosses would be so comfortable with being delegated to. This wasn't about who the boss was, but about the end goal. We had a powerful team."
>
> *– Lindsay Gibson, RIM, former senior marketing manager*

And that's what it's all about. A powerful team. Together, we were going to make sure that, first and foremost, BlackBerry was the product of choice and, secondly, (not that I'm competitive or anything) that our particular RIM team, in partnership with T-Mobile, would be the ones to deliver it! But I still had some resistance to work out. Even though I felt working with the Oprah show was a no-brainer marketing opportunity that should be grabbed without hesitation, not everyone at RIM felt that way at the time. Because this was a very new opportunity, we had no benchmark for RIM's potential return on investment for a give-away program like this one. After all, giving away 350 devices with a market value of $399 (US) each, along with monthly service fees valued at $69, wasn't pocket change. Hence the need to provide some answers to other internal leaders who wanted to understand the program's targeted cost, expected return on investment and timing since we hadn't launched full-scale in the retail segment yet.

MARKETING LOVE

Reactions like this aren't that surprising in a non-linear profession like marketing. Making the right marketing decisions aren't always black and white. They often require a real good sense of what is driving the consumer, some intuition and a sixth sense on how to connect with people at an emotional level. Excellent marketing goes far beyond just creating a need for your product; it creates an absolute love for your product. It's something Kevin Roberts, CEO Worldwide of Saatchi & Saatchi, a global company that helps other global companies build brands, calls creating "lovemarks."

In his book, *Lovemarks: The Future Beyond Brands,* Roberts discusses where successful brand builders need to go and where tremendously successful brand creators have gone. The future of marketing products, he says, is a place where brands and products have a relationship with their consumer. Think of the instant impact of these brands and you'll know exactly what he's talking about: Roots, The Body Shop, PlayStation 2, Starbucks, iPod, Rolex, IKEA, Barbie and Oprah.

> "...the way you relate to the market is, in many respects, making manifest that which is fundamentally intangible. It's not about the cost per thousand, or the rate, or what you are charging for this product. It's the way it feels, the way it represents itself, and then the way it either does or doesn't live up to those representations.[1]" – *Alan Webber, founding editor of* Fast Company *magazine commenting in the book* Lovemarks

Final decisions can sometimes boil down to people, emotions and instincts. They make for a very dynamic, but also unpredictable, reality. So I did my best to turn the people and emotions into numbers to satisfy the naysayers (there always seem to be some in the crowd) about the potential success of this program. Once I did some quick math and researched the impact of "Oprah's Favorite Things" show on other companies' featured products (a company's stock can rise the day she announces her picks), along with TV-viewing ratings, I could safely say, in black and white, that even if the giveaway BlackBerry 7230 devices were put in desk drawers or used as doorstops after three months of free service, this opportunity would offer something money couldn't buy – the testimonial of one genuine powerhouse of a celebrity like no other. To have one of the most powerful brands in the world stand behind our product was, well, enormous, in particular when the target market of this testimonial was focused on the very market we were heading right into. It didn't take long to convince even the small handful of skeptics that by passing up the Oprah opportunity, it would take an extraordinary amount of money, advertising dollars and marketing savvy to get the same kind of visibility for our newly launched BlackBerry 7230. We didn't have a benchmark to measure the return on investment, the monetary impact or device 'activations' (devices sold that are actually signed up for service) that would come directly from a marketing opportunity such as this, but one thing was for sure, this would be an investment in future return.

THUMBS UP

About two weeks into this project, we finally got the thumbs-up from our partner at T-Mobile. (Okay, so maybe I threatened him a little by telling him that, one way or another, RIM would provide a program for Ms. Winfrey, even if it meant dropping the opportunity off on my colleague's desk who happened to work with T-Mobile's biggest U.S. competitor). And because we had been working behind the scenes, my team was already prepared to meet the show's demands. Lindsay and I already had our complete tactical plan in place, details mapped out, special boxes designed, giveaway logistics sorted, etc. By the time we received the call from Oprah's producers that they had chosen our device, we were already rocking.

So far so good, except for one thing. As the saying goes, don't assume anything, and unfortunately we had. There we were, excited about working with Oprah's team and looking forward to being a part of the show. In fact, I had even been making arrangements with our CEO to get him to free up his calendar so he could make it to the show. I couldn't believe it when we were advised that only one of us would be permitted to go to Chicago, and we would not be sitting in the studio along with the audience. We were lucky to be sitting in the 'greenroom,' a backstage reception room for guests where you could watch the show on a screen. *What!?* We were giving away thousands of dollars worth of product and the team funding the product is not allowed to go? So I had a big decision to make: Which one of us would get to go to the Oprah show – me, the boss, or Lindsay, the person responsible for our program's execution?

When you've combined forces for project success, there will be opportunities for the spotlight. Sometimes you can share the spotlight, but sometimes you just have to hand it right over, even if that's tough to do. As tempting as it was, this was one of those times when the spotlight had to be handed over to the person managing the details instead of the person in charge. I was sending Lindsay to Chicago and I would have to watch from the sidelines. It made sense – Lindsay had been managing so many of the frontline details and logistics to make this happen that she needed to accompany the devices and launch the give-away program with the attention it would require.

OPRAH'S GREENROOM

Show time. The stage was covered in gifts, piled about 10 feet high. The audience of only hundreds sounded like thousands as they reacted in an absolute frenzy, some bursting into tears once they'd discovered they were actually on the show of all shows – "Oprah's Favorite Things." The noise was so loud that you could barely hear Oprah as she tried to introduce the products to this frenetic crowd. No question, it was out of control. And since I couldn't attend, Lindsay had specific orders to send me 'play by play' e-mails from the greenroom on what was happening every minute of the taped show.

After a short while, Oprah finally got to our product on her table of incredible gifts. And here's how it sounded: "LOVE IT, LOVE IT, LOVE IT, LOVE IT, LOVE IT!" She went on and on about how much she adored the BlackBerry, its capabilities and how she has personally benefited from having this product in her life. She showed video clips of these so-called housewives, keeping track of their busy schedules, their careers, kids' sports schedules, personal to-do lists and spouses' work calendars. This sure didn't sound like a device for a TV-watching 'domestic engineer.' It looked more like a power tool for working women who juggle family, careers and their personal lives. Oprah spoke for another few minutes, describing RIM's fantastic product, but it seemed like forever (at least that's what it felt like when I saw the show after it finally aired). And on top of it all, our partner company, who coughed up the free three months' service, was thanked graciously by Oprah for its part in making this giveaway happen. This was definitely turning out to be a win-win opportunity. No company could afford to pay for advertising like that.

While the show was being pre-taped, the e-mails started pouring in from Lindsay. One of them really caught my attention: "Oh my God!!! She said it wrong!!!" Lindsay was panicking from Oprah's greenroom as she watched the talk show host in action on the screen. I could almost feel the horror in her e-mail. "What are you talking about?" I shot back an e-mail. "OMG [oh my God], I can't believe she did that! Oprah called our company R-I-M."

For those who don't know, it's pronounced acronym and all, "RIM" – one word, one syllable.

I almost fell off my chair with the next e-mail. "Angela, I'm going to find the producer right now. She needs to get Oprah to re-tape that segment. I don't want to get fired!"

I told you she was enthusiastic. I recommended that Lindsay let Oprah do her thing, and that we, at RIM, would get over the slight misnomer in exchange for the wonderful job she was doing. Lindsay didn't get fired. In fact, quite the contrary, she expanded rapidly, from an inexperienced marketing manager to my marketing team co-leader. I would rely on her for the next few years to support me in launching some tremendous programs at RIM.

And then there was my partner with the U.S. carrier. I still remember his PowerPoint charts, outlining our quarterly successes for our next marketing success meeting in Seattle. Oprah was noted at the top of his marketing successes list, as one of the programs his team led that had a big impact on their company's past quarter and year. People were patting him on the back as we walked the halls of his company, congratulating him on the Oprah 'coup.' If only they knew we had to twist his arm for that whopper of a success! But why spoil his glory; at the end of the day, we did this together.

By sharing the spotlight with Lindsay and our U.S. partner, we all won in the end. The project was an incredible success for our team and our partnership. Our company had delivered a new device that would succeed across the business and retail channels, and bring some great new marketing programs to the table. And, in terms of people, well, every one of us benefited in wonderful ways, by combining forces and being a part of this unique, once-in-a-lifetime opportunity.

Combine forces. Create the synergy between resources and skills and be ready to share the spotlight, even if it means giving up a chance to sit in Oprah's greenroom.

The principle: Combine forces for synergy and strength

"Every one of us gets through the tough times because somebody is there, standing in the gap to close it for us." *– Oprah Winfrey, television talk show host and publisher of* O, The Oprah Magazine

You might be able to take on the world by yourself, but how far do you really want to go? This principle is about accepting that, as the leader, no matter how much confidence you have in yourself, bringing others on board as co-leaders can bring you to a whole new level.

It's about having the personal inner strength and confidence to let go of your ego so you can focus on the greater good of the goal and bring in or develop other key players of the team so that they can support you in achieving your goals more quickly. By developing co-leaders, you enable people to make decisions, take action and lead projects of their own, empowering others to be their best.

It will take a combination of strength and humility to allow others to share the spotlight with you. But the light will shine much more strongly when others are up there with you.

And while you're focusing on greater goals and putting your ego aside, interestingly enough, in a selfish way you will increase your *flexibility, agility and abilities.* And at the same time, you'll be able to fill in the gaps and buttress your weaknesses – something many leaders don't have the foresight to do, mostly because they fail to admit their weaknesses first. By creating space so others can expand their responsibilities, you'll be able to leverage your resources and focus your skills where they'll add the most value. When you focus your skills in the right places, you grow yourself at the same time.

BIG RETURN ON INVESTMENT

Although my team believed that the Oprah marketing opportunity was an investment in future return, we weren't certain of the exact results this program would manifest – only that it would likely bring some kind of return as we expanded in the marketplace. Like our investment in this product, investing in the development of a co-leader or a second-in-command will also provide you with great future returns.

◄◄ **Rewind** *to Chapter 04, "Know Your People," to read more about getting 'people intelligence.'*

The impact may be somewhat intangible at first, but I promise you that the results you can achieve with a great 2 i/c are exponential. Once you start experiencing the flexibility that you gain from focusing on your own strengths, or the freedom you earn to take on more challenges, or the power you receive with the additional brainpower you work with, you'll see how this relationship has the potential to become enormous!

Combining forces is particularly powerful today, when the pace and speed of attaining goals and objectives are getting faster and more furious. You can't discount the power of having a co-leader. In this environment, you're required to have a wide range of strong skills. Chances are you're going to need a second pair of hands, eyes, ears, another brain, another point of view. Then you can keep up!

It's time for the 'icons' who are lonely at the top to move over and make way for the power duos and combined forces who are in it for the greater goals and greater successes. Look at one of the most leading-edge, fast-paced industries today – the high-tech industry – and you will find reinvention of the corporate hierarchy with co-CEOs, co-leaders, creative titles or no titles, and a 'flattened' organization, where people at all levels are valued for their significance as the idea-generators of tomorrow.

Remember, you can do it alone, but how far do you want to go? What you can accomplish with a co-leader will likely be far more powerful than going solo.

> "Strange as it sounds, great leaders gain authority by giving it away.[2]"
>
> *– Vice-admiral James B. Stockdale, Congressional Medal of Honor and survivor of the Hanoi Hilton*

How to create synergy through a co-leader

The second-in-command (2 i/c) mindset started for me back in boot camp. From Day One, we were trained (or should I say brainwashed) to assign a 2 i/c to any project or task that we had to lead with a team. Be it leading a special project, mission, team, whatever, one of the first things we did was assign a 2 i/c. Why? As nasty as it may sound, the military is a business where conflict, terrorism, peacekeeping, war zones and technology glitches are part of reality, so you need to plan for the worst. And you need to plan for the possibility that you may not be with the organization in the long-term, with various postings, missions, promotions, intercontinental moves coming up every year. In such cases, an immediate successor and seamless transition are of paramount importance for the team and the mission.

The concept, however, is extremely transferable in the business world. Having a 2 i/c or co-leader has an incredibly practical application as well. Two heads are always better than one. I can look back almost 20 years (oh boy, there's that reality check again) to boot camp and the tasks I had to execute to justify my point. I know I may not have passed my training if I hadn't appointed a right-hand person to help me think through my missions. I can look back 10 years ago, to the benefits of assigning my dispatcher as my 2 i/c when I was an operations manager of a trucking fleet, or making my customs specialist my right hand when I was managing export operations around the world. I might have been the leader and the ultimate decision maker, but I was always better off with input from my 2 i/c, who was usually well connected to the front lines where the action was, or to a subject matter expert who I needed to rely on. Regardless, one more body seemed to equate to 10 times the brainpower and the input.

Strength through co-leaders is a practical and valuable mindset that has served me extremely well as a business leader. Formally or informally, permanently or temporarily, no matter what I'm leading, a co-leader seems to have always surfaced to become critical to my overall success, in any organization.

But before you consider expanding your leadership strength with a co-leader, consider this: You are about to enter the 'partnership zone.' Some might liken it to a marriage where you will have wonderful advantages if the dynamics are right. You'll benefit by growing a relationship with a partner who will help you believe in your initiatives, support your decisions, determine the course of action, challenge your narrow mindedness and bring an entirely new perspective to your project. Of course, with any partnership, there is always a flip side, such as having to compromise, or getting into heated debates that sometimes conclude with disagreement. Hopefully, it doesn't end up in a divorce.

Reality Check: For better or for worse

A co-leader or second-in-command (2 i/c) is not just someone you delegate work to, or simply someone who supplies another pair of hands and legs. Your co-leader should become your confidant(e), your extended eyes and ears, someone you will lean on during bad times and soar with during good times. A great 2 i/c will complement your strengths and weaknesses, and be able to fill in the gaps. He or she may even become your future succession plan. This is no average team member – this relationship is much more intimate.

syn

Like any successful partnership, certain factors will be important to the success of this team, including trust, open communication, mutual respect and honesty. As the leader, you will need to balance humility (and share the spotlight) with strength. But all teams need to be led and all organizations need a leader, so someone will need to be driving the bus and someone will have to make the decisions – and it will be tougher when those decisions get tough. But you are, after all, the leader.

> "A hundred times every day I remind myself that my inner and outer life depend upon the labors of other men, living and dead, and that I must exert myself in order to give in the same measure as I have received and am still receiving." *– Albert Einstein, renowned physicist*

CASE STUDY **Co-CEOs or DuWops**

Have you ever heard of a highly successful company being run by two leaders, or co-CEOs? Of course I'm a little biased, but Research In Motion, creators of BlackBerry, is an amazing example of what can come from a powerful duo. Mike Lazaridis, the inventor and brains behind the BlackBerry device, has been called a quirky, and to no one's surprise, geeky technical guru. He gave up almost half of his company before it became public to the genius strategy and salesman he brought on board, Jim Balsillie. Jim is a strategic thinker on the sales and marketing side, who worked closely with the analysts on Wall Street. He has led RIM's changing sales strategies from a direct-sales model to a carrier-based sales model, using big carriers, such as T-Mobile and Cingular, to expand the company's reach. The model turned the sales side of the company upside down for a brief period (my perspective) but opened the doors of opportunity for RIM to really reach the masses and become mainstream. Together, the pair has moved the company beyond Canada, beyond Wall Street, and into the global marketplace, providing e-mail access to almost every corner of the planet. I had the opportunity to work closely with both of these leaders on different occasions – very different leaders with different ways of thinking. The success they achieved as a team was immense. One can only wonder: Had this partnership never materialized, would either of these leaders have found themselves on *Time* magazine's 'most influential people in the world' list? Or is this strength a result of their combined force?

Let's flip to an entirely different industry, to another product I can't live without: the all-important lipstick! And apparently there's an entirely new breed on the market that I need to get my hands on. According to friends of mine who love it, the product Lip Venom from the company DuWop is a spicy, tingly gloss that enhances lips' "natural color and shape," all through essential oils. Who'd have thought that cinnamon, wintergreen or ginger would become essential ingredients? But when beauty is on the line, we ladies will resort to anything, I guess.

This nouveau lipstick brand was created by a wonderful team, who is going gangbusters in an extremely competitive industry (product cycles may only last months) with its focus on 'what isn't out there.' These two Italian makeup artists, known together as DuWop, each worked their way up on Hollywood sets, crossed paths in 1998 on the set of the NBC series *Profiler* and are now delivering pretty, enhanced pouts to the lips of America – who needs collagen when you can go *au naturel?!* Christina Bartolucci, who handles the creative side of the business, and Laura Deluisa, who takes care of the business aspects, call themselves the "beauty world's mad scientists," working away in the lab to deliver a multimillion-dollar makeup empire. This duo seems to have concocted a solid product – their partnership.

Start combining your forces for great synergy. Here's how:

1 Believe in the 'greater goal'

To bring someone on board or assign someone on your team to support you, you must get one thing straight: Without this person, you won't be able to accomplish your end goal or achieve project success in quite the same way. Everyone needs support. Once you can park your ego and accept your need for support to get to the next level, you'll be in a more humble position to appreciate where your co-leader can add value. The Oprah project is a great example of this. This was a high-profile, never-before-executed project that landed in my lap. In retrospect, I suppose I could have grabbed it, involved my team behind the scenes and kept all the glory to myself – and I've worked for many a leader who does exactly that. But I can assure you, you can only get away with that for so long. Combining forces is a principle I believe in deeply, and I really believe that the success of what you can achieve with a team, and the inner growth you experience from that success, is far more rewarding than standing on a pedestal alone! And besides, I'm a social creature. I like company. Share the spotlight, spread the wealth and have much more fun.

CASE STUDY **When you're leading history**

I've had the opportunity to discuss leadership (among many other fascinating things), with a tremendous community and corporate leader, Jan Chaplin, president and CEO of Canadian General-Tower Ltd. Jan represents the fifth generation of a family business, North America's leading supplier of flexible polymer coverstock for the automotive and swimming pool industries. And if you know anything about the automotive industry in North America, it's one volatile industry – slight changes in a large car manufacturer's business or demand can impact company leaders in a major way, up and down the entire supply chain. Jan Chaplin takes the accountability of leading a century-old family business very seriously. Running this company is not about her, but rather about the greater goal and success of the company. I suppose leaders in most companies lead to achieve success, but Jan's modest approach, along with her confidence in empowering the leadership team while filling very big shoes, seems extraordinary. She describes an environment where the spotlight is shared with people at all levels in the company. I remember her describing how a less senior employee in one of her departments was able to fill a management 'gap' for some months. Within a short time frame, he rose through the ranks to become the leader of the department and one of Jan's right-hand men. Jan's philosophy: "Let them feel the reins." She also believes her leaders should make decisions that have impact, even if it means they will experience some failure along the way. That's what building a strong team with better right-hand leaders is all about. And when your greater goal is ensuring the continued growth and success of a multimillion-dollar family business with a long tradition of successes, surrounding yourself with other strong leaders is, in itself, a strong leadership strategy.

2 Fill the gaps or expand the strengths?

Just like any marriage that has a greater chance for success when you know and understand yourself first, you might want to take a *personal inventory* before you combine forces.

◀◀ **Rewind** *to Chapter iii, "Lead Yourself First," so you can examine yourself and recognize your leadership strengths and where you'll need support to get to the next level.*

More importantly, examine your weaknesses. Obviously, our weaknesses are what tend to get us into trouble. If you're a strong planner or visionary or entrepreneur, you know where your project or company needs to go, but maybe you don't like the details and aren't interested in numbers or finance. Well, those numbers will likely be what might bite you right in the derriere. Put aside the ego and join strengths with a right-hand man or lady. Face your weaknesses and fill in your gaps with someone else's skills. To simulate innovation, Steve Jobs, CEO of Apple Computer, the creator of iPod, reminds his employees that 'real artists ship,' meaning that delivering working products on time is as important as innovation and killer design.[3]

3 Share the spotlight

Are you going to be okay with relinquishing some control to get your 'baby' off the ground, whether it's a design, product, company, charity benefit or whatever? If not, it'll be tough to establish the right partnering dynamics for success. But if you're willing to hand over the reins and share the spotlight with your co-leader, anything is possible! One incredibly successful team who I think manages to share the spotlight well, despite the

RIGHT BEFORE YOUR EYES

Don't get too caught up in what you think the perfect co-leader should look like because they come in many packages! Young and inexperienced or more mature and very experienced, you never know what talents people can bring to the table. And sometimes you can't get fussy because you might not have a choice.

When you don't have a choice of team members or resources to support you, don't despair, you might discover one of the best right hands working with you. One of my most interesting co-leader experiences was not with someone I chose, but someone who landed in my lap. That was the case back in the war zone in the former Yugoslavia. A demanding and definitely out-of-the-ordinary leadership experience, I was tasked as part of an on-site reconnaissance team to come up with a deployment plan for a large peacekeeping contingent in less than 10 days. And I attribute some of my mission's success, and my initial ability to cope and even laugh in what was a somewhat terrifying environment, to an odd and extraordinary character – Marion Ivanovich.

On that first day, as I sat in the lobby of Hotel Daruvar, Croatia, contemplating where I might start my mission, in walked Marion. God love him, with his straggly hair, scrounged up combat clothes, boots that didn't quite fit and satchel slung over his shoulder. He announced that he was here to volunteer with the peacekeepers, to help in any way he could. He had nowhere else to go. Quite frankly, no one was really sure what to do with him, and at a first glance, I didn't think he would have any skills I could use. But I could never let a potential resource sit idle for too long, so I grabbed him quickly before any of the other reconnaissance officers decided to use him. At the very least, Marion could sit in my car and read the maps for me while I tried to navigate my way around on my first day in this war zone.

Where do you start when you have less than 10 days to determine how, where, who and when to receive trainloads and millions of pounds of equipment, while overcoming obstacles like the ongoing war zone, broken transportation lines, limited ability to communicate, bombed airports and runways, destroyed roads and bridges, mined railways, and on and on?

By the end of that first day, Marion had become many things: my translator in both languages (English and Croatian), an administrator, setting up meetings, and note taker when meeting with influential national contacts who were uncovering useful intelligence regarding transportation issues, road and rail conditions, customs requirements, routing, dangers and potential partners. At one point, he fulfilled the role of publicist, arranging with Reuters and the BBC reporters when they could take pictures of 'the lady captain,' or "Captain Andela" as the papers were referring to me.

Perhaps the funniest role Marion would play was that of loyal protector. By the time we walked into our fourth meeting, I heard Marion telling the president of a powerful national trucking company quite emphatically that, no, I was not the secretary to the captain, I was the captain. And no, he did not think it would be a good idea for me to have another shot of Sliivovica or Slivovitz to get the meeting started (a whole other story!).

Who would have guessed that, within a few days, my scruffy 2 i/c would be paving my way and demanding respect for me as I steered through this very male-dominated culture! He was worth his weight in gold.

ergy

media emphasis on 'lead singers,' is the *uber* rock group U2. Leadman Bono, along with band members 'The Edge,' Adam Clayton and Larry Mullen Jr., have all shared the spotlight – interviews, articles, and on stage – over the last three decades. They approach their art and business as a real team. I wouldn't doubt that their team dynamics have heavily influenced their decades of success and strength as one of the world's greatest rock bands and global influencers.

> "The hardest thing to do is to stick together, mates, family, marriage, business, bands. It's like resisting gravity...it's like King Canute sitting in his chair trying to talk back to the tide...but you can, and we have, and we will turn the waves around...the alternative is too predictable...you rid the room of argument... you empty your life of the people you need the most."
>
> *– Bono, U2 special edition poster (iPod 2004)*

Leading without greed

"Don't break your arm patting yourself on the back!" I would get that advice from Jim Balsillie, RIM's CEO, every once in a while when my head seemed to be getting a little big. When you have confidence in yourself as a leader and have proven yourself, you shouldn't take the pat on the back alone for your team's achievements, nor should you feel the need to criticize or put others down. You'll be in a position of inner strength. When you're motivated and fulfilled, you should lead from a position that will bring out the best for you and the team. Share the rewards – give your team members exposure and let them receive the pats on the back. Bring people up. That's the best way to wield your power as a leader.

> "The group will not prosper if the leader grabs the lion's share of the credit for the good work that has been done...the group will become deadened and unresponsive if the leader is critical and harsh.[4]"
>
> *– The Tao of Leadership*

Even when you need a co-leader, you might be relying on individuals who wouldn't normally be your first choice. You might have to 'grow' your 2 i/c or cultivate co-leaders across different teams. Stay open-minded; your next co-leader might be closer than you think. Volunteers, university students, young business minds, the administrative assistant in the next office, or even a scruffy no-longer-employed victim of war – great co-leaders can come in unique packages.

And they might be sitting right in front of you!

4 Chemistry is key

When you do have the opportunity to choose someone to support you closely in your leadership capacity, consider strongly the chemistry between the two of you. This is another one of those 'soft' areas that can be somewhat elusive. In fact, there are books on how to meet someone with the right chemistry. There's a reason: how you connect with a right-hand man or woman will be important. The better the connection, the better you'll be able to lead and succeed together. Do you understand how that person thinks, what motivates them? Do they seem to understand you, respect the way you are and how you make decisions? Do your personal styles align or conflict? Chemistry is key for longevity.

Combining forces requires the ultimate in trust and loyalty for each other. But don't confuse good chemistry with how well you get along. There is nothing wrong with having strong differences, and I always think some good 'creative abrasion' (see point #5) is healthy, even when you're the leader. It keeps you both on your toes.

Think about it. You will be empowering, delegating, and handing off responsibilities to that individual. In many cases, they'll be filling in your gaps, acting on your behalf. How can you entrust parts of your leadership if you don't have that power of connection? Business chemistry – a combination of connection, trust, respect and a few other elusive concepts, will be key to your relationship. And your relationship with your co-leader will ultimately impact your success.

Chemistry is key!

syn

5 Go for creative abrasion

Remember how I said combining forces with a co-leader might be compared to a marriage? Well, at one point in my career, I used to share my office with one of my co-leaders. I'm not sure if it was the tight quarters we shared or the fact that we were leading some intense international projects, but we often found ourselves in some very heated discussions. We would debate how to do things, how we might approach a partner we had to work with, or what kind of program was required for a product launch. Furious scribbling on the white board and loud discussion was always part of the dynamics, as well as a great deal of respect for each other's skills. I remember someone popping their head into the office and saying, "You guys sound like a married couple. Lots of bickering going on in here!" My co-leader piped up and said, "Who's arguing? This is creative abrasion! This is how great new thinking starts." He was right. After duking it out for a while, we would have all of the issues on the table, from several different viewpoints, and come to a far better conclusion, having gone through the experience. Enjoy friction and opposing viewpoints. Have the confidence and the humility to accept different points of view. It's one of the most powerful gifts a good co-leader can add to the equation.

RED FLAG **Avoid favoritism**

Be careful that appointing a trusty co-leader does not lead to the perception of favoritism among other members of your team. Until you are ready to officially declare a co-leader, understand that, as you expand this individual's responsibilities, how you connect with this co-leader (through breakfast meetings, lunches, continual closed-door sessions) may create animosity between team members and disrupt the fine balance you've fostered until now. It's all about everyone on the team feeling that sense of value and knowing where they fit in. When you leverage that co-leader, be careful not to minimize everyone else's contribution. Continue to emphasize that the whole team is valuable, no matter what, and encourage everyone's growth and input at the same time.

Come together

The world is coming closer together in so many ways. The more we understand and get closer to people and cultures around the world, the more we understand that humanity's behavior as a whole isn't that much different from one another. From organisms to communities to big business, things come together in much the same way – through growth, success and expansion.

"Social groups of any kind are like living cells in that they are formed around a nucleus or a common denominator that links the individual parts. In the world of technology, the phenomenon of the Internet joins the lives of thousands who share common objectives or interests, creating a global community. On a more intimate scale, it might be an individual, an ideology, a practice, or project that brings people together and strengthens the sense of community."[5] Ma Deva Padma

---

What's in it for you...and your team?

Do you want to become a force to be reckoned with? Appointing a co-leader does not have to mean losing yourself as a leader, losing control, power or your leadership edge. Quite the contrary. It means taking your mission to places it may never have gone. But it does require a delicate balance of inner strength *and* humility. As the leader, you are ultimately accountable for certain results because you may be the only person with the authority to make the decisions.

What's in it for you? Can you really keep your footing as a leader while elevating someone to become your co-leader, your right hand? It's interesting how one of the world's most influential, successful brand-building billionaires sees it. He is well aware of his personal strength. But he has combined that with mastering delegation and empowerment as part of his own succession plan so he can continue to get bigger and bigger. According to Richard Branson, the daring guy with the beard who founded the Virgin empire, you have to have a master plan.

"As much as you need a strong personality to build a business from scratch, you also must understand the art of delegation," he says. "I have to be good at helping people run the individual businesses, and I have to be willing to step back. The company must be set up so it can continue without me."[6]

You can only go so far alone. When you do decide to combine forces, here's what's in it for you and your team:

✓ **Expand your reach. And then some**

Simply put, a great co-leader can give you double the arms, legs and brainpower. You'll be able to accomplish far more, in a shorter amount of time. As a team, you'll be able to take greater strides and reach greater heights. Additional leadership support can re-energize and revitalize by strengthening unity and growth within the team. The results and support you'll achieve with your team will take you to new and otherwise impossible heights.

✓ **Flexibility, agility and ability allow you to be selfish**

On a more practical and even selfish note, this principle can serve a wonderful purpose. Having a right-hand man or woman will increase your flexibility tremendously. I realized as a military officer that one of the greatest advantages in having a 2 i/c (or personal succession plan) was that I increased my flexibility and ability to pursue my own personal goals. I was able to volunteer for those career-advancing missions, take lengthy professional development courses and grab some of those great opportunities that came along. I was never 'tied' to my role or job. I made my own 'personal freedom' plan.

✓ **Earn respect and loyalty**

By allowing others to experience overall success and be an integral part of it, they're growing (personally, in areas like loyalty and trust). You're expanding and opening your own doors through others' growth, and earning respect and credibility for it.

✓ **Create a succession plan**

And *voilà*, you've created your own succession plan! Want to move on, take on bigger and better things, expand your responsibilities, your team, your company? You can't do any of that without a succession plan and someone to step up to the plate and yes, sad but true, replace you! Think of it this way: If you don't have someone who is able to fill the gap that your departure will create, how are you going to jump onto those bigger and better projects that are just around the corner?

Not long ago, I had made the decision to put my exciting high-tech career on hold for a while to take the time to write this book. I remember my leader at the time asking me who could fill my position once I left. My answer was simple: "Don't replace me. Promote two of my team players who have been doing a wonderful job." His response: "You can't have been doing your job as a leader for the past two years if you don't need to be replaced!" I made it clear how wrong he really was: "I've been doing exactly what a leader should be doing – empowering, expanding and growing the skills on my team."

Don't be threatened by creating strength and leadership around you. Just set your sights even higher.

Reality Check: Behind every good leader is a co-leader

Although the saying goes something like: "Behind every good man there is a great woman," I obviously look at it a little differently. I'm a firm believer that behind every good leader there is a co-leader. Why would you want to do it alone, anyway? Where's the fun in that? Everyone needs a wingman.

What's next?

You've already taken the leap; you've been leading teams. What's it take to get to that next level in leadership? Now you will get more value in taking the time to know your people, developing loyalty and trust, and empowering them.

But what's that really about? Where do you want to go as a leader? Making a difference socially or being a huge business success? Maybe doing a bit of both.

No matter what your choice is, being a 'change agent' by having an impact on people and the world around you requires a whole new pace in which we have to live and lead. In fact, it's a real 'hot seat' and it's tough to avoid. It's in your best interest to get a grip on how to lead when things are moving rapidly, so you can grab every project you want by the horns. Who wants to miss out on opportunities because something has whipped right past you?

Get ready to take on your 'big goal' with some targeted 'mission-critical' leadership strategies.

Hindsight is 20/20

Spotlight hog

Don't be a spotlight hog. Be bigger than that. Do you really think you're standing on that pedestal because you did it all by yourself? You might be holding the torch, maybe because you put the money into the pot or your neck on the line. But did you really get there without a coach or some great moral support behind the scenes every step of the way?

Have you ever been on a successful team that has achieved some success and the leader stands up and takes all the credit? How did that make everyone feel? What was the result? Anger, resentment, frustration, and probably a desire to work with another team.

On the flip side, think of how it feels when a leader stands up and says, "You know, I couldn't have done this without the support of XYZ." The end result? Pride, loyalty, respect and motivation to achieve even greater goals as part of that team.

Share the spotlight. Share the success. One thing you won't have to share is the loyalty, respect and admiration you'll receive as leader.

ergy

syn

ACTION PLAN

Synergy through co-leaders

1 BELIEVE IN THE GREATER GOAL.

- Put your needs aside, step back and focus on what needs to happen to achieve bigger goals
- Assess your strengths and skills, then fill in the gaps

2 THE ANSWER IS USUALLY RIGHT IN FRONT OF YOU.

- Remain open-minded on your quest for a co-leader
- Don't get fixated on a person's experience or existing skills so much as their potential, enthusiasm, initiative and energy

3 SHARE THE SPOTLIGHT.

- Celebrate success with the group who got you there
- Reap the long-term rewards of team loyalty and motivation

4 DON'T RID THE ROOM OF HEALTHY ARGUMENT!

- Balance your strength and confidence with humility
- Accept different ways of thinking

ergy

INTEGRATE

LINK YOUR TEAM TO THE MISSION

One life, but we're not the same
We get to carry each other

One, U2

INTEGRATE

Get the good at warp speed

Left and right hand work together

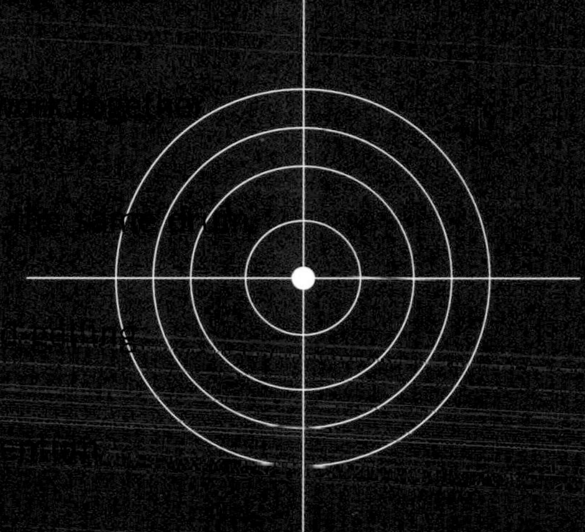

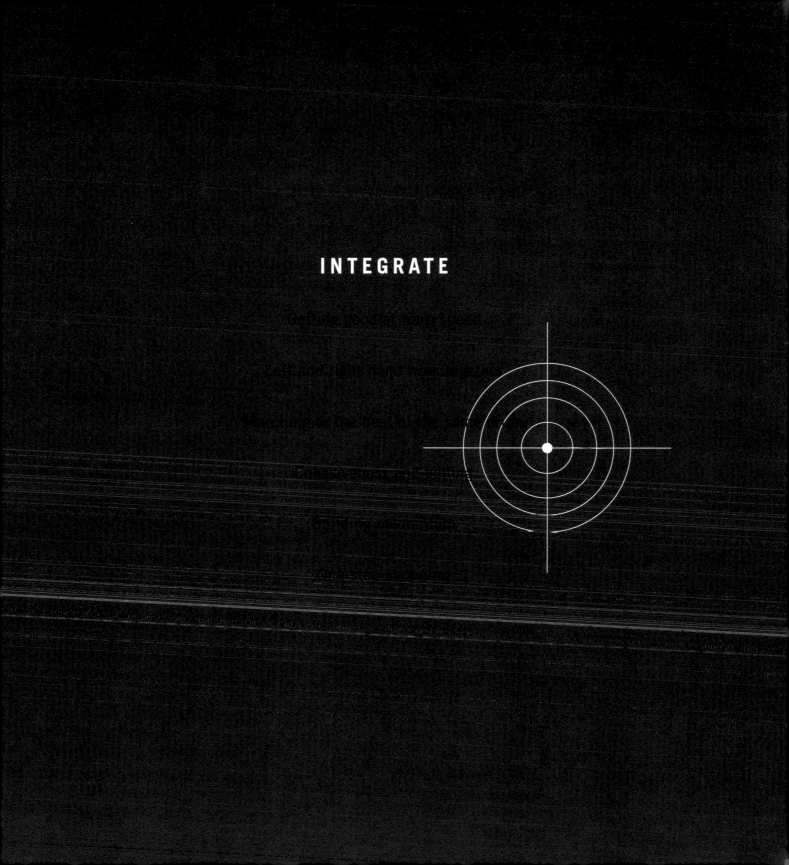

Leading at warp speed

Fast, faster, warp speed! This has been the progressive pace of my career to date. At first, I thought the military was crazy for its continual change, breakneck speed and new missions, coming at me every few months. Well, it was nothing compared to the high-tech industry in the late '90s and early 2000, when dot.com explosions were the norm and IPOs were all the rage. Often led by kids, companies that were unheard of one day would go public and be worth millions the next. When I worked in the industry, I couldn't walk into my office without one of my colleagues filling me in on the latest start-up company that was going public and some grand scheme on how we could get in on the ground floor!

So there I was in the midst of the high-tech explosion living the high life. And why not – the opportunities were limitless for those of us in the industry who were willing to step up to the plate. So I did just that, and found myself on, yet again, another adventure in life and leadership.

Three years after joining Nortel Networks and at least three positions later (did I mention things changed fast?), I accepted an opportunity to move my family to Northern Ireland for a short-term assignment with the Global Logistics Strategic Business Solutions team I worked for. My North American colleagues thought I was crazy, probably because I was a single parent with a preschooler and another son in Grade 1. But I grew up as an air force kid who moved every three years of my life and went to a dozen different schools, so my boys did not get much sympathy from me. We packed up, Game Boys and nanny in tow, and headed for a new life in Europe.

As we headed through customs in London Heathrow, I turned around to watch in horror as my nanny was taken away by customs agents and thrown into a 'paddy wagon' used to transport illegal aliens to some holding area until they got them onto flights home. Later, after discovering that her passport had been stamped with a large 'X,' meaning she would never be able to return to the United Kingdom again (I still have nightmares about this scenario), it occurred to me that sometimes things move way too fast! We hadn't had the time to get her work visa in order and, instead, took the chance that since Canadians could travel freely within the United Kingdom for a period of six months at a time, it might not be a big deal for her to support my little family abroad. It doesn't quite work that way, I learned, since a nanny is officially an employee, and therefore requires the extensive documentation that any of us needs to work overseas. "Oh dear," my boss Sandi Pitcairn, leader of our Global Logistics team, said upon hearing the news. She paused for a minute to consider my dilemma and then got back to business: "So what are your goals and objectives for the next few months?" This was high tech in the good old days, when things were moving so fast we barely noticed the bumps in the road or had time to really consider the impact of changes to our plans.

EVERYTHING WAS MISSION CRITICAL

This mission and my new position were going to be extremely exciting! Nortel was living and breathing the 'first to market' philosophy, which essentially meant we had to beat our competitors and get our new products out to consumers first. The company was yet again redefining itself in this brave, fast-paced new world. Every time we expanded our product lines or merged with other companies, it meant a big shift in how we did business. And this time, we were trying to integrate teams across the global marketplace to focus on 'end-to-end' business solutions with end-to-end product teams. Teams were being created to handle a new product through the many stages of development, from the time it was only an idea right through to delivery to the end customer. The goal was to create a more integrated and cohesive team called the Business Operations team, representing all areas of expertise. It would be my job over the next six to nine months to determine *how* our global logistics organization would integrate all of our areas of expertise (from customs to export documentation to packaging, shipping and transportation) into this new Business Operations team concept. Once we defined this new business model, we would simply 'cut and paste' it for use in other market regions around the world. These

integ

models meant we gained speed. The more you can repeat and apply stuff instead of reinventing the wheel, the more time your company saves by using these already-established best practices. Being first to market is all about speed.

And that's where team integration becomes critical. It's critical in any environment, but particularly in a complex business environment where you're launching high-tech products globally. One team member needs to know what another is doing so he can plan accordingly. So, for example, product designers need to appreciate the logistics implications of moving product into a third-world country far away from its manufacturing headquarters. It's usually the unexpected things in a product's supply chain that delay the deal or impact the revenue – things like the electrical components that require certification to import the product. It's not usually the 'rocket science' that causes delays, but rather the packaging or paperwork.

A well-integrated team could mean the difference between landing multimillion-dollar deals – or not.

Integration *unplugged*

I'm sure you've been involved with some events or projects where it isn't quite clear who is responsible for what tasks on the team, or metaphorically speaking, where the left hand doesn't seem to know what the right hand is doing. It happens often when different people aren't communicating in a situation where they should really be working closely together. It results in confusion, frustration and possibly an impact on the overall success of the project.

Improving that situation comes down to a couple of simple things: clarity and communication. You can't have a cohesive team that is linked to the mission without them.

As a leader, in order to effectively integrate your team with the overall mission, you'll need to clarify who is doing what, how they are doing it and then communicate this to the entire team. In turn, your team must be able to answer: Who, what, when, how, why? Is everyone clear *on what needs to happen, what is the situation or mission? Who is responsible* for doing what? Does everyone know *how* things are progressing? And is everyone clear on how they need to get their job done? And last but not least, do team members know *when* things must be done to meet the goal?

rate

This sort of integration can be very beneficial to small teams and complex global teams alike. For instance, I have had a small team of experts supporting me in every aspect of producing this book – from editors, to graphic designers, to copy editors, advisors, and marketing and sales reps. Over a six-month period, we grew from a team of two people to eight people. Although many of the people on the project run their own companies and have never met each other in person, everybody's work has been interconnected. For example, the writing has impacted the editing, which has impacted the copy editing and the design. And everything in the production of this book has impacted the timeline, which has impacted the marketing and sales of the book. It's been just as critical with this small, remote team that everyone place the same degree of importance on the timeline and goals of this book launch as it was with the team responsible for the high-powered global product launches at Nortel. If the team wasn't marching to the beat of the same drum, then this book would not have launched on time.

DEVIL'S IN THE DETAIL

During my period in high tech, just like in the air force, logistics was often an afterthought. We were definitely not considered part of the 'front lines' and often not consulted until after the initial phases of a project, when it might be too late to avoid problems. In the telecom world, that sometimes meant that the engineers would design big telecom gear to sell around the world, only to discover that the logistics experts couldn't fit the rather large vertically standing bays on the only cargo aircraft able to fly to some South American country where the multimillion-dollar deal had been sold! No longer an afterthought, logistics was finally becoming a competitive 'weapon' for this type of cutthroat competitive market.

An integrated team could ensure that experts like logistics specialists were brought in, in the design phase, well before the product had been built. It made a lot more sense. In my job, there were many intricate details involved in moving complex high-tech gear to more than 125 countries that could very well impact design (such as size, for instance).

To get started, I would plant myself and my boys, less one nanny, in Monkstown, Northern Ireland, where Nortel Networks had a leading-edge fiber optics manufacturing facility. What better place to get integrated than where the concept and design all happen. I also spent some time in Versailles just outside of Paris, where we had a similar need to integrate our logistics team with the new business concept. This plant built global systems for mobile communications technology, otherwise known as GSM and GPRS technology. (If this acronym doesn't ring a bell, it's the technology that allows millions of people around the world to use their cell phones and receive e-mails on handheld devices on tiny little islands in far off places. It is ubiquitous.)

COHESION = CLARITY + COMMUNICATION

Getting familiar with manufacturing plants and their many product teams meant a lot of travel to places like Paris, Istanbul, Rome and London (Yes, I know, I had a tough job!). I had my work cut out for me. To move our logistics requirements up to the front end of the business, where the concept and design occurred, we needed to be taken seriously by the engineering and product experts. These product teams needed to understand what we did and how we could add value to this overall integrated team.

How do you establish credibility, value and rapidly integrate logistics expertise in newly forming teams who barely have their mandate figured out? There were a couple of key things I needed to do over the next few months:

- **Establish clarity of purpose** – I needed a clear definition of what our team's role would be across the various product launch teams.

- **Align everyone with the big picture** – When did we need to get involved with the product launch team? Who would we work closely with? How did our role support the overall goals? What did this mean for individual team members?

- **Establish outcomes and results** – What were we accountable to deliver?

PULLING A TEAM TOGETHER – FAST

I returned to Canada about six months later, expecting a little R&R after this intercontinental move. But the universe had a different master plan. Instead, I was on another airplane and heading west, this time to Silicon Valley, California. Intent on dominating the global telecommunications industry, Nortel had gone on a $20-billion shopping spree during my absence in Europe, using highly overinflated stock prices to purchase a dozen smaller technology companies. The goal was to use these companies to round out our product offerings and beat out competitors like Cisco, Ericsson, Lucent and any other telecom giants out there with the latest technology.

Over the next few months, I was to be rewarded for my risk-taking and European stint with a real mission-critical opportunity – becoming a key member of our mergers and acquisitions integration team. Talk about being catapulted into the front lines of our business! With 12 new companies added to Nortel, I had a mandate to deliver a 90-day plan on how to integrate these companies, their people and processes within our supply chain. My integration planning skills would be put to the test...and then some!

And what a test. In my many years as a leader, I have had to pull a lot of teams together and lead many a diverse crowd. However, I can honestly say there is nothing tougher than trying to integrate extremely different companies and get them working together, especially when one is an enormous global company like Nortel and the others are small entrepreneurial start-ups. The differences in company culture, processes, and most of all, people (let's face it, people are what success depends on) and how they worked together as a team – were enormous. The new team meetings were quite entertaining, to say the least. We had different ways of doing things, organizational structures, IT systems, and goals and objectives. How was I going to get

integ

clarity of roles, alignment with the big picture and agreement on our joint deliverables when we were not working from the same sheet of music?

I had a good plan on how to integrate. The fun was going to be in the execution. It's always in the execution. And the execution was going to get even more challenging.

> **HIGH-TECH INTELLIGENCE**
>
> **Eat your own dog food!**
>
> Eat your own dog food has become a mantra at software giant Microsoft to describe the company's belief in leading by example – with their own product. Microsoft's philosophy is that employees must know their products intimately – testing, using, living and breathing them all before these products make it to consumers on the street. It's an important process for employees to believe in themselves and in the products they've helped create, and it ensures that they understand intimately how the product performs, so that they can relate entirely to the customer experience. In other words, lead by demonstrating principles you expect your team to use. Believe in yourself. Believe in your product. Eat your own dog food.

INTEGRATING VAPOURWARE

The news release announced yet another company purchase with some leading-edge 'product' that Nortel had purchased: "Nortel Networks to acquire all-optical switching pioneer Xros for US $3.25 billion…Revolutionary 3D micro-mirror technology provides key building block in creation of all-optical network."

Of all the teams and products we were going to have to integrate over the next 12 months, this one would be the most fascinating. The Xros optical switching technology that the news release was referring to didn't even exist yet. Funnily enough, that was not so uncommon in an industry where things were moving at warp speed. In fact, we had a name for nonexistent product, and it resembled some of the other product terminology in the industry, such as, software, hardware and firmware. It was called vapourware. And vapourware was not that easy to integrate into a supply chain, basically because it didn't exist yet. But that didn't mean I was off the hook. We still had to come up with a plan on how and where we would move this product, even if we were not guaranteed final dimensions or actual components, which were important when shipping product internationally. We needed to know every detail so that when this so-called product did finally exist, we were ready to get it to market. First.

One small company, one big bill. I was sent off yet again to California to come up with a 30-60-90-day plan to integrate the people, processes and technology of the new company, Xros, into Nortel. I showed up at their head office expecting a buzz of activity and a busy lab and/or manufacturing area where the technology was being produced. Instead, I was brought to some vacant office space in an office building, and after a few meetings, was given a tour of the lab. My first observation – not a very big space, not many people. Second observation, where was the product? Out of the corner of my eye, I noticed two big bays, big gray cabinets that were common in the telecom industry to house the 'guts' of a company's technology. These cabinets were filled with intertwining red and blue rope. Yes, rope. Apparently these were the prototype bays. Where was this hot new technology that Nortel had just paid $3.25 billion for? I was brought over to a table and shown a box full of hundreds of tiny mirrors all reflecting light off each other – the prototype for the photonic switch. This was the closest I had ever been to rocket science. The first thought that came to my mind was, "Holy cow, I can hardly wait to see what the baggage handlers are going to do to the boxes we'll be labelling with "This side up, extremely fragile," as they get tossed into cargo compartments when we start selling the product around the world! It was a good thing that our company was starting to integrate logistics expertise at the design phase of the product. Sure enough, months later when we first went to trial with this product, logistics, specifically transporting the physical product, became the prime issue. The hundreds of tiny mirrors made the end product so fragile it was almost impossible to transport safely. I understand that being first to market with the hottest, latest technology is critical. But when you can't ship it, what good is it?

▶▶ **Fast forward** *to "Use 'One-stop Shopping' With Stoplight Status" on page 171.*

Yep, this was integration in the front lines. There were so many companies and teams to integrate in our next quarter's revenue that we could barely keep up with the workload. And then there was this little gem of a project. Where do you start and how do you integrate 'vapourware' or a non-existent product into your busy supply chain?

What a dog's breakfast. And it was now our job to get all the kinks worked out. One thing was for sure, we certainly needed to 'eat our own dog food' and test the entire supply chain before we started shipping this puppy!

The principle: Link your team to the mission

"Activity, activity, speed!"

– Napoleon Bonaparte, French general and emperor, April 1809

Getting products, services, solutions, books, whatever, out in the marketplace faster and better than anybody else – this is the new era of buzz phrases like 'first to market' and 'just in time,' in other words, making things happen faster than sometimes humanly possible.

In any work environment, but more so in a mission-critical one, your project and team success will be contingent upon how well you integrate your team of individuals with the mission. Linking your team to the mission is one surefire principle to help you get and maintain team integration and cohesiveness. Everyone will know what they are doing, who is doing what, and that will bring clarity and a sense of value and accountability to each team player involved in the project. Can you imagine playing on a soccer team, or any sports team for that matter, and not being clear of who your goalie is, who the forwards are, who is the team captain or coach? Or what about playing on a team that doesn't understand the overall game plan?

Players, on any team – sports or not – need to know who is responsible for what and the overall objective of the game or mission. With sports, the objective is pretty simple: to win. Even so, there's still information players need to know, such as: What are they playing for (for example, the last game of the season for a title)? What's the situation? Who is the leading competing team? How is the team going to outsmart the other team? What's the plan?

The benefits almost seem obvious. How can any team work well together and achieve goals if they are not well integrated? Therein lies the challenge for any leader. An integrated team does not happen by magic or by osmosis. A leader plays an instrumental role in pulling all the pieces together.

Tying your team to the mission is about creating the 'gel' that connects the pieces and keeps them all together – it's about creating a cohesive and integrated team. Then you can face the speed and the inevitable changes together in a much more coordinated manner!

Create the gel, face the speed and get dynamic.

How to link your team to the mission

"The effective application of the troop-leading process at the platoon level is of paramount importance to tactical success. A superior tactical plan at the task force level will fail if it is not understood and executed properly at the platoon level.[1]"

– Captain David S. Davidson, USA Force XXI

integ

Good team integration requires a triple focus:

- Getting the team aligned with the mission or the big picture
- Connecting the team players together
- Ensuring clarity, communication, cohesiveness

Here are some steps you can take to ensure that you link your team members together, and to the mission:

1 Line up with the big picture

You have to have clarity to create clarity. What is your big picture and where does your team fit in? Making sure your team works well as a cohesive unit requires your ability to see and share the big picture.

Each and every team player must understand the overall goals and objectives. So, the tactical plan must be understood at your team's level, or the platoon level. Just as in the captain's advice above, you can have a superior plan at the executive level, but if the troops don't understand it, execution fails. Better understanding of the plan by the team will support a more integrated team.

Reality Check: Get clarity

You won't always have the luxury of taking over a job where goals or even your role is defined. If that's the case, use initiative and start defining it yourself! If you're not sure about your team's goals and objectives, do your best to get clarity and create a sense of direction. Ask yourself why your team exists, who benefits from what it accomplishes, whose support do you require to be successful? Talk to your leaders, clients, customers and stakeholders about their goals; talk to your team about their roles. And don't forget to bounce this direction off the people you're working for, your own boss. Find out where the organization is going and where the company is going. What are the goals for the next quarter or year? Align the general function of your team with some of the bigger-picture goals.

Once you've established some clarity and received 'buy-in' from your leadership team, you'll have a better, integrated team.

▶▶ **Fast forward** *to Chapter 09, "Connect the Front Lines and the Big Picture," for more details on how to keep the team and the objectives connected.*

Create your own goals

There have been times when I have moved into a new role and not been given clear goals and objectives, or my role has been ill-defined. You'll likely experience this if your organization is going through a change in direction or shift in overall mandate. Or if you're taking over a team that is more focused on day-to-day operations rather than long-term business strategy.

For instance, when I left the military, I had a brief stint in the transportation industry, where I led a large team of truckers who had to deliver telecom equipment around North America in tractor-trailers. My role as operations manager was very focused on day-to-day operations, and I wasn't provided with any specific team goals. But our company goals and objectives were focused on improving the fleet safety record (accidents were incredibly expensive and impacted our bottom line) and overall fleet cost management, which impacted profit margins.

> "Reality is something you rise above."
>
> – *Liza Minelli, entertainer*

CASE STUDY **Team buy-in with goal setting**

As I developed my small management team of four plus me (two dispatchers, two administrative support assistants), I made sure to involve them in developing our goals and objectives. In fact, I involved our entire team of 50-plus, everybody right down to our part-time drivers. We had monthly team meetings to open up the lines of communication and inform everyone of what was happening on the front lines in our business. These meetings also helped keep the drivers in tune and linked to what was going on with our company and our customers. It also gave the entire team an immediate forum to deal with important operational issues, such as which trucking team on which shift left empty pizza boxes in certain cabs.

rate

Our big picture soon became clear to the entire team. Here's how one of our dispatchers described the impact:

"I remember when you implemented regular team meetings and incorporated mandatory training for the drivers. These meetings were met with much cynicism from the drivers who were doubtful about your role. You arranged for key people to provide updates at the meetings, as well as key people from our dedicated customer. The whole tone changed. Suddenly the drivers felt that their roles were being given the respect they deserved and they were given a voice in the overall operation rather than being limited to their daily runs. Overall communication improved and they started to feel more comfortable in approaching you with ideas and issues. They started to help each other out and came together as a group."

We developed goals to improve our team safety records and to reduce the cost of fleet operations. We had some impeccable drivers and some accident-prone operators who had bad driving records. We needed to get to the bottom of how to proactively improve the safety numbers as well as cut operational expenses. We also started to focus on variable fleet costs with things like fuel consumption management and minimizing downtime, which could cost the company tens of thousands of dollars per customer if they weren't managed properly. Since we were the largest Canadian team and fleet of our U.S. parent company, a team focus on improving operating costs meant we could make a big difference to the bottom line.

2 Get everyone on the same page

The clarity and higher visibility that you provide when you share information and communicate effectively will ensure that your team is marching to the same beat – the team may not be marching to a tempo but it's still a beat, and that's the important point. In other words, the insight you give your team about company goals will help everyone understand the pace and direction you're heading toward.

Now you need to get the team marching in step to that drumbeat. You want your team moving in the same direction toward the same goals at the right time. That is, you want to create a 'best practice' to ensure that your team can proactively move toward team goals and reactively manage actions or issues that come up along the way. Right?

The simplest way to get your team on the same page and linked to the big picture is to share information and encourage information flow between team players. Some of the ways to start that 'gelling' and linking your team to the mission includes:

- **Kickoff meetings** to introduce new team members, current goals, changes in business priorities or whatever information needs to be passed on
- **One-on-one chat sessions** to get each team member's individual perspective on the strengths and weaknesses of team members, as well as input on their own skills and where they fit within the team
- **Team alignment meetings,** or meetings whose only purpose is to align the team to the mission. You may want to do this sort of thing so that team members can introduce their roles and goals to each other – to provide inter-team visibility. This is particularly useful if a new project is being introduced.

◀◀ **Rewind** *to Chapter 04, "Know Your People," for more insight on how to successfully line up individual skills with the job.* And ▶▶ **Fast forward** *to Chapter 09, "Connect the Front Lines and the Big Picture" for some quick steps on connecting your team through communication.*

Vague is vogue

Instability creates 'gray areas' and 'gray' is something we all need to get used to. Because it's not going anywhere. So the sooner we get used to working and thriving in gray, the better.

"Today has a very temporary quality about it. Predictability is passé, vague is vogue. The ability to improvise has become an essential skill. We must learn to bob and weave. To bounce whenever change hits. To pivot...flex...operate in a fog. Instead of futilely trying to stabilize the situation, we must learn to exploit instability."[2]
– Price Pritchett and Ron Pound, organizational change agents

integ

3 Use 'one-stop shopping' with stoplight status

A couple of things are common in the business world today. Almost everything new is project driven. And most projects are led by people who don't have much experience with integrating cross-functional teams.

The reality is that your team players may have very different skills and highly differentiated roles. In fact, they may not actually have much to do with each other. But there is some connection, some overarching purpose that they're on the same team, otherwise there wouldn't be much need for them. Make sure you keep hammering home that purpose as often as you need to in order to keep people connected, either by holding monthly team meetings or daily meetings for mission-critical situations. Because on the front lines, it might not always be so obvious. It's very easy to get lost in the day-to-day tasks.

A 'visual' update is also a great way to provide people with the clarity and connection to establish cohesion. People often respond well and remember visual cues such as a 'one-stop shopping' report known as the 'stoplight status.' It works especially well if you have your entire team integrated and working together toward a specific goal that needs to be delivered by a certain deadline.

Here's what type of information can be incorporated into this simple (usually a spreadsheet) stoplight status document:

- High-level company or organizational goal(s), objectives, the project or mission
- Key players on the team
- Key functions or areas of expertise required to support the goal
- Important tasks and milestones for each function
- Deadline(s)
- Person responsible for each specific task

A picture's worth a thousand words

Here's the best part: progress for tasks and milestones is color-coded, and color is a language that everybody understands. Red means 'look out, this is critical to our success,' green means 'good to go,' and yellow means 'the task or milestone is at risk in some way.' The report paints a quick picture so everyone can get an instant view of progress.

Perhaps the biggest benefit of this visual for a project leader is that it will help him or her manage accountability. No one likes having a red stoplight symbol beside their name or on their project. It means the project is in trouble and at risk. Using a red light symbol certainly keeps the team on top of the big issues, and will encourage those who are responsible for the task to get it back on track. It encourages discussion around who will have to do what to mitigate that risk. People will work together more closely to get that red light icon off the page. But if it wasn't there, if no one had any visibility on the issue, where would you be?

When you create an environment of accountability, team members have direct ownership for the project and take pride in the effort and outcome. And believe it or not, people want to own a piece of the pie or project.

STOPLIGHT STATUS REPORT

A simple document can help keep your team tied to the mission:

Project xxx:		Objective(s):		Team members:	
Functional Area	**Task or Action Item or Milestone**	**Owner**	**Target Date**	**Target Status**	**Comments**
Marketing	Create a big event to launch our new product	John	Yesterday		
Product Management	Deliver a commercially ready product	Jane	One month ago!		
Sales	Get purchase orders for product	Joe	Every day!		We need orders. Where are the orders?

CASE STUDY Keeping it simple

It's easy to get lost in the overwhelming detail when managing different experts and a tight timeline. Using a stoplight status report or a color-coded visual update is not only very simple, it's extremely versatile and can be used with any team, in any industry, no matter the experience.

After using a stoplight status document while working for other companies, I introduced it to my team when I started working for Research In Motion (RIM). People related to the color-coded tasks and employees immediately understood the quick view of tasks in such a simple format. So it was a great tool to use with our business integration projects for international product launches. Before I knew it, the report was being photocopied by other departments throughout the company. The reason was simple – it's simple.

It's simple enough that when Andrew, one of my senior managers at RIM moved on, he introduced it to the new industry he was joining. He was going to be leading a very complex project and launching a multidisciplinary primary health-care clinic. Andrew used this status tool to communicate with physicians, nurses, social workers, dietitians and frontline administrative staff. And working with a group of people not accustomed to traditional project management methodology and tools, such as work breakdown structures, Gantt charts, scope change control measures and other more traditional concepts, he found this report the best and simplest way to integrate his team and tie them to the mission. Here's what he had to say about using it:

"We have found that in the health-care field, the use of simple 'stoplight-style' status reports are an extremely helpful tool for communicating key project activities to stakeholders. Stoplight reports add a simple red/yellow/green indicator of status: green is happy, yellow is a problem that needs fixing, and red means the project element may be out of control. This one-stop-shopping document is really useful if you have to communicate important information to team members who may have little prior experience with big implementation projects. The net result: high-profile projects are delivered on-time and all team members are able to contribute in major ways."

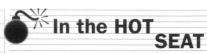

In the HOT SEAT

INTEGRATE + COMMUNICATE + EXECUTE = MISSION ACCOMPLISHED

Integrating your team successfully with the mission's objective is just one part of a three-part leadership strategy I use in my workshops. It provides new leaders with a simple and powerful approach to 'hit the ground leading' when they're facing a mission-critical project. If you find yourself 'in the hot seat' and leading a fast-paced project, combine the Action Plans from this chapter, plus Chapters 09 and 10 (highlighting the actions: integrate, communicate and execute, respectively) to help you establish a solid mission-critical mindset. These simple strategies are the fundamental basics you need to help you succeed with your team in the hot seat. To ensure you get the most out of these simple leadership strategies, it's critical that you don't use each of them as a stand-alone actions. In other words, you really need to apply the ICE (integrate + communicate + execute) actions versus just the I or the C or maybe the E.

Visit our website at www.iceleadership.com or www.hittheground leading.com for information on the ICE model and powerful tools to help you integrate, communicate and execute.

"To be in the All Blacks is about loving what you do. It's about caring for each other... That's the beauty of playing in a team. You have 15 guys who all have one goal in mind rather than a set of individual goals. A collective goal. The aim is to be successful. The aim is to win and to do everything you can to make yourselves better players and better people."[3]
– Sean Fitzpatrick, former captain of the New Zealand All Blacks rugby team

integ

What's in it for you... and your team?

Believe it or not, integration is an area that is not that well managed – for many different reasons. Organizational change or new team goals can put a team in limbo, where team leaders are not sure of where or how they fit into the new organization. Good team integration requires good communication, which is another stumbling block for some team leaders.

Here's a good analogy to highlight this very point. An orchestra conductor's strength lies in his ability to have every musician, with a multitude of talent and skills on different instruments, from percussion to strings to winds, come together at the right place and the right tempo, to deliver music to our ears. Can you imagine the noise we'd hear if he didn't? It makes me think of some of my children's music class recitals.

One of the fundamentals for a well-integrated team is linking the team members and the mission by communicating effectively, sharing information and using simple visual tools.

At a recent leadership workshop I did with some of the front-line leaders at Microsoft (the software giant who has provided the world with tools to communicate and integrate with), the principle of team integration was a big topic of conversation. In fact, at the end of the day, as the participants and I were reviewing what they found to be the most beneficial factors to add to their leadership action plan, better team integration and improved ability to manage those responsible for the tasks (accountability) were two of the top responses. Simple tools help make team integration simpler to manage.

Here are some team benefits to being linked to its mission:

✓ **Everyone will march in step**

Sharing a common goal, understanding timelines and working together to meet objectives will help your group become more congruent.

✓ **Get more love in the team**

When people clearly understand what their job and their buddy's job are, and how they tie to the bigger picture, there will be more peace and less anger. No one will be tripping over anyone – a huge cause of frustration on projects. People will respect each other and work together better.

✓ **Balls won't be dropped**

There will be less confusion around who is doing what and when, and that will help to improve accountability.

✓ **Keep focus**

The stoplight status report will help you direct and focus duties, which in turn will create the energy to keep things moving.

✓ **Keep it gelled in critical times**

One of the best ways to excel through fast change is to have a 'gelled' team. And good gelling comes from good integration. When you have to do a right-angle turn, it's much easier when your team has been working together.

✓ **Security and value**

Organizational restructuring and job insecurity cause an intangible erosion of morale, motivation and well-being. And this results in lost momentum, lower productivity, and employees hiding in their office cubicles. People just don't feel warm and fuzzy anymore, so you will have to work extra hard at keeping everyone together to re-instill some of that momentum and establish new objectives. Keeping everyone in the loop will get them out of their cubicles and ready to approach the next mission. And, you can bet, there is another mission waiting for you and your team around the corner.

> "It takes one, just one
> And then one follows the other one
> And then another follows the other one
> Next thing you know you got a billion
> People doing some wonderful things
> People doing some powerful things
> Let's change and do some powerful things
> Unity could be a wonderful thing."
>
> – *"Unity," Black Eyed Peas*

rate

Hindsight is 20/20

If you don't know what's going on...admit it

One of the worst things you can do when things get tough is avoid meeting with your team. But it's a very common leadership response. When change sets in and the workplace becomes a 'danger zone,' everyone starts hiding in their cubicles and closing their office doors. The result is a fractured and anxious team who will not be ready to respond when new direction is finally handed down.

Unfortunately, over the years, I've been stuck in the middle of organizational changes, right-angle turns, merging teams and endless downsizing. For example, while I served in the military, our military bases in Canadian Forces Europe were closed down and then the forces were faced with a reduction program. When I worked in high tech, my 'high-tech high-life' and jet-setting around the world with Nortel came to an abrupt end when the dot.com bubble burst. I faced many a day reorganizing my team, calming the chaos, handing out Kleenex and trying to reinject some level of energy and forward momentum into a team that had ground to a sudden halt.

After one particular episode of high-tech downsizing, we lost 40 percent of our immediate team players. And within a couple of months, we would add to those cuts one vice president and a couple of other executives from that same team. That left me and one other director standing with the remnants of several teams. I ended up picking up the pieces and the team players of one of these now 'leaderless' teams and joining them with my team, which was still trying to get back on its feet from the downsizing just two months earlier. The other executive and I had a tough road ahead since we both needed to figure out how to get this team functioning together.

Within a two-day period, we had pulled our teams together for a conference call (our team was located across North America) to communicate what had transpired and to assess where we were in terms of recent changes.

But apparently that was not enough, and the team appeared to be lost. Later that day, I had a knock at my office door from one of the sales managers. He was quite concerned that the 'right hand didn't know what the left hand was doing.' The sales director and I did not appear to have a plan to get our teams working together.

He was right. The rapid changes in the company and the leadership team created a lot of anxiety and uncertainty. We needed to keep communicating with team members and pull them together even if we didn't have that much to tell them.

Keep this in mind. When you're dealing with a lot of change or a mission-critical project, it's just as important to tell your team you don't have all the answers yet. Sort of like "we don't have a plan, but we have a plan to have a plan – and here it is."

So we set up another conference call to tell the entire team that we still did not have all the answers yet. We shared our next steps so they didn't feel disconnected or left out: we were meeting with executives to get their view on immediate priorities; we were visiting with customers to brief them on team changes. We held brainstorming sessions to make sure we fit the right people and skills with the newly established priorities.

Getting out in front of the team and admitting that we didn't have all the answers yet gave each team member a lot more comfort about their jobs and roles than if we had kept meeting behind closed doors.

Be up-front with the entire team. Don't be afraid to admit you don't have all the answers.

integ

Outside the corporate BOX

SEVEN SECONDS IS ALL YOU NEED

Talk about mission critical. If you think delivering a project in three months is a tight timeline, can you imagine a competitive environment where more than 20 team members are integrated to the point of absolute precision and success comes down to seven seconds or less?

Formula One (F1) racing teams have a seven-second 'competitive weapon' called the pit stop – a special pit where race cars stop for refuelling or any rapid maintenance like tire changes, before they blast back onto the main track. And these pit stops are manned by extremely well-trained, well-integrated teams. Can you imagine leading a pit-stop crew where millions of dollars in winnings can be impacted by your team's performance? The precisely timed, millimeter-perfect choreography of a modern pit stop is vital in helping teams turn their racing strategy into wins.[4] Here are some of the key elements to keeping this team well integrated and winning:

• **Team *strategy*** – Car performance and 'stop' strategy is evaluated throughout the race in real time by team strategists – when to make a pit stop is a strategic decision that can win or lose a race.

• **Team *communication*** is vital to success – The team manager listens to all team radio communications and 'scrambles' the pit crew (read: gets the team into position – fast!). Then the race engineer tells the driver when to pit, and everyone works together to get the car in and out of the pit within seconds.

• **Team *integration*** – More than 20 crew members participate in the modern day Formula One pit stop. They all must work in unison to service the car in a matter of seconds, from the lollipop man (who communicates significant information to the driver via a big lollipop sign), to the 'jack' man who lifts the car, to two crew members who operate the refuelling rig, and the three crew members on each wheel!

Within seconds, the car is on its way. Hopefully with a split-second competitive advantage over the other racers for a first-place finish and a multimillion-dollar win.

What's next?

Get ready for it. Something is coming just around the corner and it will challenge you and your team. And leading through challenges is a lot easier when you have your team working together as a cohesive unit.

Integrating your team successfully goes hand in hand with powerful communication strategies. How many people are you leading? Where do they all work? How quickly do you have to get the message out to them? Big or small teams, local or global, there are some really effective and really simple ways of getting the message out.

Effective leadership requires more than just getting the message 'out.' Important information needs to get out, ideas have to flow back to you, data needs to be shared, and situations need to be anticipated.

Three-dimensional communication is where it's at.

rate

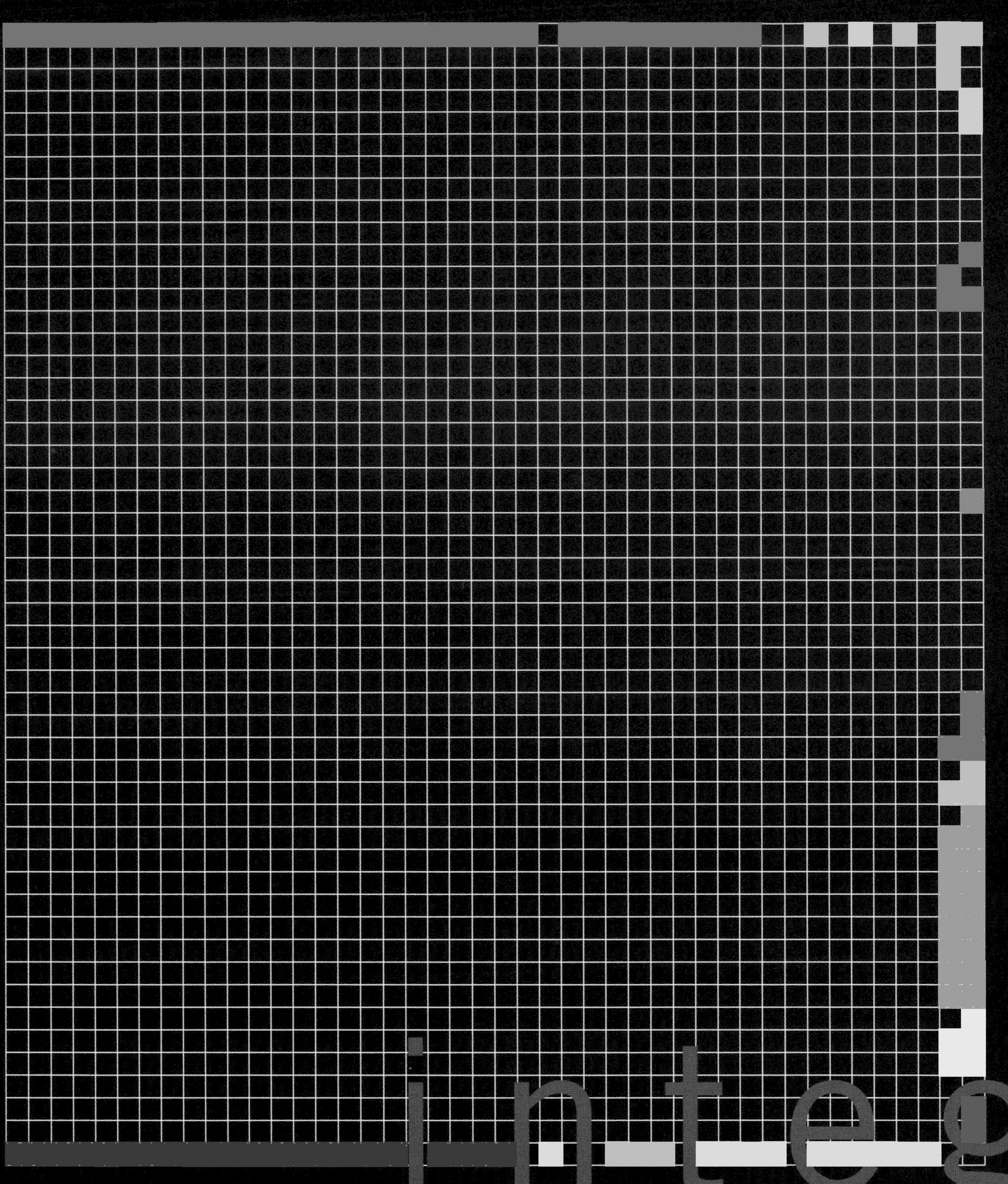
integ

ACTION PLAN

March to the beat of the same drum

1 GET USED TO WARP SPEED.

- Fast, changing and complex are key elements of the environment in which you'll be leading

2 GET CLARITY AND CREATE CLARITY.

- Get clarity on your big picture and accomplishments within the team
- If you don't have it, create it. And then get buy-in

3 LINE UP YOUR TEAM WITH THE BIG PICTURE.

- Share information on specific projects, goals and timelines
- Involve your team in the development or creation of goals, and brainstorm on how the team can align with those goals

4 USE ONE-STOP-SHOPPING TOOLS.

- Provide the team with a visual reference for updates
- Manage accountability and ownership with the stoplight status strategy

rate

CONNECT THE FRONT LINES AND THE BIG PICTURE

The beautiful lull, the dangerous tug
we get to feel small from high up above
and after a glimpse over the top
the rest of the world becomes a gift shop

Gift Shop, The Tragically Hip

COMMUNICATE

The communication fusion

Stay 2 steps ahead

Think in 3 dimensions

2 up-1 down communication

Informed and in sync

The Monday morning meeting

Monday mornings. Ugh. For most of us, Mondays start with a sense of doom for the work that lies ahead, but that doesn't stop many of us from rushing into the office early to get a head start on the work week. Well, if you work at Research In Motion, the Monday a.m. rush exists for an entirely different reason.

Yes, you get that same sense of overwhelm, but it's brought on for reasons other than you might expect. At RIM, the Monday morning rush is about taking part in a sales and marketing ritual – the 'Monday morning meeting' or the 'MMM' as it's otherwise known by employees. Your mission: get to the second-floor cafeteria – capacity of about 75 – and snag a seat before the other 150 or so employees attending get there. This was definitely not a day to wear stilettos. It's hard enough to get motivated on Monday mornings, let alone start the week in a crammed two-hour meeting. What could possibly compel me to make this ritual?

There were plenty of reasons, especially if you wanted to make it in this company. One of them was that the meeting was mandatory. But another key motivation was to get updates and views from the top – our CEO and COO who led the meeting shared weekly words of wisdom.

There are approximately 600 hundred people around the world on RIM's sales and marketing team and all of them are invited to participate at the MMM – *and* expected to provide an update of their weekly activities. Our global employees (hundreds of them) joined the meeting via teleconference to provide us with their updates on the penetration of RIM's leading-edge wireless handheld device, BlackBerry, in various market regions. Rank is of little importance at this meeting. One by one, everyone, from a new inside sales coordinator to a senior vice president, had the opportunity to take the microphone that circulated the room and share information.

When I first started working at RIM a few years back, I heard lots of discussion each Monday from colleagues who had just attended the lengthy session. For some reason I had this notion that the meeting was 'optional' and was quite pleased with myself that I chose instead to use my early start to prepare for the coming week. But after several months, I discovered that I was actually supposed to attend the meeting too. I could no longer avoid the MMM.

At this point, I hadn't met our CEO, Jim Balsillie, now considered one of the most influential men in the world by *Time* magazine – pretty powerful stuff considering some of the other recipients of this prestigious recognition have included Oprah Winfrey, Bill Gates and Dan Brown, author of *The Da Vinci Code*.[1] I had, however, heard some great 'Jim stories' around the water cooler – not surprising, given his growing status as a global icon. Along with the BlackBerry inventor, Mike Lazaridis, who started the company and designed the product, Jim had come on board as the financial strategist and sales mastermind. Together, they have co-led the company and its evolving BlackBerry from the not-so-sexy, 'bull-frog' device to one of the coolest wireless handheld products on the market today. (Okay, I admit, I have *drunk* the 'BlackBerry Kool-aid' as they say and I might be just a little biased.)

Jim puts a great deal of value on the Monday meetings to foster the company's ongoing success. Here's the thing: Once you step into RIM's MMM and speak into the microphone, you no longer 'fly under the radar.' Nope, you are now on his radar, and that means skipping the Monday meeting is no longer an option, as I learned when I made the bad decision of opting for yoga class over the MMM. Sure enough, I received an e-mail on my BlackBerry from Jim by 8:06 a.m., delivering his message short and to the point: "Where are you?" Thank God we hadn't designed the built-in camera BlackBerry yet. Jim would not have been impressed with my downward dog pose instead of my upward update!

INFORMED AND IN SYNC AT THE MMM

So I made my first appearance at the MMM, and the timing couldn't have been better. I had recently been tasked with a new project, and this was an excellent opportunity to provide an update to the sales and marketing organization. After only a few months with the company, I had already gone through a reor-

commu

ganization and was now reporting to our COO in a new role – to establish a professional services organization. I now headed up a team that would generate revenue based on services rather than product sales. It was a new initiative for the company.

When I got to the meeting, dozens of people were already lined up against the cafeteria walls, but I saw an empty seat and headed right for it. First on the agenda, a teleconference update from both new and existing teams around the continent. Then, employees began to pass the microphone around. After what seemed like an eternity, it finally made its way to me. This can be an intimidating experience – for the brief moments that you speak, all eyes and ears are on you. I gave my update on the project, the progress we were making, our 30-, 60- and 90-day objectives and some potential upcoming issues. You don't often get an opportunity to brief your executive team or business units as well as so many employees all at once, so I was taking full advantage of my time with the mike. Little did I realize, I was now going to have that opportunity again and again, in fact, every single Monday.

Eventually the microphone made its way to its last stop, Jim Balsillie. He gave a quick briefing on the competitive landscape, our product road map and some new partnering strategies the company was working on. He then provided a big-picture view of the company plans and progress, launching into other markets around the world. In about two hours (I didn't say this meeting was short, did I?), I had a current and complete view of RIM's sales strategies and key goals.

When the meeting ended, I packed up my notebook quickly to try and squeeze in a quick trip to Starbucks, but Jim was heading my way. "Angela, I don't think we've met. I'm Jim Balsillie." Like I didn't know! "It was good to hear from you today. I'll come by your office sometime to hear more about how the project is going." And he meant it.

In fact, over the next few years, I would have lots of opportunities to chat with Jim about my team, our particular front lines, marketing programs and product launches with one of RIM's largest partners and distribution channels. Jim has a habit of 'popping' into your office or your team meeting and joining right in. He has an uncanny ability to keep it all connected – from high up above.

Through the MMM, Jim had orchestrated immediate access to information at all levels of his organization. By stepping out of his office and doing drop-in visits with all members on the team, he stays on top of what's going on, on the front lines.

I'd say this is a pretty clever strategy to stay informed and keep the rapidly growing teams in sync. But then again, you don't become one of the world's most influential leaders by accident, do you?

The principle: Keep your front lines and big picture connected

> "In Iraq, generals admit that the captains and lieutenants often know more about how to combat the insurgency then they do. It is, they say, a platoon leader's war.[2]" – Time *magazine, May 2005*

We're moving at warp speed these days – so fast, things can be a blur. Leaders today are in the midst of a communication evolution, where things are happening so lickety-split that strategy and planning are happening almost at the same time as execution. To succeed at this pace, you have to work extra hard to stay on top of it all. However you manage, it's critical to connect your front lines and your big picture.

Business models tend to change frequently to stay in line with the rapidly changing business world. Partnering strategies, product delivery models, supply chains and organizational structure can all impact company goals and objectives. To accommodate shifts or a change in company vision, team leadership, and the roles and skills required to support the changing mandates, must also move in a continual state of evolution.

That's why meetings like the MMM at RIM are great (I never thought I'd admit to it) – one-stop shopping to stay in the loop. Whether you're an entry-level administrative assistant or a vice

CONNECT THE FRONT LINES AND THE BIG PICTURE

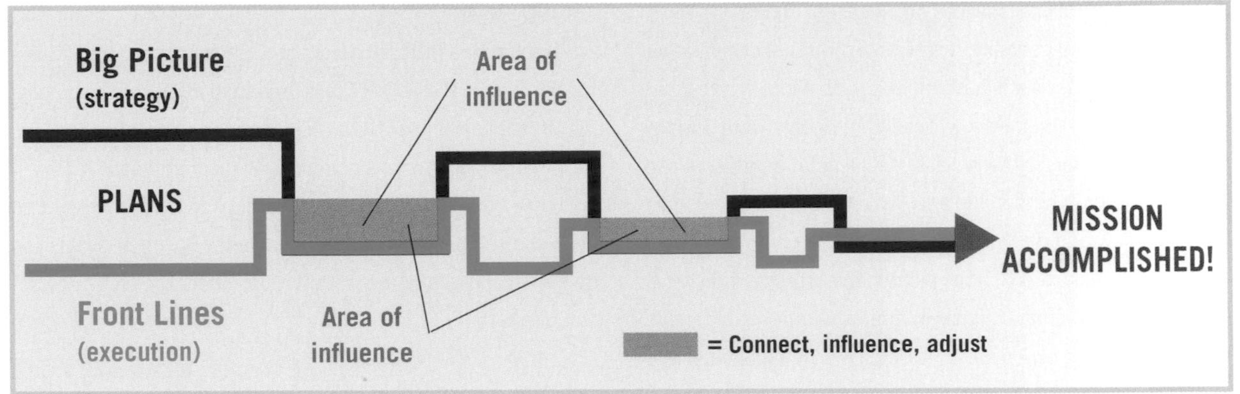

president of sales, you need to keep in touch with the big picture, understand clearly what's happening on your front lines, and if you're a leader, make sure there is a continuous flow between these two layers.

The big picture is where strategy happens and the front lines are where execution occurs. Now think of them both as 'mutually symbiotic.' Each process needs the other to succeed. A big-picture vision must be executed, or it doesn't become reality. By the same token, without that vision, the front lines can head in entirely the wrong direction. Each process influences and benefits the other.

This concept can apply anywhere. My (life) partner, Tom, despite having more than a full-time job running a manufacturing company with two other partners, decided a couple of years ago that he really wanted to build a luxury home. No small feat in itself, but Tom doesn't do things 'small!' Before he could start building the house and executing his dream, he had to have a vision. What type of area did he want to live in? What property was available that would match what he was looking for? What kind of house did he want to build – contemporary, traditional, two-story, bungalow? All of these considerations were rolled up into his vision. Once he nailed them all down, he was ready to execute – find the land, hire a designer and bring in the tradespeople to build the home. He found the perfect lot, but then discovered that he was required to build a house of a certain size on that lot. He needed to adjust his vision and his design…and his budget. As Tom moved from the planning stage to the execution stage, his experience on the building site and front lines started influencing his big picture. Tom's initial vision to build a smaller home in less than a year changed significantly as the reality of working on the front lines, with designers, tradespeople and the municipality, influenced his vision.

Whether it's building houses, starting companies or launching products, planning and execution go hand in hand and need to be continually updated to maintain that continuous cycle of success.

FRONT LINES INFLUENCE THE BIG PICTURE

As a project evolves, strategy and execution gain more accuracy and clarity – and the cycle of updating the plans and the execution continues. Once you start turning plans into reality and the reality on the front lines unfolds, the big-picture vision may require tweaking. So it's important to understand that the big picture around you is going to change direction. Everything about planning and execution really is dynamic.

That big-picture direction will always, in turn, influence execution. As plans become reality and execution unfolds, that process will influence the strategic direction. This cycle exists as long as your project is alive.

Think about what would happen if you had your team lined up to deliver some new departmental initiatives and then the vi-

comm u

sion of the company changed direction. As a result, this particular initiative is forced to change too. You wouldn't want to lead a team focused on goals or objectives that are now obsolete or not lined up with an outdated big picture, would you?

To lead effectively, it's your job to keep on top of that big picture (strategy) and front lines (execution) relationship. That means stepping out of your daily operations and poking your head out of your cubicle or office to see what is going on around you. Go to other team meetings to check out what's happening or attend information sessions on new initiatives in the company. Attend external trade conferences and keep up-to-date on industry initiatives.

> "When I fly, I want to be the smartest sonofabitch [sic] in the sky. I want to know who I'm up against, what they're flying, where they are, what they're carrying, and what the ground threats are. I want to know everything, I want it right, and I want a minimum of surprises....Situational awareness is not found in a manual or a top secret report, but every fighter pilot has it.[3]" – *James D. Murphy, F15 pilot and president of Afterburner Seminars*

Don't you want to be the smartest son of a bitch in the sky?

How to connect the front lines and big picture

Keeping it all connected is actually not that difficult to do. You can take your entire team to a whole new level with two simple concepts. They are:

1. Tune into the three dimensions
2. 2 up-1 down communication

TUNE INTO THE THREE DIMENSIONS

What we're going to talk about is really a *communication fusion,* a 'nonlinear' or three-dimensional approach to keep everything connected. You need to think beyond what is going on in your line of fire – above you, beside you and around you. This involves communicating in a whole new way.

Maybe you're a sales manager or director of a large corporation. Or an entrepreneur and president of a start-up company, or a politician who represents a large number of constituents. You might even be considered one of the most influential people in the world. It doesn't really matter. Successful leaders understand how to connect the big picture to the front lines. They think in three dimensions. They work at staying two steps ahead. They treat communication as a proactive process.

Here's what to do to ensure a three-dimensional connection:

1 Get outside your box

Don't just think outside the box – climb right outside of it. What's happening outside your team or your department? How about the business world outside your company, your customers, the competition, economy, here and internationally? Believe it or not, these things can quickly impact your team on the front lines. How much time do you spend getting acquainted with the world outside your four walls?

2 Anticipate change. "What could this mean to me?"

Have you ever noticed how some people in your organization have a real knack or even a 'sixth sense' for knowing what's going on around them? These individuals look beyond their own cubicle – they're in touch with change and forecast things before anyone else does. They're in tune with the three-dimensional world around them – the horizontal teams, the vertical organizational hierarchy and the external world. For example, they hear news of a large deal with a new customer in another country and immediately think about what this might mean for the company, either the need to create a new team or at least a few new positions to support the change. If you're anticipating change, such as a new political party heading the federal government, it might trigger a personal interest with the national budget and you could forsee the impact it could have on programs that affect your industry.

nicate

Keep your eyes wide open. Stay in touch with changes outside your company and continually question what those changes may mean for you and the organization. You'll be more aware, agile and, ultimately, better prepared for potential impact.

CASE STUDY **In-flight intelligence**

In the air force, we used to have this expression called *situation awareness*. Flying at the speeds fighter pilots do, they have to be keenly aware of what is going on around them – not so much so that they can *keep up* with the speed at which things are changing in the sky around them, but so that they can *anticipate* what is coming their way; they have to 'check their sixes' for bogies and bandits and know instinctively what's going on, on every axis. Three-dimensional awareness (or lack of) is a matter of life and death. It's sort of like staying in tune with the big picture but at a more acute gut level.

We might not be moving at Mach 1 or the speed of sound in business, but things are definitely moving at a rapid pace. Accurately anticipating what's coming is a powerful leadership strategy. That's where thinking in three dimensions really pays off! Why? Because you can prepare your team for upcoming change, or even better, jump at an early opportunity. Preparation and foresight always lead to a greater chance of success. Staying in touch with what's happening in your company or with your customers will keep you on your toes and thinking ahead all the time. And if you're thinking ahead, you're more likely to come out ahead.

3 Gather friendly intelligence

What about other teams or leaders within your company? How well do you connect with other groups? We can get so wrapped up in our own deliverables that we stop paying attention to what's going on around us. Take the opportunity to participate in other team or department meetings. Better yet, get your team players to participate and then report back to the group on new initiatives and where you may be able to collaborate or synchronize goals.

And then there's your company's intranet – obviously a great place to gain intelligence! Be proactive, seek out info, company announcements, new partnerships, alliances, product launches, or new teams that have been created. How can you leverage this information? Consider this example:

I recently met a sales clerk, Mark Davenport, at the Virgin Records Megastore in Union Square in New York City. I was looking for a 'naked' CD collection – a compilation of very cool, chilling lounge music. He knew immediately what I was talking about, whisked me down a few flights on the escalator and then proceeded to 'up-sell' me on several other chill CDs that he raved about. When I asked Davenport how he knew so much about music, he laughed and said this clerk job was just a sideline gig. He used this position for intelligence-gathering and getting real-time frontline information for his full-time job – running a music consulting company and agency for world renowned DJs and hip-hop musicians.

▶▶ **Fast forward** *to Chapter 12, "Push Your Envelope," to read more about one of Davenport's hip-hop superstars.*

4 Share it, don't hoard it!

Believe it or not, some leaders sit on very important insights that their team could benefit from without even realizing it. Now that you have a good handle on how to think and lead with a three-dimensional awareness, it's important to share that information with your team members to keep everyone on the team aligned and synchronized.

Sharing your knowledge can be as simple as forwarding an e-mail that has been sent to you from your boss or someone in another department. But it also means having the foresight to gather all of that very useful information that you take for granted and pass it on, for example, when you attend meetings that others don't, or you have privileged conversations with people your team might not have access to. Ask yourself this: What information do you have that will benefit others?

Keeping your team informed of simple facts can mean the difference between a bunch of people that report to you versus a 'cohesive and well-connected unit' who understands how they fit in with your goals and those of the organization.

commu

Reality Check: Beware the right-angle turn

I will never forget an e-mail that I and 80,000-plus employees received while working for Nortel Networks, one of the world's largest telecommunications companies. Sent by then-CEO, John Roth, the e-mail was entitled, "The Right-angle Turn." It contained details of how Nortel was making a large strategy shift in its core competency and product line by merging with a company called Bay Networks from Billerica, Massachusetts. As a manager of 25 people in global export operations, my immediate reaction was "this won't mean anything to us and shouldn't have any impact." Within two months, both companies were merging resources and our global logistics team went into a tailspin. Reorganizing and downsizing impacted every single one of us in no time flat. Never underestimate the seemingly innocuous changes within your company.

2 UP-1 DOWN COMMUNICATION

Now that you're looking at things from a new vantage point, what can you do with it? You can leverage a 2 up-1 down strategy to communicate effectively.

Better awareness = better preparation. For everything.

1 The 2 up-1 down strategy

This strategy is almost an unspoken rule in the military. The military chain of command is probably one of the best at getting information out across departments or between layers of its organization at lightening speed. Using the fan-out communication process (often used with rapid response or emergency teams), information is transmitted right down to the front-line team leaders (platoon commanders, captains or sergeants), ensuring they are connected to the mission's big-picture vision. Let's put it this way, when the military doesn't do this well, the consequences can mean life or death.

The key to the success of the 2 up-1 down concept is that *every leader* is responsible for ensuring that his/her team has the information about what's happening in at least two organizational levels above them. Transposed to the business world, this means that your team will need to know what's going on at their level, your level and your boss's level. As a team leader, it's your duty to keep your direct reports (people who report directly into you) completely informed of any news, goals, objectives, and organizational or leadership changes. In the military, that means that a platoon's sergeant should know and communicate what's going on in the company and in the regiment. In business, it means the inside sales coordinator on the sales team needs to understand what's happening in their own business unit, other business units and other departments.

The reverse must also happen. You need to ensure that the leaders who are two levels above you have accurate insight into your team's progress on goals, objectives, projects and missions. Think about it: How effective can a military platoon be if it doesn't understand what their regiments' goals or the battalion's objectives are, as they head off into some new territory to fight the latest battle? How effective will your team be if they are not in sync with the department's or company's direction?

CASE STUDY **2 up-1 down, air-show style**

One summer, as a young lieutenant, I had an exciting task. I was responsible with my team for coordinating the logistics efforts for an international air show that would be held that summer at our fighter base. The best part was the feature act – the Frecce Tricolori, an Italian aerobatics team that has a reputation for the most spectacular, risk-taking air show. To plan for this big event, I used the 2 up-1 down communication strategy – pretty common in the military – for the final month of planning. I would attend air show coordination meetings that involved all support teams, including air traffic control, air safety, suppliers, vendors, food services, accommodation providers, etc. At this meeting, we reviewed the big-picture vision for the air show with all of the organizations and vendors so that we could coordinate all parts of the event effectively. Immediately following these strategy meetings, I organized a more tactical session: a recurring weekly logistics meeting with the key players on my team who were responsible for pulling together the details for the air show. There, I updated my team on the ground displays, such as aircraft, company booths, military equipment, air demonstration teams, number of participants expected, marketing and PR activities, and many other details. The team was now in sync with the latest big picture. I, in turn, received updates on the logistics plans, tactics and execution that my team was leading, and was able to bring that update back to the air show planning sessions.

Within two hours, from our top-level wing commander (the CEO of the base) to the troops, from the strategy developers and vision owners to the front lines, everyone was connected.

Reality Check
Good communication = big impact

2 up-1 down communication sounds simple, doesn't it? It should. Would you believe that team and organizational communication is one of the key reasons why projects fail, yet it's one of the most simple leadership actions you can get good at? In fact, some major IT project surveys point to 57 percent of projects failing because of poor communication[4] – with an impact that costs billions each year! Research by global consulting firms, such as Watson Wyatt, indicates that companies with effective communication strategies can increase shareholder value substantially, compared to those companies with inefficient communication practices from management.[5]

No doubt about it, how you communicate with your team will impact frontline execution and big-picture results!

2 The 'all-hands' meeting

RIM's MMM is a great example of how a successful high-tech CEO keeps his team informed and connected every week. The meetings began in the earlier days of RIM when the sales and marketing team numbered in the dozens, in contrast to the now-hundreds of participants.

A simple weekly update, with information flowing both up and down, is easy to get started (and it doesn't matter where your team is located). It's critical in ensuring that everyone is on the same page and it can provide great visibility for your team.

CASE STUDY **Virus-hunting**

How does anyone in the computer virus software industry ever catch up? Imagine how fast-paced and ever-changing the world of virus-hunting is – once you finally develop a strategy for one virus, another virus has likely already started wreaking havoc. Symantec, a top-notch computer virus hunter, works hard at keeping the team in sync. Virus-hunting is a tough business – the work is never done and the market can shift 30 times a day. Being well-connected in this industry is an absolute must, and can mean the difference between a devastating virus on the loose and the next global solution. *Fast Company* magazine describes the challenge for the mastermind behind the scenes:

"Weafer [leader of Symantec's virus chasers] and six of his lieutenants are sitting around an oval Formica conference table for a weekly security briefing; several remote locations are looped in by speakerphone. There's a rapid rundown of the threats everyone's dealing with, and that provides an opportunity for Weafer to ask lots of questions and make sure the various sites are acting in sync."[6]

This team might be scattered around the world, but the all-hands meetings combined with a 2 up-1 down style of 'lieutenants and generals meeting' on a weekly basis is what it takes to stay on top of the next threat.

Leading from 20,000 feet, acting from 200 feet

Today's leaders need to be aware of global issues beyond their day jobs, generating revenue or delivering products and services. Our one-time gigantic planet is shrinking by the day as issues that once seemed to be on the other side of the planet are now right in our backyard. We've already seen the influence of rock stars, actors, politicians and everyday people who take a conscious, unified stand on such issues as global warming, AIDS, the effects of weather patterns (tsunamis, hurricanes) and possible pandemics like the avian flu – all of which continue to threaten us no matter our wealth, location or position.

So when you're thinking about the difference you want to

commu

make as a leader, don't just think local – think about making a global difference. Check out The Earth Charter Initiative being implemented through the UN-mandated University for Peace in Costa Rica. This global initiative addresses the biggest picture of all – the world we live in, what's happening to it and how each of us needs to make a difference. So next time you are considering the big picture, think 'real big picture'...like the world we live in. Then do what you can in your environment to make a dent in this global situation.

> "Every one of us can make a contribution. And quite often, we are looking for big things and forget that wherever we are, we can make a contribution.[7]"
>
> *– Wangari Maathai, Earth Charter Commissioner*

Outside the corporate BOX

HOW A POP DIVA STAYS CONNECTED

What does it take to pull together one of the most high-energy, awe-inspiring two-hour musical performances that has a Cirque du Soleil flavor, bagpipes, skateboarding and some real sexy edginess? It's not news that Madonna is a multitalented, highly powerful business woman. She's renowned for paying meticulous attention to detail – costumes, choreography, production. She's also known for being intimately involved in her own concert tours – from the vision to the execution. Her Re-Invention Tour 2004 was just another fine example of her ability to glide comfortably back and forth between visionary and executioner. With her mind-boggling track record of incredible success, is there any reason to believe her Confessions Tour 2006 will be any different?

A successful tour like the worldwide Re-Invention Tour, or all of her tours for that matter, requires leadership at every level. That includes frontline leaders such as show directors, tour production directors, lighting specialists and music programmers. How do they make it happen?

Preproduction planning, choreography, rehearsals and crystal-clear distinction of roles and accountability with every member of the team. And, of course, it wouldn't be possible without Madonna's demands for perfection.

What are Madonna's results when she masterminds the connection between her big-picture vision and the front lines? Hundreds of thousands of thrilled fans who receive a super-stimulating barrage of powerfully choreographed sound, light, dance and music. That and a lot of cash.

The front lines:

- 1 queen of pop
- 20-plus performers
- 55 tons of ground equipment, including sound, lights, videos and speakers
- 18 semi-trailers carrying equipment, including a turntable stage
- 750,000 fans attending the performances

The big picture:

- 1 two-hour performance
- 56 shows across North America and Europe
- 897, 214 tickets sold
- $124+ million, gross revenue [8]

nicate

What's in it for you... and your team?

By now, you probably see the importance of keeping you and your team in tune and connected three-dimensionally. Everyone benefits when their team leader is informed, in sync with what's happening in an organization and, most importantly, sharing that information.

I remember one of my senior managers once telling me how much he appreciated the e-mails I forwarded to him and the insight I shared at our weekly team meetings. Maybe I've been brainwashed as a military lieutenant about the importance of sharing information and not hoarding it like many leaders do – my training has taught me that success can quickly turn into failure when useful information isn't relayed to the team.

Here's how sharing info will impact your team positively:

✓ **Keep informed**

Keeping people up-to-date about their environment ensures a greater understanding of what's going on outside of their box. *What other projects do they need to know about? What new partnerships has your company made?*

✓ **Add value**

Greater team and organizational awareness ensures that people are better aligned and that they understand where they fit in and how they impact team goals and objectives.

✓ **Empower**

Understanding how a team member's job lines up with overall organizational goals encourages personal accountability and empowerment.

✓ **Foster change**

Keeping your team apprised of upcoming or potential changes will better prepare them when things do change. *Are you gaining new customers? Where is your product going?*

✓ **Reduce in-the-box thinking**

You want people to be two steps ahead, so give them a big-picture perspective. In turn, this will stimulate innovation. *Do you inspire your team to think creatively about how a new company's initiative will integrate with your goals and objectives?*

✓ **Connect strategy and execution**

The more aware the team, the better able they are to make decisions on the front lines. Team members will better understand how they are impacting the strategic direction. *If you asked one of your team players, would he be able to tell you exactly how his role ties in with the latest strategy?*

Better informed employees = better performing employees!

> "What are ya gonna tell them?
> No more than I have to, if that!"[9]
>
> – *Chili Palmer, from the movie* Be Cool

THE FLIP SIDE

Sharing information is such an important part of keeping the front lines and the big picture connected that I think we should look at this from one more angle – the consequences of not sharing information with your team. I've seen a couple of different reasons why a leader might do this:

1. Knowledge is power – Some leaders believe that by keeping good information to themselves, they will be more valuable and knowledgeable than the majority of the team.

2. Inside the box – Some leaders can be so absorbed with their immediate task at hand that they forget to look at what's going on around them.

I've been at the receiving end of both. Very different motivations, but, ultimately, the same results. By not keeping your team informed, you could get caught with your pants down.

Some leaders believe their job is more secure if they appear to know more than the rest of their team. Or they've positioned themselves as a 'subject matter expert' and don't want to threaten their perceived value.

Keeping knowledge to yourself may make you powerful for a short time. However, once things start happening at a faster pace, you may not have the time to update your team, leaving members to perform essential tasks without all the info. Be prepared for devastating consequences in this case.

When I lead a team, I want them to know as much info as I do (except sensitive information I need to keep under wraps).

commu

Hindsight is 20/20

Don't get caught with your pants down!

I was recently asked to speak on leadership at a wonderful annual conference by a highly enthusiastic university team of business students. As usual, I arrived well in advance to make sure we had all the technical aspects of the presentation worked out.

Most of the key organizing members, however, were all busy running around and although I was seated at the head table during dinner, they had little time to eat, let alone fill me in on the schedule. I was eventually told I'd be speaking sometime between dinner and dessert, but that seemed to be a two-hour process.

I had no choice but to go with the flow. Before dinner was over, I headed off to the change room to get into a G.I. Jane outfit – a prop that went along with my talk. Well, no sooner had I taken off my dress pants to put on my gear, I heard words that would equate to any keynote speakers' nightmare…"Angela, are you in here? You're being introduced on stage right now. Are you in here?"

The organizers of this high-energy event were so consumed with the minute details and what was transpiring on the front lines, that they neglected to look up at the big picture – the overall flow of the evening, as well as the status and presence of important guests. It's always important, no matter what your role is, to get your head out of the sand (I love that ostrich analogy!), so that you don't miss out on the important things going on around you. The organizers' lack of focus on the big picture impacted the performance of participants (like me) right down the line.

Talk about getting caught with your pants down!

The more of us that have good awareness, the more smart heads out there to keep an eye on the tasks our team should be doing and assess change. In turn, I get more and better ideas from my team. Not only should you surround yourself with smart people but with informed people.

RED FLAG **Need-to-know basis only**

No matter what industry you work for, classified or sensitive information needs to be shared carefully. When assessing whether information should be shared, military team leaders generally use the rule on a "need-to-know" basis; that is, they assess whether information that is shared will improve operations and team awareness, or if it will have a negative effect. What is the impact if someone on the team shares the info with someone they shouldn't? Will this impact morale in a negative way? While passing on information is a powerful way of keeping your team connected, sensitive information must be shared using a 'need-to-know' filter.

What's next?

Consider this: You've been approached by your boss with what seems like an impossible project. Impossible, but still an extremely exciting challenge. You know it would take you to a different level, both in terms of personal growth and level of experience. But you can't help but think to yourself:

- How am I going to do this?
- Where do I start?
- No one else has ever done this, so what do I need to do to get it done?

Breaking new ground is all part of leadership and it's something you can be good at. You just need to develop an 'execution mindset' and get *ready for the leap!*

Successful execution when you're leading at warp speed (and most of us are these days), comes down to some key things, including preparation for execution. It's a simple approach and mindset you can adopt with your team to get ready for when the 'rubber hits the road.'

In the pages ahead, we'll look at a team of people who move at the speed of sound (seriously) to see how they prepare for the successful execution of their missions. When you're flying by the seat of your pants, *preparation* is often what makes the difference between a successful mission and poor performance.

nicate

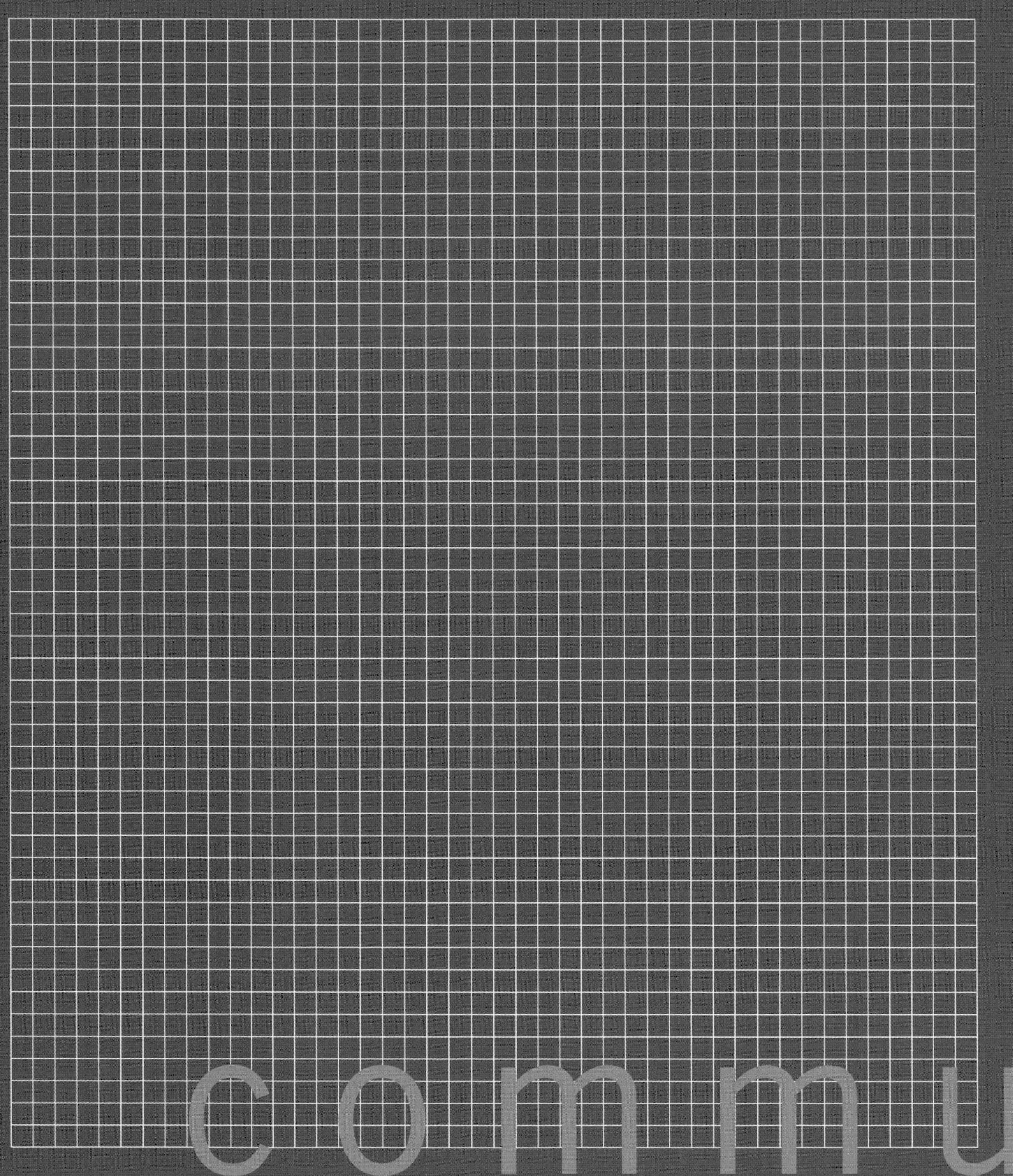
commu

ACTION PLAN

Communicate 2 up-1 down

1 PRACTICE EXECUTION EVOLUTION.

- Direction will change and you could get sideswiped
- Keep your team's skills and project/work objectives lined up with changing company goals

2 TAKE TIME TO CONNECT.

- Pop in for visits, walk around the office, sit in on meetings

3 TUNE IN THREE DIMENSIONALLY.

- Think big picture, be aware of what's happening around you, beside you, above and below you

4 USE THE 2 UP-1 DOWN COMMUNICATION CONCEPT.

- Keep your boss and your boss's boss updated
- Make sure your team is visible
- Feed your team big-picture scoop

nicate

EXECUTING QUICK, DIRTY AND SOMETIMES FLAWED

There's only so much you can learn in one place
The more that you wait, the more time that you waste...
Are you ready to jump?

Jump, Madonna

EXECUTE

Make it happen

Plans into action

Quick, dirty and simple

Thrust and vectors

Flawed execution

Yanking and banking

"Hard right. Hard right!" the pilot was yelling into my helmet intercom between hard breathing and the usual grunting. There we were in an air-to-air combat mission, which for most of us non-aviators would equate to a bunch of fighter jets flying right toward each other. In reality, this was a training mission for NATO pilots to practice their flying and combat skills. We were 10,000 feet above Europe in 'low fly 7,' a dedicated military flying zone. There were 'friendlies' and 'bogies' (good guys and bad guys, respectively) assigned all over the sky on this beautiful sunny September day, and I could barely keep up with the U.S. F-15 eagles or German Tornados buzzing around us.

This might sound like a scene from the movie *Top Gun* or one of Xbox 360's latest war games, but it was actually a day in the life of a fighter pilot. This was the real thing. And my neck was killing me, physically hurting, as I tried to keep my body from getting flung around in the backseat of a jet while the pilot pulled and turned hard on the aircraft stick (otherwise know as 'yanking and banking'), which typically produces extremely steep turns, dives or rapid climbing in the supersonic jet fighter F-18 we were flying. Suddenly, we banked over hard and fast in a steep turn, and I saw the g-meter, a flight instrument that indicates gravitational force (g-force) on the aircraft, climb rapidly to 7+ G, so seven times our body weight was being pulled with the aircraft while we flew at hundreds of miles an hour.

With this amount of g-force on the body, you can expect your blood to move down to your legs and away from your head. Needless to say I was no exception and my vision started going a little fuzzy. My training as a backseat passenger was all coming back to me – now would be a good time to do the M1 maneuver, an anti-g-force 'straining' technique that keeps the blood flowing in your upper body (read brain) and prevents small 'stars' from appearing in your eyes. I kicked in with the M1 maneuver, a combination of a good ab workout and holding your breath and grunting (it's a very unladylike maneuver), just in the nick of time. It was time to get back to the bogies and keep my eye on what was going on around me.

So how does a girl like me end up a fighter pilot for the day? I mean, these seats were a hot commodity among us pilot wannabes since the air force only had a certain amount of two-seater jets to begin with. You have to have friends in the right places, in my case, a couple of fighter jock buddies from my training days in boot camp. What pulled me to this experience had a lot to do with my aviation background. I grew up as an aviation enthusiast and already had some flying experience, so one of my first priorities as a lieutenant was to get trained in high-altitude indoctrination, a three-day course where you spend your time in ejection seats and a high-altitude chamber to learn about the flying equipment, the physiological effects of flying in supersonic machines, ejection procedures, and all sorts of other exciting things. All of this so I could be certified to just ride in the backseat as an observer! No wonder these fighter pilots need so many years of training to get qualified to fly these aircraft.

Soon after completing my three-day training, I was a privileged passenger along for the ride on this air combat 'mass attack' mission, led by one of Canada's top guns and historical fighter squadrons, 416 Tactical Fighter Squadron (TFS). With so many jets buzzing around this airspace, and all of us appearing to be flying directly into each other, I didn't have a clue what was happening. What was happening from the pilot's perspective, however, was the execution of a well-orchestrated mission. It was a mission that took several hours to plan, with each of the pilots on the team playing an intricate part in the planning process, attending many briefings just two hours before the flight to review all aspects of the mission.

BITCHIN' BETTY

Isn't it funny how the things that appear so effortless, are often very complex when you really get behind the scenes? This was one of those experiences. It takes the incredible coordination of so many variables to be able to fly these missions – airplanes are flying at the speed of sound and $35 million worth of state-of-the-art equipment is being used, yet these pilots are almost

exec

'at one' with their aircraft. Finally, after all of the planning and skilled aerial maneuvers for what seemed like hours, the mission was called off. We had fulfilled our training objectives for the day. As I sat in the backseat, absolutely wiped out, I could hear the pilots chatting on the radio about the completed mission and, another important matter, what was for lunch. Just another day at the office for them. But, then, just as I was relaxing and no longer worrying about keeping an eye out for enemy aircraft trying to shoot us down, 'Bitchin' Betty,' the annoying cockpit voice kicked in to warn my pilot to be aware of the current altitude in which we were flying. Apparently we were flying low enough over the hills that he needed to pull up to a higher altitude, or reset the radio altimeter. No, nothing about flying these jets was simple; in fact, nothing about orchestrating the mission was simple. It all came down to a lot of training experience and a lot of planning and preparation. That's what made it appear much simpler.

> "An idea can be as flawless as can be, but its execution will always be full of mistakes."
>
> *– Brent Scowcroft, national security expert and recipient of the Presidential Medal of Freedom*

Once our four-jet formation landed smoothly, and the aircraft were taxied to the hangars, I couldn't help but think to myself how these fighter pilots have an absolutely amazing day job. It doesn't get any better than having your morning coffee and jumping into your jet for a little air-to-air combat. We parked the jets, the canopy of the jet lifted, and we unstrapped g-suits, parachutes, helmets and other bits and pieces. My 'fighter jock for the day' experience came to an almost ungraceful end, as my legs were so wobbly from the tough flying that I practically landed splat on the tarmac!

FLYING BY THE SEAT OF YOUR PANTS

After reviewing the aircraft tapes, the 'friendlies' (we, the Canadian pilots), had come out on top. A little friendly competition among the squadrons and nations is always nice, so declaring that your team has the best top guns and got the most bogies during the mission is all part of the fun.

> "You don't concentrate on risks. You concentrate on results. No risk is too great to prevent the necessary job from getting done."
>
> *– Chuck Yeager, first pilot to fly faster than the speed of sound*

After such a mind-blowing experience, I found myself driving down Germany's autobahn back to my desk job, thinking that it would be tough to go back to the paperwork grind. But something occurred to me on the drive back. In addition to all of the very specific training my colleagues and I received throughout our military professions, the ability to execute or 'make it happen' was second nature to many of us. In the military, executing is not a trend or buzzword; it is a way of thinking and acting that, over time, has become a way of being. How *apropos* that I had learned on that day the 416 Squadron's Latin motto, *Ad Saltum Paratus,* which dates back to their Second World War days, and translates to "ready for the leap." Because in essence, that's what leadership and execution is all about – preparing and planning for the unknown. And then getting on with it.

The principle: Get the execution mindset

Most of us will never lead a 'mass attack' mission like that of a pilot responsible for pulling together supersonic jets for an air-to-air combat mission, but wouldn't it be powerful to know that you have the ability to make things happen? That you have the mindset to get things going, get a team organized to move a project forward and deliver key goals and objectives? If all of this speaks to you, then you have the execution mindset.

This principle is about being able to turn plans into reality in a short time frame. And I believe it's one of the most powerful skills you can arm yourself with as a leader. It's needed everywhere. It applies to any team, business, industry or organization and can be used in many ways:

- Building your own business
- Creating a new sales team
- Organizing a fundraising event
- Developing a marketing program
- Building a house
- Launching a product
- Planning a trip

Without successful planning and execution, goals can't be achieved, teams can't move forward, products can't be created, and missions can't be accomplished.

In the military, we were taught to develop the execution mindset by planning, preparing and using tools and checklists. We learned that successful execution is often about what you do *before* you begin turning your plans into action, because once you get going, those plans are likely to change anyway.

Even though developing the execution mindset might initially seem daunting, once you learn an effective leadership approach and get the right tools in place, you can execute almost anything. I learned my best execution lessons in boot camp at 22 years old. The important part is that I practiced what I learned, and put the same tools into practice for the next 20 years.

> "The most effective way to do it, is to do it."
>
> *– Amelia Earhart, first woman to fly solo nonstop across the Atlantic Ocean*

Take fighter pilots, for example. They train for years to learn to fly complex multimillion-dollar aircraft, and they study tactics and flying strategies. But it doesn't take them years to understand how to *plan and execute* a successful mission. Whatever the mission, they will approach its execution in the same way every time by following a set of best practices and steps so that they can develop an effective plan, communicate it, align the team with it and then execute it.

The same successful approach to execution in the sky works on the ground, in business and anywhere. The approach is key.

Execution *unplugged*

In its simplest form, execution might be defined as "the ability to get things done."

But in reality, execution can go a lot further. Execution is fundamentally based on your ability as a leader to take a plan and turn it into reality. However, you don't often get a well-laid plan handed to you on a platter by your leadership! So, guess who needs to come up with one? You'll need to take the ideas your team develops and come up with the strategy to make the plan yourself.

On a much bigger scale, execution can also become the power of creation. Executing and taking action will lead to a transformation of your team and organization. For example, I recently met two young entrepreneurs who are starting up a charter aircraft service in southwestern Ontario. They have the skills to fly aircraft, have invested lots of money in the business and bought an airplane to provide the service. But they have to execute their business plan successfully and get that airplane flying as many hours in a day as possible to ensure a certain profit level. Here's where the transformation comes in: Where these two entrepreneurial pilots are today in terms of their skills, knowledge and business wisdom is not at all where they will be tomorrow, next month or a year from now. They are learning by the day about marketing strategies, launching a product, how to seek financing, connecting with business associations and partnering with others to grow their business. There is no question that, as they make progress through this phase of execution and bring their vision into reality, they will be transforming – themselves and their business!

KEEPING IT SIMPLE

Executing doesn't often require complex charts or graphs or plans. In fact, too much 'process' can bog down your progress. But it will always require effective leadership, as does almost every principle we've talked about in this book, from 'the buck stops with you' (accountability) to 'linking your team to the mission' (team integration).

I believe in keeping it simple when you can. And by 'simple' I mean keeping the process simple – all the process in the world will not replace good leadership. I have had to rely on some pretty rudimentary methods to execute some fairly complex missions in the past. Most of the deployment planning I did for the UN mission in the former Yugoslavia was developed from simple checklists (documented in standard operating procedures for air and rail moves), to-do lists and task lists. I didn't have a laptop computer or cell phone with me; what I did have were hand-scratched notes in my platoon commander's notepad, kept in my combat pants pocket. That was my project plan for the next few months. My handwritten plans and lists guided me on a daily basis through the complex execution of determining how we could best move the contingent of army troops and their equipment across countries and into a war zone in a matter of days. Team meetings, briefings with business leaders, situation reports (sitreps), status reports and, most importantly, a list of all actions required. You can have all of the plans in the world, all the fancy process you want, but without any *leadership and action,* you don't have execution.

> "I don't give two hoots in hell about 'theory' or 'strategy.' I like 'doing stuff.' And I'm drawn to people who like 'doing stuff.' That is I'm obsessed about THE WORK ITSELF. Work that matters. Work you can brag about. My mantra: It's WOW Projects, stupid. (Or else.)" *– Tom Peters, management guru*

Keeping execution plans simple is just as effective in the business world as it is in the military, especially when you're moving rapidly. Even though I have had formal project management training and I'm adept at using a lot of technology, for me, successful execution of any project always comes back to the same things: an execution mindset that combines effective leadership skills, sharp focus on objectives, the energy to 'kick-start' a team, momentum maintenance throughout the project, and the confidence and know-how to apply some simple best practices to lead you in the right direction.

RED FLAG **The execution dilemma**

The ability to make it happen still remains a roadblock for many leaders. It takes courage to jump into the deep end, as you face new challenges and forge into the unknown, blazing new trails. And it's that unknown that often stops leaders from executing – fear of failure, of not knowing the answer or appearing like you're not quite sure of what you're doing.

Get over it! Whether you and your team are developing a new program, introducing a new service or trying to reach performance goals, execution is all about making things happen. The difference between a leader who can execute and one who can't get a team engaged is not about knowing 'how.' The difference lies in the leader's mindset – if one believes they can make it happen and relies on her confidence, leadership skills and best practices, she can put anything into play.

So don't let that fear of the unknown or the 'new' stop you in your tracks. Having the mindset is half the battle.

> "Success is often achieved by those who don't know failure is inevitable." *– Coco Chanel, fashion designer*

How to get the execution mindset

With two decades of execution experience (how time flies!), I've had a lot of opportunity to practice and witness the execution mindset. The impact of good execution was really visible in the early 1990s during Operation Desert Storm. My role as logistics officer in Europe had been rapidly refocused to working specifically on deploying the Canadian fighter squadrons to the Persian Gulf. I recall watching as, within minutes, my major (my boss) turned one of our logistics offices into a full-fledged 'command post,' equipped with call logs (for every phone call, fax, message and task we would receive) and a white board that became our instant deployment plan, complete with a priority list of aircraft that had to deliver thousands of pounds of equipment to the Persian Gulf in a matter of weeks.

Our plans changed a million times but it didn't matter. His execution mindset and his great example of getting things moving, getting the team organized around priorities and using very simple tools got the rest of us off our duffs. We didn't worry about the 'how' but the 'what' to reach our goal.

Here are some of the steps you can take to develop your execution mindset:

1 Create your own execution doctrine

It's tough to know where you're going on a road trip without a map. Knowing where and how to execute is similar – it helps to have a road map, or some sort of template. And that's one of the first things I learned in the military – the value of having a standard approach and then choosing what you need out of it. Any good military approach or way of doing things is documented in a standard operating procedure (SOP). SOPs help create a standardized process, based on tried-and-true practices. With these as a guide, you'll know where and how to get started. The mission I described earlier took just two to three hours of preparation before the actual flight, using a 'fighter force tactics' manual, a mission-critical information document, and to-do lists for every element of the mission.

I was lucky. I was trained to use a simple execution framework back in boot camp in my early twenties. Over the years, as I've gained experience, I have taken that simple framework (which documented an outline of key steps required to set up and implement an operation or military project) and have added some depth to it. Years later, I use the same simple approach. The only thing that has really changed over time is my experience and my level of confidence.

▶▶ **Fast forward** *to the Execution Intelligence box on page 200 for a simple execution framework.*

"The more you know about the tactics you need to line up for your mission, the easier your big picture is going to be. SOPs help you get started at a tactical level." *– Lieutenant-Colonel 'Slider' Gagné, commanding officer, 416 Tactical Fighter Squadron*

CASE STUDY **Executing at the speed of sound**

How do leaders in the 'hottest' seats approach their missions? Whether it's to provide rapid reinforcement for other squadrons, patrol the sovereignty of a nation or intercept enemy aircraft, fighter leads, those responsible for leading teams of fighter pilots in executing their missions, use a Fighter Force SOP. This type of SOP is a standard operating procedure that defines the best practices and steps that a team of pilots should take to prepare effectively when executing a mission. Here are a few of the elements in this SOP (unclassified, of course!):

- **Timings checklist** – This timeline identifies the specific timing, key tasks or milestones required from the start to the end of the mission. When things are moving at such a fast pace, every step is critical, right down to the minutes. So why not document actions to be taken before take-off that are mandatory in making this mission successful? For instance, the SOP 'take-off time minus 10 minutes' requires that the aircraft should be taxiing down the runway 10 minutes before departure.
- **Briefings checklist** – This communication checklist incorporates key things that must be included in the team briefing: objectives, training rules for the mission, alternate mission (backup plan, important data points like minimum fuel levels).
- **Formation duties** – This list assigns key duties to synchronize the team with the mission. For pilots on the team, this covers information like mission plans, weather info, coordination of intelligence briefings and area maps.

Timelines. Communication. Team duties. I'll bet that each of these categories could apply to any team project you've completed. And that's the power behind an SOP like this.

According to Lieutenant-Colonel 'Slider' Gagné, commanding officer of 416 Tactical Fighter Squadron (a good friend from my days in uniform), there are many advantages to an SOP like the Fighter Force SOP used by Canadian Forces pilots and team leaders. Each and every mission will present an entirely new experience and adventure, but the SOP provides a common approach:

- A tool for rapid planning
- A consistent planning method across teams or squadrons
- Team synchronization for each new mission or exercise

exec

2 Make it quick and dirty

How you come up with a plan to execute can be as simple as using a white board to identify the 5 Ws and 1 H (who, what, where, when, why, how) or as complex as using Gantt charts and full-fledged project management processes.

> "In the majority of cases [where the CEO fails] – we estimate 70% – the real problem isn't the high-concept boners the boffins love to talk about. It's bad execution. As simple as that: not getting things done, being indecisive, not delivering on commitments.[1]"
>
> – *Ram Charan and Geoffrey Colvin,* Fortune Magazine

The straightforward approach works well with my keep-it-simple philosophy of execution. People understand simple checklists, so that means you'll be able to get them involved with a plan and mobilized toward goals much more quickly. And these days, in any business, speed is one of your biggest competitive advantages.

Besides, when you're faced with a fast turnaround to implement a project, the simple approach might be all you have time to do. And there's nothing wrong with that if it achieves the goal. The execution path from start to finish, from concept to completion, begins with some very simple questions.

Reality Check: SOPs on *The Apprentice*

When asked how his military skills may have helped him succeed in becoming one of Donald Trump's winning apprentices, one thing stands out for Kelly Perdew: "One specific thing I implemented was a standard operating procedure for acting as project manager. I solicited input from all the team members and created a 20-point standard operating procedure checklist…I implemented it on the second task, and we won the next five."[2]

Getting started – What's your mission?

- What's the situation?
- What needs to get done?
- What part does your team need to play?

The timeline – How much time do you have?

- Hours, days, weeks, months?

The approach – What's the task and how can you break it up into manageable chunks?

Big problems or plans are made easier when broken down into manageable parts. Ask yourself:

- Does it make sense to break the project down by the time you have available, or by key milestones or phases that need to be achieved?
- Time: Week 1-2-3
- Phase: Phase 1-2-3
- Milestones: Concept – Design – Test – Implement
- What big things need to be done by when?

The key tasks

Once you've identified the key phases, list the tasks:

- What are the key tasks you need to accomplish within these phases?
- What resources or expertise do you need?

Answer these questions and you will have the beginning of a framework and checklist for your execution plan. Slow and steady may win the race, but when time is of the essence, quick and dirty gets the job done. Identifying what needs to happen, when and by whom, provides you with a road map and a way of checking progress on your project, goals and objectives. The last two steps help you pull it all together.

3 Document the plan

Once you take a quick and dirty approach to gathering information, use it in a framework that delivers the tasks and timelines to your team, simply. One way to do this is to use the stoplight status report in Chapter 08.

◄◄ **Rewind** *to Chapter 08, "Link Your Team to the Mission," for a quick review of this visual document to help your team see what has to be done, function by function, to reach a goal.*

EXECUTION INTELLIGENCE

Create an SOP

What do you get when you merge military operations orders (a checklist of essential areas that are critical to mission success) with a business product introduction process (a chronological process that some companies use to launch their products)?

Answer: The best of both worlds.

The simple checklist below takes some of the important elements to plan a successful military operation, and incorporates them into the phases that are necessary to launching a product or service. The beauty of having an already established checklist like this is that you get to pick and choose what works best for your situation.

Here's a framework you can use to create your own SOP:

Situation

What is the critical business need?

Mission

What do you need to do to support the critical business need?

Execution

How will you break this problem down? In phases? Stages? By time? It's up to you!

Once you've determined the best way to approach the execution phase (by phases or timelines), you need to outline key activities and the timeline for each phase.

Phase I – Define or concept (your mission, your product, your service, your goal)

- Define the business environment
- Define the initial resources and expertise you will need
- Gather information
- Develop a high-level, general view of your timeline and list the important milestones along this timeline
- Conduct and document a SWOT (strengths, weaknesses, opportunities, threats) analysis

Define the communication strategy – who, what, when, where, why, and how to communicate with whom. Include who *not* to communicate with.

Following Phase I of your execution plan, you'll obviously need to brainstorm and map out some additional phases as I have suggested below.

Take a look at www.iceleadership.com for more tools and tips on how to execute today.

Phase II (Plan or design)

Phase III (Implement or build)

Phase IV (Lead or commercial readiness)

4 Put three-dimensional communication into action

Every SOP and checklist I've mentioned that supports execution requires that you identify some sort of communication strategy to go along with it. How are you going to communicate execution strategy to your team? How about executives, key stakeholders, customers or clients? Will you have meetings or communicate your plan in writing? What if your team is working remotely? This is where applying the 2 up-1 down communication strategy – linking organizational goals at least two levels above you (front-line leaders/boss), directly to the team players just below you – is very important. Poor communication is often a prime reason for failed execution.

◄◄ **Rewind** *to Chapter 09, "Connect the Front Lines and the Big Picture," for details on how to establish an effective communication strategy for your execution plan.*

If you're wondering how you can start taking action and get some of your strategies in gear, think of the three simple concepts we've reviewed in the past three chapters:

- Integrate
- Communicate
- Execute

Make up an effective and easy-to-apply leadership strategy when you need to make it happen, whatever 'it' might be!

Reality Check: Execution is flawed!

Execution is a hot topic these days, and it should be. Companies, teams, every kind of organization needs people who can execute. But does it have to be flawless? Perfection seems to be the preferred benchmark when you're executing, but it's a benchmark that I don't particularly believe in. Unless, of course, we're talking about matters of safety and security, where lives might be at stake. Trying to achieve standards of perfection in a process that is entirely dynamic is completely unrealistic. As your plans turn into reality, things will change, plans will change. Don't worry about being flawless so much as generating momentum to achieve your goals. Execution needs to be more about 'thrust and vectors' and less about achieving perfection (See Red Flag for details.)

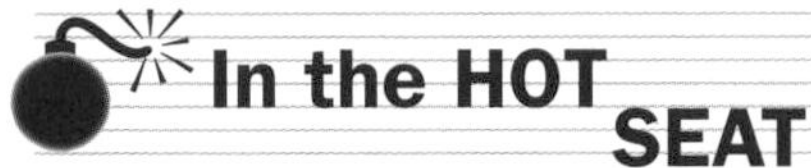

USE ICE WHEN YOU'RE IN THE HOT SEAT

The projects you're executing might be tough, but the approach you use doesn't have to be. This three-part leadership strategy is a powerful approach to hit the ground leading when you're facing any type of mission-critical project. Consider this strategy the beginning of a critical step in successful execution – your execution doctrine:

Integrate + Communicate + Execute = Mission-critical leadership strategy

- **Integrate:**

Keep your team tied to the mission – ensuring that your team is connected and integrated with the mission means you've established well-defined roles, clarity of individual goals and objectives, and a clear understanding of the big picture and mission.

- **Communicate:**

Clarity of the plan, big picture and details through clear communication is critical.

Updating the team and any other key players on the plan keeps everyone on the same playing field.

- **Execute:**

Break your problem down into manageable execution phases to keep you on track and moving forward. Having a checklist, template or framework of important steps, tasks and milestones helps you think, plan and execute quickly.

Visit my website at www.iceleadership.com or www.hitthegroundleading.com for information on the ICE model to *integrate, communicate* and *execute.*

"Most executives have embraced mission, vision, and values to communicate the ends for which companies compete. Still, something is missing: the doctrine that provides the integration between ends and means – how companies compete." – Mark B. Fuller, Fast Company *magazine*

"Speed up. Cover more ground. Put your faith in action – in mobility – and maximize your personal productivity.[3]" – *Price Pritchett and Ron Pound, change management consultants*

What's in it for you... and your team?

Once you have your plan and you're ready to execute, it's time for the fun stuff – turning the plans into reality.

There is a real positive force that comes from a leader who knows how to turn plans into reality. Keep in mind that I'm not saying that such a leader knows all the answers; I'm saying he or she has the mindset. Execution is not about having the answer – it's about having an approach!

Getting your team organized and executing creates energy. A team with energy moves things forward, generates action and, ultimately, reaches milestones.

RED FLAG **All thrust, no vectors**

We used to have this expression in the air force to describe leaders who displayed a lot of energy, took lots of action, but had no particular direction. They always seemed to be spinning their wheels but their tasks weren't tied together and therefore they never seemed to move things forward. We would call this having "all thrust and no vectors," a term that was coined from one of our jets, the CF 101 Voodoo, a beautiful rocket ship that didn't fly all that well.

Execution is not about making people busy for the sake of making them busy. Execution is about mobilizing forces and taking action *with* forward direction. In other words, making sure you have thrust and vectors.

The success of execution is in the preparation, planning and mobilizing of the team for phase I. You can build complexity into your mission by adding more phases, milestones or processes. Don't get too bogged down by phases II and III just yet. Plans made too far in advance are likely to change anyway. But energy and direction will carry the team through all the detours.

Outside the corporate BOX

THE FIVE-MINUTE LEADER

Jet-setting is great but there is a tough side to being an airline pilot. At least this is what I tell myself when my brother, Brendan, calls me from Bangkok, Athens or Mumbai, on a four-day layover!

Brendan is an airline captain with Etihad Airways Airbus 340, who flies intercontinental passenger jets. He works all hours of the day and night with a crew of 13 relative strangers, people he may not work with from one flight to the next. His mission, in a short amount of time, is to create a sense of cohesion among this team and fly about 225 passengers thousands of miles, safely, efficiently and comfortably, while facing the common challenges of long-haul crews, such as boredom, fatigue and jet lag.

There are thousands of crews like Brendan's carrying hundreds of thousands of people through the sky, something many of us take for granted.

Crew members receive months, if not years, of training to make their jobs look simple. Their jobs require memorizing drills, practicing their skills in simulators, passing practical and written tests and conducting final 'release checks' before flights.

Once they're in the air, the flight crew members are expected to maintain high standards – standards that come in the form of SOPs for every role – from flight attendant to captain. Here's how Brendan describes the impact:

"The SOPs allow me to climb into the cockpit with another pilot I have never met and complete all of our tasks with the minimum of communication and briefing. Yesterday, I flew with a French first officer I have never met, a cabin manager from India and the rest of the crew came from seven different countries. We are all trained to follow SOPs."

exec

✓ **Momentum builds motivation**

A good plan means people know where and how they fit in. Having that knowledge translates into a team that can take the right kind of action to move things forward. That forward momentum will help get the energy level of the team and the project up, and there is nothing better for morale. Another interesting by-product of momentum and motivation is a sense of value. People like to be where the action is, where the energy is, and on a winning project.

✓ **Confidence and respect**

So you and your team are achieving goals and your execution plan is coming together. Team players are feeling good about what they are doing and the value they are adding to the project. In fact, you might even have team players from other teams seeking you out, interested in getting on board with your project – its progress could generate excitement among other departments or organizations.

I can remember all of the 'take-charge' leaders I worked for when I was a young lieutenant in the air force, particularly on some of our mission-critical projects. My operations director at Nortel, where I worked years later, had the same impact on me and my team. On one occasion, this decisive and visionary

Hindsight is 20/20

"You have 20 minutes to execute"

If I can learn to execute, anyone can. I was 22 years old and hadn't led a single thing in my life, yet I was being introduced to the 'art' of execution in boot camp. Week after week, my fellow soldiers and I were put through the test to see if we had what it took to be a leader. Initially, some of these tasks were mini-missions that lasted a mere 20 minutes. There was barely time to think, let alone accomplish our goals. As we progressed over the weeks, the missions became increasingly more complex and could literally last for days. Having an approach and a framework to guide us through rapid actions became instrumental to our success.

I will never forget my first leadership task – I had to build a helicopter landing pad. I was given 20 minutes, seven officer cadets, a pile of equipment and a notepad to accomplish this goal. After the sergeant had given me my orders, I sat down for at least five minutes, overwhelmed and with absolutely no idea of where to start. But I eventually moved from this frozen state and started delegating tasks for the next 15 minutes. Unfortunately, I did a poor job providing specific goals or milestones or getting updates from my team. Before I knew it, my time was up and the sergeant was debriefing me on why I failed the task. Failed the task! I'd never failed at anything in my life up to that point. I failed for one simple reason. I did not execute. And that's a painful lesson to learn when your sole purpose in the world of boot camp is to execute.

WHAT DID I DO WRONG?

- I let the task overwhelm me and I didn't know where to start. Because of that, I failed to get the team mobilized and moving in a forward direction.
- I failed to use the simple execution planning tool we had been taught – simple checklists really work!
- I didn't communicate with the team – no one was sure how we were progressing or how others were doing.

Despite my failure, it was the perfect 'kick in the pants.' I had a very quick lesson on the value of executing in future missions. And if you're going to fail, you might as well get it over with at the beginning of your career, no?

leader directed us to gather facts, data and our top three goals in the next five days so we could understand and evaluate the competitiveness of our business model immediately. This was a critical step to keep us two steps ahead of our competition.

When the meeting was over, most of us were in awe of his confidence and matter-of-fact manner. And it gave me the confidence and trust in him that most leaders seek. There's something to be said about a leader who knows how to anticipate where to go and takes the right decisive action to head the team in the right direction even if the exact solution has yet to be determined.

✓ Choices in life

When you can execute, you can make things happen. The very nature of the execution mindset is about growth, realizing your potential, using your talents and making what's possible real. With every new project you execute, you learn new things. You gain courage and confidence in your ability to make things happen, and you'll become more empowered. Professionally, people will trust in your abilities to get things moving and make a difference, and that means more opportunities and bigger and better projects will come your way. With more projects comes choice. And having a choice is as empowering as it gets.

What's next?

Great plans are important, but if you don't deliver, don't make things happen, then you'll never be able to move your team and business forward. Being able to execute effectively is your *competitive advantage*. It will give you the edge you need as a leader, and open a lot more doors leading to more choices in your career and life.

More choice, more opportunities. What more could you ask for? Well, how about being able to access your exponential potential, that unseen web of opportunities and connections at your finger tips? Then you can *really* start to make things happen!

We all have the potential to do some pretty powerful things. Why not access it?

ACTION PLAN

Get ready for the leap

1 THE MINDSET: THINK 'MAKE IT HAPPEN' AND IT WILL.

- Think 'yes' instead of 'how'
- Don't get caught up in knowing the answer – it will come

2 USE SOPS AND CHECKLISTS.

- Rapid team coordination comes a whole lot easier when you know where to start
- Get 'execution readiness' with a checklist to manage timelines, communication, resources and milestones

3 QUICK AND DIRTY WORKS.

- Ask yourself key questions to get started – What's the situation? What's your specific mission?
- All big problems can be broken down into manageable chunks

4 DON'T FORGET TO ICE!

- Integrate, communicate and execute

ute

ACCESS YOUR EXPONENTIAL POTENTIAL

Tell me did the wind sweep you off your feet
Did you finally get the chance to dance along the light of day
And head back toward the Milky Way?

Drops of Jupiter, Train

THE FORCE

The ripple effect

Access an infinite amount of possibilities

Resourcefulness

Follow the energy

Authentic connection

Beyond networking

A series of fortunate events

I'm sure you're familiar with the business term 'networking.' In fact, you've probably had professors at school, work colleagues or friends expound upon the virtues of networking. 'It's not what you know, it's who you know' is a common phrase that really captures the essence of what networking is all about. Apparently, according to many of my business friends, I'm a good 'networker.' Superb, some might even say. But I'm not so sure.

Before you continue reading, I want to make it clear right off the bat that this chapter is not about networking. It's about something much more. It's about accessing a 'force,' one that seems to be a combination of energy, momentum, passion and, maybe even at times, magic. And when you do access it, it can take your 'networking' to an entirely different level – if you have the right approach. The more life experiences you have, the more you realize you can create your own 'fortunate events,' especially if you get good at accessing this force. So when you're in the middle of some mission-critical project, or changing direction completely in your career or life, or just out gathering information, you have the ability to take a linear opportunity and access it exponentially, something I call 'exponential potential.'

Now don't get me wrong. There is no doubt that it is important to network – to get out and meet people to expand your list of contacts. No one succeeds in business without help from others. But the problem with networking is the approach. Many people network with a 'what's in it for me' attitude. They wonder 'how can I use this meeting or this contact to my advantage? If you can do something for me, then I might do something for you.' And here's where I see the problem – if you make networking entirely self-driven or self-serving, you won't get nearly as much out of it as you can. With that 'linear' approach, I believe you can only go so far.

But you can take your ability to network to a whole new level by keeping in mind a couple of things. First, minimize your agenda. Replace the 'what's in it for me' thinking with an 'I'm genuinely interested in meeting anyone and everyone' approach. And secondly, be open to helping others who have that passion or personal drive without expecting something in return. The 'receiving' will always come later if you give just for the sake of giving. Become interested in people – who they are, what they do – and be willing to share some of your knowledge or resources to help them. By doing this, you move from creating a linear 'give and take' opportunity to a world of 'exponential potential' – where doors, networks and people open up for you just by connecting on a genuine level.

And that's what this chapter is about – accessing your exponential potential. Using the positive 'force' that you have created by taking a genuine interest in people.

Exponential potential *unplugged*

Simply put, your exponential potential starts with the belief in yourself and your ability to connect with others who believe in you – family, friends, colleagues, associates or even strangers who you may meet fleetingly. With no expectations of rewards or personal gains, you can provide opportunities to help others reach their own exponential potential. That approach will turn your networking opportunities into genuine connections. And that's when the world will open up even more to you.

To be successful in expanding your network you have to start with conviction, a focus on where you are going without a steadfast route on how to get there. Having an attachment to how things must happen and what you expect people to do for you can result in trying to force a path. Conviction and belief, combined with energy, focus *and* flexibility, allow you to have more freedom to let the path unfold. Sit back and watch as the web starts spinning, information is gathered and opportunities or answers flow back to you. I'm not suggesting you sit on your duff – you do have to maintain focus and energy – but you can let the process flow. Each and every contact you make will generate momentum. Sometimes, you'll only have pieces of the puzzle or a resource that may not be exactly what you were looking for, but it'll get you one step closer to where you are going or want to go. Energy, focus and the right approach allow the ripple effect to set in as one thing leads to another.

Looking back, I realize that I have had some seemingly

insignificant introductions over the years that have eventually led to some huge stepping stones in my career in one way or another. These connections may have led to some success, or some extreme change in my career path. And they did not necessarily come from a premeditated plan to network.

CHANCE MEETINGS MIGHT MEAN BIG JOURNEYS

So how have some of my 'chance meetings' over the years shaped my destiny or helped me experience an entirely different level of potential?

It usually starts with an innocent quest for information; I'm stuck and I don't know how to get started. Maybe you're about to set some dream in motion or start something new and exciting. Maybe you're positioned to lead a groundbreaking project or accept a once-in-a-lifetime position. Maybe you're going to start up a business, but you haven't got a clue on how or where to start.

Let's start with where I'm at this immediate moment. Writing and marketing this book – a great example of a chance meeting (or two) that has led to a big journey. Sometimes it's a good thing not to know exactly what you're getting into or you may never take the leap! I can't pinpoint the day or time in my life when I made the decision to write a book. But once I began the process, it quickly became all the exciting things I just described: a dream, a groundbreaking project and definitely a once-in-a-lifetime chance (because I may never do this again) to create a product for my new start-up company. But as with any big change, my decision to write this book was met with some skepticism. In fact, I remember my mother's first, thought-provoking question to me: "But dear, what on earth do you know about writing a book?" she asked in her crisp British accent. My mother isn't known for mincing words – she usually gets to the point. And she had one. It caused me to stop and think for a minute or two. She was right, what did I know? Not much, as a matter of fact. This was one of those choices in life that came about not because it was logical or along my career path. No sir. This was about as nonlinear as it gets. But it came from accessing some exponential potential – a vast network of support and people giving back far greater than I could have ever imagined. All because of a series of fortunate events.

> Beyond your physical self, beyond your thoughts and emotions, there lies a realm within you that is pure potential; from this place anything and everything is possible. Even miracles. Especially miracles.[1]
>
> *– Deepak Chopra, cutting-edge spiritual leader*

NETWORK VERSUS EXPONENTIAL POTENTIAL

My brother has a different way of looking at how I got onto this book-writing adventure and the incredible connections that seem to have evolved out of this journey. He has always said my potential to take on great challenges and succeed has come from my wonderful business connections. Connections that he believes I have cultivated not because I am a tremendously skilled 'networker,' although it might seem so to the untrained eye. "No," he says, "it's because you like parties, Ange." Well, he's not necessarily incorrect. And he should know – as my younger sibling, he was often sweet-talked into helping me clean up the house before my parents returned after one of my 'half the high school' parties. All older sisters did that, right? However, what he is really getting at is that I do enjoy socializing and meeting people. That same interest in others can energize your network and take it to a different level.

Enjoying people, socializing, resourcefulness or living life to its fullest, call it what you want. I like to believe that this type of 'connectivity' results in a boomerang effect that is driven by a genuine connection with people, an approach that involves sincerity and giving back with less concern of receiving something in return. And the 'boomerang' can come back in many different ways – luck, new contacts, new business, important information, anything really.

If we could put this potential force into really simple terms, a formula even, it might look something like this:

Exponential potential [force] = resourcefulness + genuine connection + giving back + a little luck

RESOURCEFULNESS, DESTINY OR LUCK?

I had my first experience with this interesting force back in the war zone in former Yugoslavia – an environment that couldn't get more mission critical. When my reconnaissance team and I first landed in Belgrade, we were wearing civilian clothing so we wouldn't stand out quite so much as soldiers. But the airport appeared to be full of military uniforms. While waiting for my luggage, I got a fleeting glimpse off in the distance of a man in one of these military uniforms, just as he was heading to another part of the airport. I noticed that he was wearing a red armband with a gold wheel on it – I would have been wearing the same armband if I was wearing my own uniform. This was an international insignia in the military world for 'movements control' or people who specialize in moving troops and military equipment around the world. Did I need to talk to him!

To be honest, although I wouldn't admit it to anyone, I was quite terrified about this overwhelming mission. Spotting this stranger, who apparently had a similar profession, made me feel a whole lot better.

I grabbed him just in the nick of time before he got lost in the crowd. After quickly introducing myself as a Canadian military 'movcon' officer, I asked him a million questions. What was he doing there? Who did he work with. What was the real situation out in the streets, or the front lines of this civil war? Upon finding out who I was and my mission, his 'pat' response was something I'd hear a hundred times over in the next few weeks. "You're Captain Mondou? Oh-oh, no one mentioned a woman was coming with this reconnaissance team. This could be a problem. But welcome to Belgrade!" Major Gimre didn't have many answers for me that day, but meeting him became one of the most strategic moves I made during that entire mission. He became a conduit or powerful connection point for many people I needed to meet.

Once we arrived at our decrepit (previously condemned) and now barely revitalized 'quarters,' we were advised that, for the next three days, we would be confined to these Yugoslav People's Army (JNA) barracks. United Nations leadership needed to determine how, what and where would be best to unleash the multinational reconnaissance teams in these warring countries of Serbia, Bosnia and Croatia. This news could have been a catastrophe for a 'movcon' officer tasked with developing a logistics strategy in 10 days. A three-day confinement meant that I only had seven days left and I hadn't even started. But the force (that energy and momentum I referred to earlier) had already started working.

Within 12 hours, Major Gimre, a Norwegian movement control officer, arrived with some excellent intelligence that would propel me into action even from my confined position. He provided me with a list of key UN contacts in Zagreb, the capital city of Croatia. These contacts could help with some of the international decision-making that would be required, and provide phone numbers for important government officials who would help pave the government and business path, and provide the official permissions we would need to get things done. Perhaps most importantly, these new contacts could provide me with the latest status on the runways we were considering as our inbound ports of entry for troops and military equipment arriving by aircraft. All of this from one fleeting handshake in an airport, all while I sat confined in 'the black hole.' If I had not run after that major in the airport, with no other goal than to introduce myself, I would have been stuck twiddling my thumbs for a few days. Instead, I had information flowing right to me.

> "I'd better not forget luck. The odd bit of luck goes a long way. We were lucky to sign Mike Oldfield and we were lucky to get hold of the Sex Pistols in 1977. We've also been lucky that people like Virgin Atlantic's unique airline service across the Atlantic, and I was lucky to survive all my balloon and boat trips![2]"
>
> *– Sir Richard Branson, creator of the Virgin brand and empire*

THE FORCE IN ACTION

Years later, while working in the high-tech industry, I would have another incredible experience that would once again strengthen my belief in the power of connecting. The tech bubble had burst, and I had decided that I needed to move to another company from Nortel Networks, where I had enjoyed some incredible years. Unfortunately, the company was going through a tremendous downsizing phase, and despite a commitment to me that I always had a place at Nortel, I felt it was time to move on.

So I decided that, while I took a two-week holiday, I would use the time to start shopping around for employment opportunities. While surfing the Net, I landed on an article about Research In Motion (RIM) and the new chief operations officer (COO) that had recently been hired. The article highlighted this man's tremendous success in the telecommunications industry, both in North America and around the world. Something in the discussion about this high-tech superstar and the company he had recently joined really resonated with me and I decided to look into employment opportunities there.

After a quick call to RIM's main line, I was connected to the company's corporate vice president of Human Resources. We chatted briefly about my credentials and he asked me to forward a curriculum vitae. By the end of the week, I had had several interviews, one of them with Mr. Don Morrison, the high-tech superstar I had read about just days earlier. This was an experience of 'mind over matter' – when you put your mind and energy into something, you can be blown away by how quickly things can come together.

I had a job offer within a week. By the time I showed up at RIM several weeks later, the corporate VP of HR was nowhere to be seen. In fact, he had moved on to other pastures the very week I showed up for my new job. To this day, I wonder about the coincidence of connecting with someone so briefly who brought me into one of the most 'happening' companies on the continent, only to disappear within a week of my arrival. How fleeting an opportunity. This job was obviously something that was meant to be. I had set some intentions and put some energy behind them. And things came together quickly, even with such a small window of opportunity. There seemed to be a bigger force working in the background, something stronger than simply my ability to network.

force

Reality Check: Networking for a higher purpose

When you're networking for a higher purpose, such as a humanitarian project or a mission-critical situation, there is no question that everyone is already driven in the same direction on a much deeper level. People generally want to help people, especially in a situation of great need. In this case, the 'exponential potential' for a network to ignite is ready and poised. But you still need to access it, and you still need to get the momentum moving forward. I remember meeting a Habitat for Humanity leader in New Orleans just a few months after Hurricane Katrina had devastated the region. I recall her describing what seemed at times like opportunity had 'fallen out of the sky' while she was trying to find land, finances and other resources to help rebuild her community after the devastation. But after watching her in action for a day, meeting politicians and business leaders and people in the street, I realized she was helping to bring those opportunities to her community. I was witnessing a woman accessing her exponential potential and it was definitely at work.

ONE THING LEADS TO ANOTHER

Chance meetings seem to be a part of my reality and I believe many of these 'inconsequential' meetings are what has led me to access my exponential potential, like my introduction into public speaking. Not something I ever thought of getting into, but it has now become something I do for a living. One day, my lawyer, a member of Zonta International (a global service organization comprised of professional and business women) asked if I could be a presenter at one of the local monthly Zonta strategy sessions. The organizers were interested in my experience working around the world and, in particular, with a humanitarian project supporting Vietnamese and Chinese orphanages while I was employed with Nortel.

My speech led to another and then another. Different organizations heard about my eclectic business background and wanted to hear more. My name was soon being passed around to other local and regional service clubs and, before I knew it, I was on a speakers' circuit, albeit an unpaid one. There tends to be a domino effect in the public speaking business, particularly with leadership speakers, since the subject is an ongoing favorite in most organizations.

My network of personal and business connections spread like wildfire – speaking in front of 50 to 100 people at a time is a very quick way of expanding your contacts and developing some great personal friendships. There was no agenda or ulterior motive on my part, other than to spread my passion for leadership and my sincere belief that it is one of the most powerful ways of seizing your own potential. I think everybody has a leader in them, and that leader can be turned loose!

SELF-PUBLISHING ROCK STAR

From these connections came perhaps the most dramatic turn on my career path to date – the paid speaking circuit. It has tied right into yet another new career platform: becoming an author.

So how does one go from wearing combat boots, to high-tech marketing exec, to author and public speaker? Exponential potential has to kick in. I'm talking about your ability to access an entire realm of possibilities through your connections, as well as resourcefulness, energy and a sincere interest in people. If you're lucky, and I have been on many an occasion, your wonderful connections lead you to someone like David Chilton, otherwise known as the author of *The Wealthy Barber.* David, to date, is Canada's most successful self-published author, and has accomplished an impressive publishing feat: Originally working out of his basement, David has gone on to sell more than three million copies of his best-selling book in North America!

Meeting an inspirational individual with this kind of a success story, just as I was considering a book-writing venture, was yet just another fluke or chance meeting I have often experienced. And it resulted from the most unsuspecting of opportunities – a free speech I gave to a local community organization. Timing is everything, they say, so I was extremely fortunate to be introduced to David just around the time he was deciding that he could no longer coach any more authors. He was just too busy, and almost every aspiring Canadian author sought his advice. But out of the goodness of his heart, he decided to coach me.

When I met David, as successful as he is, I found him to be an unpretentious individual with a deep-down genuine interest in helping people. In fact, he calls it the 'impact quotient' and measures his own fulfillment by helping others achieve their potential and dreams. I also found him to be one very energetic, 'high-octane' individual. That first meeting went by at warp speed as we exchanged a million questions (mostly coming from David). Questions like: What was my story? My background? Did I like to travel, speak publicly? How was my family life? There was a lot of ground to cover. Luckily for me, I've received continued support from David over the past couple of years as I embarked on this self-publishing journey. I don't think I will ever forget this very valuable piece of advice he shared with me:

"Angela, I have full confidence in you being very successful with your book. The only way you won't be successful is if you screw up! And in that case, you will only have yourself to blame!"

Now that sort of puts it into perspective, doesn't it? Thanks David. Did I mention he has quite a sense of humor?

> "Don't worry about making a fortune – make a difference! Reach out and help as many people as you can. Personal success is a natural by-product of helping others to reach their goals. Forget all the tricky stuff and remember this: Be nice!" *– David Chilton, self-publishing guru and author of* The Wealthy Barber

Chance meetings, the power of connection, networking and people giving back – all of these things add up to yet another important stepping stone on my path. That, and a big dose of luck or something like it. There certainly seems to be an intangible force at work at times. I can't tell you how many people I meet who let me know how lucky and privileged I am to have such a self-publishing success like David Chilton coaching me behind the scenes. Believe me, I know.

We all have access to incredible opportunity. And you will be surprised at how people – in many different ways – will help you access your potential. We all have a network available to us, but your approach to your network will determine how far you can take it. Remember, it's all in your approach.

BEYOND NETWORKING

I know you won't be surprised when I tell you that, somehow, despite my isolation as an author, banging away at my keyboard day after day, I ended up in a television commercial. As with so many other opportunities, it led to even more. This time, it led to seeing my face on a coin! How does one end up representing Canada's peacekeepers and war veterans on the face of a newly minted Canadian coin? From yet another fleeting meeting and a fortunate event. (More on this in the Case Study that follows.)

CASE STUDY Lights. Camera. Action!

Talent this way – there were signs posted all over the place that directed us to the right studio. I followed the signs to the building where we would get fitted for our wardrobe, have our hair styled and makeup applied. It was only 7 a.m. and apparently we were already behind schedule. I had two stylists fussing over my hair and makeup, and the wardrobe manager straightening the medals on my jacket. "Can I get you anything for breakfast?" another woman asked me. "We have hot meals, scrambled eggs, or do you prefer something healthy, yogurt and granola?" Breakfast was being served to me while I was being made beautiful. Hmmm, I could certainly get used to this pampered lifestyle. Paris Hilton, eat your heart out!

How I got to star in a television commercial is yet another unbelievable story. I had just joined the Canadian Institute of International Affairs (CIIA) and was attending an evening presentation with a couple of wonderful speakers – university professors from Wilfrid Laurier University's Centre for Military Strategic and Disarmament Studies. The topic that evening was the military's plight to keep up with our global peacekeeping commitments. As I sat in the crowded room, I noticed a military uniform in the far back corner, and once the very thought-provoking presentation was over, I ran over and introduced myself. Once a military member, always a military member. So I had a brief chat and exchanged cards with this military public affairs (PA) officer who worked closely with many civilian organizations.

Several months later, I received a call from this gentleman. The Royal Canadian Mint was unveiling a newly designed and minted 25-cent coin to commemorate the 2005 Year of the Veteran. And it had contacted The Department of National Defence for names of authentic peacekeepers and veterans who could be featured on posters and in a television commercial that the Mint was making to publicize the new coin. The PA officer wanted to submit my name. For the first time in my life, I would have an opportunity to be on a poster and billboards. (Okay, so I wasn't getting paid the same as those GUESS models, but still, this was an opportunity a girl couldn't refuse!)

I was not selected for the poster but instead was called weeks later to audition for the role of 'peacekeeping hero' for the national TV campaign. Unfortunately, the timing was very bad. I was in the midst of moving my family home on the day of the audition.

I didn't know much about casting agencies and major production companies; apparently, being provided with two days' notice is one day more than most actors get.

So I apologized for not being able to make it to this casting call and hung up the phone. My partner, Tom, overheard the phone conversation and insisted that I call the agency back immediately and get back on the audition list. After some discussion about whether he was okay to manage the mayhem of moving day on his own, I called the casting agency back and it paid off. I ended up getting an honorable role in the commercial, which portrayed me as a Canadian peacekeeper. But more significantly, my profile, along with the profile of a wonderful Second World War veteran, appeared to merge on the back of the coin. (I have to say, I take great pleasure in telling anyone who cares to listen that Her Royal Highness, the Queen, is on the back of my coin!)

◄◄ **Rewind** *to Chapter 05, "What Goes Around Comes Around" for more on the Juno Award-winning director who directed this commercial and Sarah McLachlan's "Into the Fire" music video.*

Who would have thought that such small events – a short speech to a women's organization and a chance meeting at an event – could lead to an entirely new career path? Doors have opened, opportunities have come my way, and my personal and business web has expanded exponentially.

After my experience with the UN mission in the former Yugoslavia, my book-writing and self-publishing adventure might be the most challenging leadership experience of my life. If past experience is anything to go by, I know it will also likely be one of the greatest opportunities I have ever mobilized.

So go ahead and take that leap. And then access your exponential potential. Believe me, it's there.

The principle: Access your own exponential potential

> "There is one thing stronger than all the armies in the world, and that is an idea whose time has come." – *Victor Hugo, influential French writer*

This principle can have immeasurable power, but how much you draw from it all depends on how you use it. For example, when you find yourself facing a daunting challenge or a difficult work project and you're not sure where to start, know that there is an infinite amount of information and resources available to you. And even better, they are virtually at your fingertips – just like the Yellow Pages! The trick is in knowing how to access them and use them.

Looking back, I owe a lot of my leadership success to something I call 'connectivity;' that is, connections that seem to work for me through people I know, people I don't know and people I didn't realize were going to cross my path. Some of these contacts can instantly become a wealth of information, supplying answers for certain projects or further contacts. In some cases, these connections have led me in unexpected directions, helping to take me down unfamiliar paths I may have never come across otherwise.

Reality Check: Use the force. Take networking up a notch

Replace the 'what's in it for me' motivation with 'genuine connection' and interest in those you meet, and you add an entirely different level of energy to the contacts you're making. Instead of arriving with a completely selfish agenda, with this approach, you'll be ready to help others. If you don't follow this approach, you're missing out on opportunities and downplaying the potential of people to get you connected to others. Connectivity isn't so much about 'working the room' as releasing the opportunities.

PREMEDITATED NETWORKING

Here's why I think we need to take a step back from the whole concept of networking to get it back on track. Think about some of the business-and-cocktail functions you may have attended. While you chat with someone who you just met, their eyes dart around the room, trying to catch a glimpse of who just walked in. You know he's wondering, "Who am I missing out on?" The fact of the matter is he has an agenda, something he needs to accomplish, and someone he wants to connect with.

So what's the result? If that individual hasn't really taken the time to connect with you because 'someone better' might be coming along, you naturally won't be very motivated to help that person. In fact, you'll probably feel a little insulted.

If you come across as having a very self-driven approach, you may very well be shutting yourself out of an incredible connection, a great opportunity and a whole network of people who can lead you to new resources and information. Remember, it's the insignificant meetings that can offer that real 'magic.' Using a self-centered technique to expand your horizons can backfire.

Here's a case in point:

About a year ago I was a keynote speaker at a meet and greet function for a national conference. There, I met a woman who calls herself 'an international networking guru.' During the meet and greet, she walked over to me, thrust her hand out and forcefully shook mine. After introducing herself, she proceeded to tell me how much I needed her help. "You need to know me! I know you're writing a book and I can connect you with anyone you need – editors, publishers, etcetera!" Well, besides the fact that I already had a wonderful editor whom I was very fond of (despite her tearing my writing apart for a year and a half!) and had North America's most successful self-published author coaching me in the background, the first thing that came to my mind was "What does this very assertive woman want?" As soon as someone tells you, "you need them," you can bet there is a catch. As the evening progressed, I saw her use the same approach several times when meeting some very prominent people. Funny thing was, by the end of the evening, she was asking *me* if I could connect *her* with two of my most-prized contacts. I guess she needed me! I found her approach off-putting and not nearly as powerful as someone who is connecting because of a genuine interest. Bottom line: I think everyone has something to offer, especially at events such as meet and greets that are set up specifically for networking. I love sharing my experience and helping others, but not if I feel like I'm being 'worked.' Had that 'networking guru' shown a genuine interest in me and my work before trying to satisfy her own specific agenda, she may actually have been closer to achieving her goals.

Take your networking to a whole new level by replacing personal agendas with a sincere interest in learning about people. Resourcefulness is critical to getting ahead, but it's important to balance your needs with being a resource to others as well.

Keep all these things in mind so you can readily access your exponential potential:

- Connect on a genuine level with people before you network on a material level.
- Help others as much as those who help you.
- Connect, network and leverage whatever you can for a greater purpose (humanitarian, crisis, etc.).

Be resourceful. Connect to people. Give back. And then experience the opportunity.

> "Giving people your full attention when they speak is the sincere person's answer to flattery." – *Anonymous*

How to create your own exponential potential

So where do you start? How do you begin to access your exponential potential and create that ripple effect of information and opportunity flowing to you?

Here's how:

1 Focus your energy. Then follow the energy

It all starts with you. It doesn't matter what mission you're on. Whether you're looking for a job, leading a business project, organizing a silent auction for a community fundraising event, or starting your own company, focus your energy and then follow it after you've determined your intentions to start building the momentum.

Setting intentions = conviction. Conviction creates energy. When you inject energy into an idea, the idea takes on roots and releases more energy. If you don't begin a project by setting intentions first, that is to determine what you're looking for or what you want to do, then you'll lack clarity.

Once you know where you're going, make your declaration to the outside world. Until you're ready to declare your intentions to friends, family, business colleagues and strangers, you haven't planted the seed!

You can set your intentions in many different ways. For example, casual conversations with colleagues will often lead you in positive directions. "Gosh, I know someone who can help you with this," or "you need to meet...." Take the case of several of my friends who have all recently made drastic shifts in their career paths. They set their intentions by starting with the 'be-all, end-all' test of inner strength – telling their families that they were quitting their jobs and heading in a whole new direction. The instant they made the declaration, all sorts of doors started opening up to set their new goals in motion.

2 Leave no stone unturned

You never know what doors will open or, more importantly, who will open them for you. The person you least suspect can lead to the most fruitful opportunity. I'm a firm believer in seizing every opportunity that comes your way and being open about who can bring it to you. All opportunities lead to new doors.

The question is: Would you recognize an opportunity if it passed you by?

Let's go back to one of my toughest environments as a leader, the war zone. Everything there was mission critical. With little time and information to act upon, I didn't let anyone, no matter who they were, cross my path without introducing myself and getting as much information from them as I could. Being resourceful in this scenario was a matter of success or failure, no in-between. From the major in the airport, to the night-shift railway master in Bosnia, to the scruffy translator I adopted, I introduced myself to all of these individuals on a sincere quest to make my part of the mission a success. It was like rapidly putting pieces of a puzzle together – everyone had something to contribute! When I chanced upon the major at the Belgrade airport, I had just landed in the midst of chaos with a huge job to do and not a clue of where to start. Major Gimre opened up some important doors for me with some simple information. And together with some energy and capabilities, I was able to carry out my mission.

Leave no stone unturned. Even the smallest rock may hold important information for you. Need more proof? How about this scenario:

Last year, I had the opportunity to meet with the senior business editor of Penguin Group (Canada), a large book publishing company about a book I hadn't even begun to write. Apparently, having an opportunity like that is not that common in the book-writing industry. How do you get to meet a large publishing house editor when you haven't even written a paragraph? That break landed in my lap through a well-connected friend at Research In Motion. He had copied me in on an e-mail to introduce me to someone he thought I should meet – Joanne Thomas Yaccato, a businesswoman who has written several best-selling books. She certainly seemed like an accomplished woman and someone I would love to connect with so I followed up with another e-mail to her. Next thing you know, we're having lunch, and before we're done, she had e-mailed her editor who she felt had to meet me.

Never leave any opportunity to learn on the table.

☯ Leadership, life and interesting connections

'Synchrodestiny' à la Deepak Chopra or Ralph Waldo Emerson's Law of Spiritual Gravitation. Both of these philosophies touch on the concept of meetings or occurrences that happen by chance, coincidence or destiny. A fascinating topic! Either way, the profound impact that accidental or chance meetings can have on your career or life can sometimes be quite remarkable. The more you believe that insignificant meetings can lead to powerful opportunity, the more you will experience it. Deepak Chopra describes this belief as 'synchrodestiny' where things come together, coincidentally some might say, at the right time and the right place. Emerson's Law of Spiritual Gravitation is very similar. One of my life's journeys took me to live and work in Ireland for a short period. Browsing around a small gift shop at The Giant's Causeway, an unbelievably windy location on the northern tip of Isle, I came across a small carving of a Celtic cross. It symbolized life's journeys and meetings, which bring a multitude of opportunities and encounters. The inscription on the back (Emerson's Law of Spiritual Gravitation) could not have been more perfect: "People destined to meet will do so apparently by chance, at precisely the right moment." How ironic that I was now reading this message in my father's homeland and in a country where chance meetings were what had put me on this planet. I felt like I had come back to where it had all started for me.

the

3 Practice business pinging

Get good at 'pinging' or bouncing ideas or questions off of others. In the submarine world, pinging is used for underwater detection of other equipment by bouncing a sonar 'ping' off of it. In the world of Internet and data transmissions, you can send a ping command that sends a packet of information (data) to another computer with a request to send the data packet back.

Pinging is a great analogy in the business world. Send out feelers in your work or social network using any means – in-person meetings, e-mails, telephone calls. Reach out and ask questions. Admit you don't know stuff and ask for help. Set up meetings with people who are experts in the subject you're interested in and ask for their advice. The more feelers you send out, the more information you'll get back. If you're going to pretend you know it all, there's no reason for people to give you the information you're looking for.

The more pinging you do, the greater your chance for return. When you hit the right spot, you might get something back. This approach is a little different than networking or connecting because you might not actually be getting out there and meeting people in person and you might not be on a specific quest for information so much as just gathering information. For instance, last year, I decided that I really wanted to take my keynote presentations up a notch. I felt they could use more *oomph*, perhaps by adding more multimedia features to my current format. But I had a budget and I wasn't sure what to do. One day, as I was having a massage (or should I say 'deep-tissue beating') with Paula, my tiny but tough massage therapist, I mentioned to her what I was thinking of doing. By the time I got home from my massage, there was a phone message for me with the name and contact information of one of Paula's clients who just happened to be in the multimedia business. And he could work within my budget and help me to achieve what I wanted.

Never underestimate the power of 'pinging' or a tiny massage therapist! Some people and some professions just seem to have the most incredible 'reach' simply through the amount of contacts they can make in a day.

force

RED FLAG I have control, don't I?

Admitting you don't know stuff and/or need help is not the same as appearing out of control. Quite the contrary. This is clever information gathering to make sure you have what you need to make better decisions and maintain forward momentum. Running around, grasping at straws, not knowing what's up or down is, well, just that. Think 'gathering information' versus 'chicken with head cut off!'

4 Going with the flow versus forcing the path

Accessing our exponential potential is a very dynamic process – it relies on connecting with others and utilizing the energy both within and around you, while keeping in mind the different priorities of all the people involved in the process. Not everyone will accommodate your timelines, so once you've made that connection, you might just need to back off, or explore another temporary route.

Can you force your timeline, agenda or goals when you're relying on so many elements to come into play? Perhaps. But you're better off setting the wheels in motion and allowing some flexibility for the path to unfold. Maintain direction, but allow some of the pieces to fall into place on their own.

Now in some cases, that might be pretty tough to swallow. Like this book, for instance. As a self-published author, I'm reliant on so many people helping me, sharing their network, connecting me with channels of distribution, contacts, book buyers, publicists – you name it. And I have incredibly tight deadlines. Am I in a position to force my agenda? Not necessarily. I would not want to alienate the wonderful support I am getting. However, does that stop me from trying to work other angles or seek alternate paths? Never. Set the wheels in motion but continue to explore other routes if your mission is critical.

Keep exploring other paths and keep as many doors open to expand your opportunities and increase your flexibility. Staying open-minded and flexible is a wise approach – boxing yourself into a specific path will only limit your opportunities for information, resources and other paths that may open up to you. Things are just moving way too fast these days to box yourself in.

In the HOT SEAT

HELPLESS CHILDREN IN A FARAWAY LAND

A few years ago, I was involved in a wonderful humanitarian project – sending containers of medical supplies, beds and clothing to orphanages in Vietnam and China. This project literally landed in my lap, because someone else had accessed their exponential potential and it extended right out to me. Catherine Mossop, a woman I had never met or even heard of, had adopted a daughter from China and a son from Vietnam a few years earlier. She was appalled at the poverty and poor condition of the orphanages. They lacked beds, clothing, medical supplies, you name it. So she returned home on a mission: to collect supplies in Canada and send them to the orphanages and children in need. Before she knew it, she had warehouses full of donated items – hospital beds, medical supplies, pharmaceuticals – and she didn't have a clue on how to move them to the other side of the world.

She led a career transition company, so she worked with a large and diverse group of professionals. She began to access her exponential potential and she managed to get a warehouse full of gear organized, packed, documented, shipped and exported to the other side of the world. This had become somewhat of a mission-critical project.

Her contacts got to work for her: someone knew someone at Nortel Networks, who brought the project to the global logistics team, who brought the project to me because of my UN experience and work experience of leading a team of export specialists.

Months later, with a team of logistics specialists working during their 'free time' and a generous corporation who footed the bill to move the containers of equipment from North America to Asia, a group of children in a land far away received so many things to help make their lives better.

"Many people said what I was trying to do was impossible and would never happen. But those who can see the invisible, have the courage to act and the passion to share can accomplish the impossible." – Catherine Mossop

What's in it for you... and your team?

If you can bring your resourcefulness, various contacts and your exponential potential together, you have the powerful ability to access a force much greater than yourself. You can expect that many more doors will open up for you, your team and the mission you're working on. How could you and your team not benefit from that?

RED FLAG **Always give back**

No one gets anywhere without someone else's help. It doesn't matter who you are or where you are. To reach your exponential potential, you'll likely require a helping hand along the way. In turn, it's our responsibility to provide support to those who can benefit from our skills, knowledge and experience – it's what you have to do. Maybe you'll offer some guidance, or maybe your part in the connection is to lead one person to another. Whatever your role, you can reap many rewards by helping to fulfill the dreams and goals of others.

Here's what could be in it for you:

✓ **More scoop**

As you start connecting your resources, you'll gather bits and pieces of the puzzle. Before you know it, you'll have a lot more information than when you started. While more access to knowledge and contacts won't always get you exactly what you're looking for, you can be certain that interesting insight and knowledge will flow your way. As you watch the big picture come together, you can decide what's best for the end goal.

✓ **Team confidence**

A boss who's good at accessing 'beyond the network' tends to be the kind of leader who doesn't get too caught up in 'I don't know where to begin' but instead just begins. Once you start to put your connections to work, your team members will experience a forward momentum and energized approach, instead of being victims of the 'deer caught in the headlights' or experiencing the usual frustration that can go with project inertia.

Outside the corporate BOX

DOGS, POODLES AND GIVING BACK!

What do you get when you mix high energy, hip-hop style, rap beat, the hottest athletes and celebrities? The '2 Live Stews,' aka Doug and Ryan Stewart. These brothers are revolutionizing sports-talk radio with their playful 'sports rap' approach and easy banter. And their audience – affectionately referred to as dogs and poodles – is increasing by the day. After just a few years on the air, a recent five-page spread in *Sports Illustrated* magazine describes the program as the number-one sports radio show in America and ESPN 2 radio has picked them up for a season. Here's betting more seasons are on the way.

I got to see these sports rap revolutionaries in action when I appeared as a guest on their show during a couple of Super Bowl broadcasts while I was working for Research In Motion. Sitting in 'radio row' at the Super Bowl with this fun and fast-talking duo, it quickly became obvious why their new brand of talk radio is spreading like wildfire across the United States. They're HOT.

So what would this rapid rise to stardom be attributed to? Ryan Stewart, a former NFL defensive back believes some key principles have led to the duo's success in a competitive business. He attributes much of his own success to the help he received from so many others.

And he hasn't forgotten the importance of giving back. Ryan spends countless hours working with local charities that he really believes in, such as Big Brothers. Here's Ryan's philosophy:

- **Just do what you do.** Knowing your limitations and capabilities is critical. If you want to accomplish something but don't know anything about the task or industry, seek counsel. You'll always find someone who knows someone who can assist you.
- **Have faith.** Belief in a higher power can help you accomplish all that you set out to do.
- **If you want to be blessed, be a blessing to others.** So many people get caught up in their own world that they forget other people are trying to make moves themselves. So don't forget to extend your support to others.

Now that's powerful – a successful NFL player now on the brink of superstardom in sports radio, and one of his priorities continues to be helping others. Ryan truly understands that he is reaching his exponential potential in part because of the genuine support he receives from the many people who believe in him. And it would appear he and his brother have barely reached the peak of their success.

✓ Two steps forward

You can put your network in motion, but it doesn't mean the answers you seek will immediately appear or be obvious. Each connection is a stepping stone, bringing you that much closer to your goals. Access everything and everyone you possibly can. The more options and information you have as a leader, the more you set your team up for success. If you had to cross a big river stepping on stones, wouldn't you want to know where all of them were before making the journey?

✓ Exponential versus linear progress

Authentic information gathering, creating 'connectivity,' using the 'pinging' strategy and generally being open-minded allows you an infinite amount of possibilities and an exponential, versus linear, path to opportunity. I always suggest having a plan, but I also caution about following it too closely or getting caught up in the black and white. Your greatest progress or opportunities may actually be in the gray zone. The energy and momentum may be coming from a completely different source.

force

Hindsight is 20/20

"I'll show you mine if you show me yours?"

Are you a networker, information broker or a connector? How you respond to this question will, in part, influence how you reach your exponential potential, because, to a certain degree, each of these roles is motivated differently. Don't get me wrong, networking and information brokering definitely has its place. And it can result in many wonderful paths crossing. Something must be said for a business skill that people spend a lot of money trying to acquire. I even have friends who attribute their inability to network as the reason that they haven't been successful when looking for a job!

Don't lose sight of how your intentions are fuelled and be careful of how others will perceive your motivations. Are you merely 'using' this contact for personal gain or do you have a genuine interest in meeting them? Are you willing to help passionate people (whose passion you believe in, obviously) who might need your support even if you won't necessarily get something out of it? Or do you believe specifically in a 'scratch my back, then I'll scratch yours' philosophy?

That self-serving attitude is the difference between contact brokering, networking and genuinely connecting, and it lacks the power of genuine connection, which seems to motivate people to help you in an entirely different way.

I have met many 'networking experts' who profess to have large and powerful contact lists – lists they will not share with just anyone. And you won't get access to any of it unless you can provide some powerful contacts in return. Of course, many people are not initially up-front about their motives for wanting to help you. I had an experience with this type of person at a function last year. It was only over the course of a few hours that the truth came out. What the 'networking guru' really wanted was access to some of my network. Her tactic? Trying to make me feel like I wouldn't get anywhere without knowing her and her contacts. What I actually felt was that she had a hidden agenda and an ulterior motive. There was no sense of respect for me or attempt to connect with me as an individual. I suppose at the end of the day I could have played the game right back: "I'll show you mine if you show me yours." But I didn't trust the delivery and, besides, who's got the time?

Interestingly enough, in a recent conversation with a lawyer friend, he advised me that some people will actually pay to gain access to an individuals' network of contacts and their insight into how to work with these contacts. He called it brokering services. So I guess next time I feel a heavy-handed networking guru coming at me, I can throw them my card and tell them I'll write up an agreement. I realize that you wouldn't want to just hand over access to your wonderful network of friends and influential people that has taken you years and lots of credibility to build. But I do think that if you approach your networking opportunities without some flexibility in the 'give-take' dynamics, you'll miss out on opportunities.

Know the difference between networking, brokering and meeting with a genuine connection. The results can be very different.

"In today's environment of thinking locally and acting globally, I have come to fully appreciate the art of networking *and* connecting. And facilitating. These are leadership traits that contribute to the expansion of many different horizons, be it corporate, social or political. It is through the spirit of connection between people that creates this expansion. Expansion means constant progress. Expansion means knowledge and knowledge is enlightenment." *– Shawky Fahel, CEO, JG Group of Companies, humanitarian and global 'connector'*

the

ACTION PLAN

Use the force

1 FOLLOW THE ENERGY.

- Have clarity on your goals and be ready and work hard to achieve them
- Put some energy into your ideas and then go with the momentum

2 BE RESOURCEFUL. YOUR POSSIBILITIES ARE INFINITE.

- Leave no stone unturned on your quest for information
- Useful information and influential contacts can come from anywhere

3 CREATE THE CONNECTION.

- Connect on a genuine 'I want to know you' basis versus a 'how can you help me' approach
- A sincere attitude will motivate those who are helping you
- An authentic connection results in an entirely different power

4 DETACH YOURSELF FROM THE OUTCOME.

- Don't get hung up on how you get there. Remain open-minded to the different contacts and opportunities that flow your way

force

PUSH YOUR ENVELOPE

I'm at the top and there's nowhere else to go
You can call me nice or you can call me CEO
Cuz if you dis I'll be quick to dismiss ya
Put you in the mailroom where I won't even miss ya

CEO, Princess Superstar

METAMORPHOSIS

Never, never, never give up!

Blood, sweat and fear

Fake it until you make it

Personal paradigm shift

Reinvention on demand

You ARE the CEO

Illegitimi non carborundum

All good expressions come from the air force. Way back in the 1980s, I had majors telling me to "make it happen," or warning us that it was "all about execution," or sharing practical advice like *"illegitimi non carborundum."* Apparently that translates into something like "don't let the bastards grind you down," so it's a particular favorite of mine these days!

To this day, my all-time favorite saying is 'push your envelope.' The expression was used a lot in the air force's aviation test environment. That's where leading-edge aircraft designs flown by cocky test pilots are pushed beyond their maximum safe limits of performance during test flights to really get a sense of what these aircraft can achieve. Aircraft have a certified (or anticipated) performance 'envelope,' which covers many facets of their flight capabilities – maximum 'G' loading, speed, height, payload, etc. When these certified test pilots push the aircraft envelope, they're validating what the airplane can really do, and it might be greater than what the initial specifications indicate. The 'cocky' part to their job comes from what they really do – take supersonic machines thousands of feet up in the sky, fly them faster than the speed of sound and throw them around to make sure their wings don't fall off – or so these test pilots have told me. By the time they land the aircraft, the pilots have pushed their own flying skills and challenged themselves more than most people probably do in a lifetime. I guess they have a right to be cocky.

> "The secret to my success was that somehow I always managed to live to fly another day." *– Chuck Yeager, first man to fly faster than the speed of sound*

When you apply the 'push your envelope' philosophy to your own life or career, you might be very surprised at your own capabilites. Personally, I find I grow most from the experiences that push well beyond the average, and they give me a sense of personal fulfillment – fast. There is no quicker way to catapult yourself to a whole new level.

I started pushing my envelope early on in life. From adventurous hobbies as a teenager, like flying, to career choices such as military boot camp, to exotic travel and an international move to Europe, I've always pushed myself to step out of my comfort zone. It might seem a little sadomasochistic to some, or perhaps unsettling to others – why can't you just be happy with where you are in life, with what you've got? To me, the answer is simple: Each time you push yourself, you'll find there is more you'll get from it. Much more. And that has been my pattern to date. Try something new, feel the fear, push through the envelope and come out the other side rejuvenated from the new experience in life.

But no experience has come close in providing me with life and leadership growth like my short-term adventure leading a team in a war zone.

Back in 1992, I was pushing my envelope at full force. I landed in a war zone in former Yugoslavia that brought out every facet of who I am – emotionally, physically and spiritually. The experience embodied what this principle is really all about – facing fear, drawing on every ounce of confidence, worrying about failure. This experience led to a huge transformation in my life.

TURNING MY WORLD UPSIDE DOWN

I hate to say it, but I asked for it. This was definitely a case of 'be careful what you wish for!' I was a young captain with a few years' experience under my belt, and I was driven and ambitious. After proving myself as a young lieutenant, I was quickly promoted to captain and awarded a top logistics officer's job in a sought-after posting in Europe. Like most career-driven people, I always wanted to get to the next level. At this point in my life, there was a lot of opportunity to do that.

Before I got to the war zone, I was having the time of my life. I was on fire! I was living in the middle of Europe, traveling the world, skiing in the Alps and wine-tasting in French châteaux. Along with all of this, I had an exciting job with lots of visibility, in part because my posting with the Canadian Forces was part of the NATO command sitting in central Europe. Our military

metamo

base became the deployment platform for most things going on in the world. Deployment coordination orders logically went through our European location, which was central to many destinations. What that meant, however, was that sometimes my world would be turned upside down. Rapidly.

For instance, just one year prior to this UN mission, I had to rapidly shift gears, from fulfilling a more routine position as an administration officer to putting on my combat gear for a six-month stint planning logistics for the Gulf War deployment of our fighter squadrons. With that came new duties, a new team and new office space located between our quickly established logistics 'command post' and the War Room – the place where leaders were briefed and strategic decisions made. Part of my new role included briefing the wing commander, air division general and other senior officers on the progress of the deployments, as well as getting the latest intelligence on the deployment and sharing that high-level view with my team. This was a whole new ball game for me, and the Canadian Forces in general.

REALITY TV AT ITS WORST

The Gulf War was no ordinary war. You might recall it being referred to as a 'high tech war,' where scenes of fighting and deployment were brought to you live, around the clock, right into your living room. This truly was reality TV, as the BBC or CNN crews took the world to the war zone.

I remember going in for one of our War Room briefings, which always began with a big-picture overview of the mission by an intelligence officer (IntO). While waiting for the general, we all had our eyes fixed on the numerous TVs airing CNN's latest report on the Gulf War. Minutes later and with a rather shocked look on his face, the IntO took his military 'top secret' message, threw it in the paper shredder, then recommended we all watch CNN for the next 10 minutes. The station's information was more up-to-date and accurate than ours!

On another occasion, I remember a corporal blasting into our command post yelling for me to look at CNN. "Ma'am, ma'am, take a look at the TV – your husband is on." After weeks of CNN reports of beaten-up allied pilots who had become Iraqi prisoners of war, the last thing the wife of a fighter pilot wanted to hear was that her husband was on TV! But there he was, climbing out of his jet after returning from a mission with three other pilots. CNN was there capturing the latest from the heroes of the allied forces.

GOING FOR IT

Within months of shifting to my Operation Desert Storm assignment, I had gained some very unique experience, and a desire to take on more. So what could be next? Well, how about another war zone? But this time I would get right into the thick of it. Soon after the fighter squadrons redeployed from the Gulf and our European teams took a little R&R, the opportunity came up.

It was now late 1991 and war had erupted in Yugoslavia. Canadian Forces Europe was tasked by the UN Security Council to plan and prepare to deploy the largest peacekeeping contingent it had ever organized. I watched for a few months as the army units on our base prepared for this next mission. Equipment was being painted white with big UN symbols on the doors. Regiments prepared for the upcoming deployment. The army base was a buzz with activity. Funny thing was, while I led the team of experts for multi-modal deployments, specially trained troops who could move military gear anywhere by any means – road, rail, sea, air – no one had come to us for consultation on this monumental deployment. So I called my army buddy, Captain St. Denis, (a good friend from my cadet days who helped me navigate my way around the army world) and asked his advice on how I might get involved in this huge operation. "Well," he asked, "do you really want to get involved with this mission, Angela?" I hadn't really thought it through, but for some reason I blurted out, "Of course! No one else in Europe is trained like we are to do this sort of thing." He replied: "Well, if you really want it, go for it. Go talk to your colonel." And the rest, as they say, is history.

Reality check: You are your own career manager

In the words of my master warrant officer back when I was just starting my career, *"YOU are your own career manager, ma'am. Don't leave your career up to anyone else but yourself. If you want a job or you're looking for a promotion, then YOU need to go for it!"* Great words to live by, don't you think? Do you really want to leave your career path, and significant choices that will impact your life in a major way, up to someone else? I was given this advice back in my twenties. It was relevant then, and with the rapid shift in the business world, it has become even more relevant today. You are your own boss.

A few short days later and I was off. Preparing for my new mission was a whirlwind of activity that included 'getting kitted' with everything from barrack boxes to a flak jacket to a weapon, (magazine, ammunition and all). I was tasked as part of the reconnaissance team, a team that would deploy into the unknown before all of the other Canadian and international troops. My job was to establish the deployment plan and develop an 'in-country' supply chain to receive millions of pounds of equipment. As I stepped onto that SwissAir flight, destination Belgrade, I had no idea where I was heading. I had stepped into the unknown before but this was a whole new ball game – unfamiliar territory in a foreign country in the middle of a civil war.

One thing was for sure, I was heading beyond my 'safe limits of performance,' right past those curves on the graph that represent the 'envelope' in that mathematical equation. I was definitely going to push *my* envelope.

SURVIVING BLOOD, SWEAT AND FEAR

For the next several weeks, I would work harder and longer than I've ever worked in my life. A typical workday was 18 to 20 hours. I really couldn't sleep anyway, because I was riding high on sheer adrenaline. I had so much to do in such a short amount of time to get a workable plan in place, and I was starting from scratch. It was difficult to get my hands on any information or intelligence, such as the lay of the land, the state of the airports, railways, roads, bridges or seaports – all of the things that I needed to know in great detail to be able to do my job.

I had landed in uncharted territories. I had a clean slate and no one really knew where to start. The stakes were high – failing to come up with a decent plan could mean embarrassment to Canada and the United Nations.

> "The more one does and sees and feels, the more one wants to do!" – *Amelia Earhart*

But there was no stopping me. One evening (or late morning, since it was about 1 or 2 a.m.), while stopping in Banja Luka, on our way to no-man's-land north of this location between Bosnia and Croatia, I begged an Argentinean major to take me in his armored truck to a nearby railway station so I could start gathering information on the state of the railway lines or whatever info we could find. The scene was almost comical. I spotted a large rail route map high up on the walls of the station, so he hoisted me up on his shoulders so I could rip it down. A man in uniform came out of nowhere and started yelling at us, for obvious reasons. Our antics at 1 a.m. in the railway station looked a little suspicious. After a challenging discussion in Spanish, Bosnian, English, and complex hand gestures, we found ourselves sitting in his office, served with Slivovitz (plum brandy), and gathering the latest information on the rail routes that had been destroyed, were mine-ridden, and those that could support some of the extremely heavy equipment I needed to bring into the country.

Long hours. Long days. Lots of sweat! And then there was this little thing called fear. We were, after all, in the middle of tremendous devastation and a nation at war. I was now way beyond my comfort zone in every way. Let's just say I experienced fear on a few different levels.

Fear of failure was a big one. Fear for personal safety. Having to be escorted to barrack block showers within the confines of the military camp felt pretty foreign to me, but I wasn't going to ignore advice like that from my senior officers. Having to gun tape bullet holes in my bedroom window of our hotel/headquarters that had been under fire also seemed very surreal. If these windows were full of bullet holes, where did that leave me in the middle of the night? On second thought, I might just sleep with my Kevlar vest on top of me!

The good thing was that I was often too busy to be afraid. Like the first night, the area around us was under mortar attack. I was so caught up in the complexities of this massive deployment that I barely had time to acknowledge what was happening that night. I received a phone call from the Norwegian team captain, who – along with his troops – had been assigned to my team, advising me that his country had ordered them to stay put in a safer location and they were not to come to our location until the fire had died down. Only then did I realize things were worse than I thought.

> "We are not provided with wisdom, we must discover it for ourselves, after a journey through the wilderness, which no one can take for us, an effort which no one can spare us, for our wisdom is the point of view from which we come at last to regard the world." *– Marcel Proust, French intellectual and novelist*

THE UNKNOWN

Whether it's a war zone or a new job, when you head into the unknown, you need to plan, then plan for the unplanned and prepare for new experiences. Almost everything I did on this mission was new to me, such as leading a multinational team of movements specialists – the team responsible for rail move operations, supply chain planning and everything from negotiating with local transportation companies to meeting UN officials. When the UN realized that there was only one of me and too much to do, I was assigned a small but energized group of Norwegians and Swedish troops in addition to my two Canadian soldiers. Being in the unknown meant leading this eclectic team through change – a lot of it. Each day, it was necessary to re-align my team with our ever-changing mission, reviewing priorities, coming up with a communication plan (a challenging task when you don't have cell phones or laptops) and assigning tasks.

I had anticipated change. When you're in unfamiliar territory you never know where you might end up. In one particularly bizarre situation, I found myself in Zagreb, the capital and largest city of Croatia. I was there to brief the prime minister's right-hand man on our plans and get 'buy-in,' support and the government influence we needed across the business sector and transportation infrastructure. Just me in my combats and two gold bars on my shoulders, sitting in the Croatian parliament buildings around a table of 20 or so newly elected officials in this fledgling government, pushing to get what we needed.

Leading in the zone

Flow: the place where mind, body and action are united in purpose. During my peacekeeping mission in the former Yugoslavia, while I didn't have a clue where to start, things just seemed to flow at times. Some things seemed effortless, even paranormal. Sometimes a challenge stood in front of me, and within minutes, the world was coming together around me to remove it. When I needed help or support, it seemed to materialize, sometimes out of nowhere. So this was what it was like to be in the zone – the 'flow' as it is often referred to in the sports world – where you've set out to achieve a goal and absolutely everything connects. That's what can happen when you push your envelope.

I made it through this war zone. I moved through the challenge, the change and the monumental task of leading through the unknown. And in taking on this challenge, I entered my own zone, the 'there's nothing in my way now' zone.

After just weeks, I emerged a changed person. I had always been confident, capable and on top of my game, but when I left behind the war zone, I came away with an intangible belief in myself, afraid of nothing and convinced that there wasn't anything I couldn't do. And I had a new appreciation for the smallest and simplest things in life. I was the CEO of the most important company ever: Me.

The principle: Push your envelope

This principle is about taking yourself to your maximum safe limits of performance, so you can gain powerful growth as a leader. Taking on those projects that 'stretch' you, as well as your resources, people and energy, will help you experience huge personal growth and get you to a level where you own your destiny, where you are the driving force in your life and career.

> Live your life with arms wide open
> Today is where your book begins
> The rest is still unwritten.
>
> – *"Unwritten," Natasha Bedingfield*

It's a powerful and necessary principle for successful entrepreneurs and leaders in any business or industry. I truly believe that applying this instrumental principle will keep you on your toes, exercise your mind and ensure you're always finely tuned to your personal strengths and passions – the things you likely want to focus on in life. But (there is always a 'but'), of all the principles to add to your leadership game plan, this principle is one of the most challenging to put into practice.

Push your envelope *unplugged*

Think you're ready to push your envelope? Although the expression 'pushing the outside of the envelope' comes from the world of aeronautics, it's very relevant to the demands of today's fast-paced business world and life in general.

During the post-Second World War era, propeller-driven aircraft began to get replaced with jets. Designers were testing new engines and performance characteristics of new models. Test pilots who flew beyond what designers and engineers calculated as possible and/or safe were said to be pushing the outside of the (flight) envelope.[1]

So what happens 'on the ground' when you start pushing your envelope? This is where the blood, sweat and fear come in. You will be stepping into a personal unknown zone – an area where you don't have much, if any, experience. You might be venturing into something that you're not even certain is personally possible. You can expect to feel uncertain, some fear (of failure, rejection, safety), and the obvious stress and sweat that goes with uncertainty or the feeling of not being 'in control.' And then there's the personal effort required – you can't move into your own adventure without a huge amount of effort!

PIECES OF THE PUZZLE

Don't panic. Once you jump in, the pieces to the puzzle will quickly start to fit together and you'll find support and encouragement from people who have taken a similar path, signs of progress and other cues that you're making everything fit together. As each piece of the puzzle is added, your comfort zone will expand. You'll start gaining confidence that you've made the right decision, or have the skills to do what you set out to do. But this time the experience will be entirely different. You're now playing on a bigger field.

SEIZE YOUR POTENTIAL

With enough practice, pushing your envelope will become a skill, even a personal strength. And as with any skill you acquire, you can apply it to all parts of your life, be it hobbies, a passion or a big career move you didn't have the guts to make before.

Pushing your envelope will help you realize that we all go into big things not knowing where life will actually take us. The key is to 'know that you don't know' and do it anyway! That's where you realize your potential. That's when you can experience the transformation that you'll carry with you into the workplace and other aspects of your life. I learned how to fly gliders and power aircraft in my late teens and early twenties. My pursuit of this hobby rapidly brought to the surface for me a deep understanding of my strengths and weaknesses, which I was able to use in my role as a young officer. Through flying, I gained skills, confidence, self-esteem and an understanding that I was capable of doing things I put my mind to. That knowledge followed me everywhere and so did the realization that I had the inner strength to face fear when I needed to. And trust me, I scared myself a lot while flying!

Once you get a taste for change, you will never go back. That sense of accomplishment, of achieving your potential and confidence in yourself, is addictive *and* 'recyclable.' You will want to use those skills to push your envelope again, so you can experience one more time the elation that goes with taking yourself to a whole new level, a new personal dimension.

LEADERSHIP STRENGTH

Sure you'll probably work harder than ever when you push the envelope. At the same time, you'll likely harness and test every other principle you're going to read about in this book and in your leadership game plan. Principles like accountability, believing in yourself, taking risks, going into the unknown, thinking out of the box, influencing others to believe in your path.

Can you see the fantastic connection here? By pushing your envelope, in whatever way, you'll strengthen your leadership muscle. It's a principle that tests and grows almost every skill and principle you will need to apply as a leader.

And when you get through to the other side of your personal test, you'll stand back and realize that you're no longer the same person you were going in.

RED FLAG **Nothing ventured. Nothing gained**

First things first. Pushing your envelope will require stretching your limits, taking on something new, something big. And facing your fear – often rooted in failure or rejection.

Women are notorious for quietly sitting back and waiting to be recognized for what they've done instead of asking for that promotion or job they deserve. The brave ones ask for what they want and are ready to face rejection head-on.

I always prefer to ask for what I want and face potential rejection, which is not always a bad thing. You find out pretty darned quickly where you stand or what might be standing in your way of getting what you want. Or you can simply wait and see what's offered. I'm too impatient for that. You should be too.

Ask for what you want. If you don't, how will you ever know what could have been? I have a far greater fear of missed opportunity than asking for what I want and not getting it!

How to push your envelope and start owning your life!

Get ready for an exciting journey! Putting this all-encompassing principle into practice starts with you. Numero uno. So set your intentions and get going.

> "Believe in love. Believe in magic.
> Hell, believe in Santa Claus. Believe in others.
> Believe in yourself. Believe in your dreams.
> If you don't, who will?"
>
> – *Jon Bon Jovi, rock star*

Some of the key actions you'll need to adopt to put this principle into practice:

1. **Never, never, never give up.**
2. **Be brave. Surround yourself with others who are.**
3. **Believe in yourself…it's contagious!**
4. **Fake it until you make it.**
5. **Make sure your drive is greater than your need for cash.**

1 Never, never, never give up

It's critical you stay committed to any new challenge. Pushing your envelope or stepping up to a new project or opportunity is going to test you in many ways. Your commitment to reaching this new personal level in your career and life will help support you through the tough times. Without that commitment, you may waiver or even give up as you face the inevitable hurdles of growing and changing.

There is no question: To get what you want, you have to be prepared to work hard. Really hard. And huge personal growth, transformative growth, will not come easy.

Relentless commitment is necessary.

CASE STUDY **Learning to fly**

Last year, while I was skiing with my two sons, I received a long-distance call from the United Arab Emirates just as I stepped into the lounge for some well-deserved après-ski refreshments. It was my younger brother calling, and he had a huge announcement. "Ange, I just greased [read: landed smoothly and beautifully] an airbus A340 onto the runway. I'm in the left seat, baby, and I thought I should call you and tell you that I have just realized my life's dream of 30 years!"

Wow! What an incredible achievement. I began to instantly reflect on what gave Brendan the push to reach his goal. Ever since he could talk, Brendan has been obsessed with airplanes and flying. As a kid, he had model airplanes hanging from his bedroom ceiling and posters plastered on the walls. Of course, growing up on air force bases has obviously had an influence on both of us. But Brendan took his interest to new heights by learning how to glide the moment he was old enough and hanging around aircraft hangars, introducing himself to any fighter pilot that crossed his path.

Finding a way

Realizing his dream meant overcoming huge hurdles throughout his life and career path. At the young age of 18, he was accepted into the military to train as an air force pilot – a huge step toward realizing his dream. But in the middle of learning how to fly fast military jets, he was released from his jet course. Unfortunately, as a teenager he didn't have the maturity to deal with the high stress levels that training entailed. He had failed his lifelong dream. It was a devastating blow.

Bound and determined, he found other ways to realize his dream of becoming a commercial pilot. He spent years living below the poverty line and in some very remote locations so that he could slowly clock up the flying hours needed to accumulate enough multi-engine hours to eventually get to the big leagues – heavy jets. In an unbelievably competitive business requiring literally thousands of commercial flying hours before you can get anywhere, Brendan became frustrated with the lack of movement in his North American flying career. So he picked up and moved to Africa to fly for the United Nations – a huge change in his life, but it was where he could start clocking the types of flying hours he would need to qualify for the bigger airplanes. Challenge after challenge, my brother remained relentlessly committed to his career path, even when many friends and family members around him thought he should give up.

Today, after 20 years of staying the course and following his dream, he sits as a captain in the left seat of one of the world's leading-edge aircraft – the airbus A340.

2 Be brave

If you're feeling any uncertainty, anxiety, nervousness or even fear with one of your career choices, well, all I can say is that you're on the right track. Pushing your envelope will push your fear button. Fear will stem from any changes you face, doubts about direction and decisions, or the possibility of not succeeding – an obvious biggie! I think the more nervous you are about your new venture, the more powerful the change you could experience at the end of it.

Nobody makes changes in their life, shifts their gears, or pushes their learning curve for accelerated growth without some angst. You're not alone.

☯ The taste of freedom

Writing this book has highlighted a fascinating life paradox for me. The decision to write this book and everything that goes with it continues to be exhilarating and terrifying at the same time. And I know it's only just the beginning. Very recently, I worked for one of North America's most successful high-tech companies. It offered tons of opportunity and lots of success, right in the town where I'm living. I had it made. But shaking up my life every three years or so seems to be a pattern of mine. So, after working in the high-tech industry for years, I decided it was time to give it up, shift gears and take more control of my destiny. I began to pursue my own dream, started my own company and wrote this book. I'm tasting freedom alright. And I'm losing some sleep. But I'm following the advice of many an entrepreneur these days – "get your dentist to make you a bite plate so you won't grind your teeth. You won't lose quite so much sleep!"

The *I Ching* or *Book of Changes*, an ancient Chinese text, centers on the dynamic balance of the opposites that we face in life. Growth is one of them:
"Growth is not an easy process; it's risky and sometimes frightening, but with courage and fortitude we become stronger, more supple, and hopefully more aware. Releasing your grip on whatever you're clinging to, whether it's an identity, a relationship, a place, or a thing, may seem impossible at first. But once you feel the truth of it all, all the way to your bones, letting go becomes easier, and can even be exhilarating. Once you disengage from habitual behavior, you'll get a taste of freedom and it will stimulate new behaviour and new attitudes."[2]

Shift your own gears

Now that my identity is no longer attached to a highly successful corporation, I no longer have someone else's powerful product to move around the world or market. Here I am finally, after years of working for others, suddenly in my own corner office with a new title: CEO. Hell, I can call myself whatever I want now 'cause I'm the boss!

With all that newfound freedom, flexibility and 'control' over my life comes some angst. I'm responsible for finding the business so that I can generate income while I'm trying to pursue my creative side and market this book. Now I'm totally responsible for my 'identity' – good, bad or ugly. Will I have any credibility as I try and stand on my own two feet? Will I be able to have the influence on my destiny that I'm looking for when I'm the CEO of me, instead of the executive of someone else's success story? I must be brave.

Balance the fear with other success stories

If you can't beat 'em, join 'em, right? One of the best ways to combat the anxiety of pushing yourself into unknown territory is to surround yourself with like-minded people. Or even better, people who have already 'been there and done that.' They'll be able to offer a unique perspective of the road you're traveling Once you make that commitment to push your envelope and head off on your new challenge, you'll be pleasantly surprised at how many like-minded people you'll meet or connect with, right at your doorstep. Friends, business associates, your lawyer or kid's coach, sometimes even strangers will say to you, "Hey, you have to meet blah, blah, blah…they have done something similar to you!"

Don't be afraid to call upon people who've done what you want to do and set up a meeting to get their insight. Or join a professional club that might bring you closer to like minds. There are so many ways to reach out and when you do, you'll be amazed by just how many others reach back.

3 Believe in yourself…it's contagious!

I discussed in Chapter 06, "Spark Creativity," the need to believe in your team in order to keep them energized and passionate. This is a case when you have to lead by example. You have to start with you. But, when you're leading yourself, you need to believe in yourself. This will be your number-one tool in helping you push the envelope and trek through new space.

One of many inspirational points that Steve Jobs, co-founder and CEO of Apple Computer (creator of iPod, a very hot-selling MP3 device), made in a commencement speech to Stanford University graduates was about the need to 'connect the dots,' even though one of the hardest things about believing in yourself is that you can't predict the future. You still have to be able to visualize where you want to go. And you've got to trust that, although you can't see the end result with total certainty, soon enough you will be looking back, connecting the dots and thinking to yourself, "Wow! I knew this was the right path and it's incredible."

Start now, one small step at a time

Have you always wanted to be a singer? Start taking singing lessons and then go find a local gig. My girlfriend has always dreamed of writing a book. In between taking her son to kindergarten and managing their home, she is now heading slowly

> Of course it was impossible to connect the dots looking forward when I was in college. But it was very, very clear looking backwards 10 years later. Again, you can't connect the dots looking forward; You can only connect them looking backwards. So you have to trust that the dots will somehow connect in your future. You have to trust in something – your gut, destiny, life, karma, whatever – because believing that the dots will connect down the road will give you the confidence to follow your heart, even when it leads you off the well-worn path, and that will make all the difference.[3]
>
> *– Steve Jobs, co-founder and CEO, Apple Computer*

down the path of writing a children's educational guide – one hour at a time, when the window of opportunity presents itself each day. That's how you start. One small step at a time. My friend's progress may be slow but it's steady. And one hour at a time, I'm watching Kelli dream and grow.

Take on a small challenge; go out and try that hobby you've been dreaming about. Or take a huge leap and head toward the big job you really want. But start somewhere. Small steps and small achievements build the internal power of belief!

4 Fake it until you make it

Maybe this is a little cliché. It tends to attract some heated debate, but I still like it. And I believe in its power.

Reality is, to get where you want to go, you have to start somewhere and you have to be able to see yourself getting there. And you might not think you have all the skills you need, but you certainly need to convince others that you do or will.

This means believing in yourself, where you can be in the future and getting others on board with you. It takes a combination of confidence, belief and chutzpah. You might need to close your eyes, hold your breath and hope for the best. I look at it like this: If it's not rocket science (believe me, in the air force and high-tech industry I have been surrounded by some real live rocket scientists), then how hard can it be? You can do it!

SCHOOL-YARD INTELLIGENCE

Fact or fake

"For many Americans, the words 'government official' and 'lying bastard' are practically synonymous. Now Colgate University psychologists report that leadership skills and the ability to deceive do, in fact, go hand in hand. And the connection begins earlier than you might think."[4] – *Psychology Today,* "Making Leaders and Mis-leaders"

When Colgate University psychologists studied the correlation between leadership skills and the ability to deceive, they discovered that similar traits existed in both preschoolers and college students. The study revealed that when children were given a drink that was sweet or tart, but told to tell people it was sweet, even if it wasn't, they convincingly deceived people. The same experiment was conducted with college students with similar results. The children who had emerged as leaders in earlier play periods were the same children who were better able to lie convincingly. Apparently superior social skills and the ability to manipulate others are important attributes to have in positioning yourself on top – even if it's the top of the nearest playground.

RED FLAG Faking it

There is a difference between believing that you can really do something versus presenting yourself as someone you're not. I'm not suggesting a con job à la Frank Abagnale Jr. of the *Catch Me If You Can* variety. However, his story (made into a movie) has some merit in demonstrating my point. Through his own confidence, Abagnale, a successful con artist, was able to convince the world that he was a Pan Am airline pilot, a pediatrician, and a Harvard Law School graduate. He was able to cash $2.5 million in checks in 26 countries before the world caught on.[5] Definitely underhanded, but he is also living proof that when you act like you believe in yourself, others will too!

metamo

5 Your drive for passion is GREATER than your desire for cash

The fuel for your fire, and the courage and confidence to push your envelope, will come from one place – your passion. No matter what walk of life or industry you look at, most successful leaders chased their passion before they chased cash. And in many cases, many of them put money aside, or took a lot of their hard-earned earnings and invested all of it into their passion – a big risk! Airline pilots, hip-hop producers (see Outside the Corporate Box below), corporate execs or humanitarians, what has kept them commited has been a passion for what they are trying to achieve, what they believe in. Not a driving desire to make tons of money first.

Start with the passion. That's how you'll sustain the energy and drive needed to reach your dreams. Energy and passion are far more likely to lead you to success. The cash will follow.

Outside the corporate BOX

SMART, FUNNY AND PLAYFULLY PORNOGRAPHIC

How do you reinvent yourself from teenage kid to Manhattan hip-hop diva while running your own show?

"Just worship her!" says *DJ Mag* of Princess Superstar. A one-woman show, this upcoming global star booked her own tours and ran her own label (The Corrupt Conglomerate) until the year 2000 when Princess realized that being both star and management would work the "nerves of even the steeliest jet-setter." So now she's focusing on being the superstar. With music mags describing her as the next edgy blonde to move in on Gwen Stefani, and after making *New York* magazine's 50 Most Beautiful New Yorkers list in 2005, it seems she's got the right focus. And if that's not enough, besides writing her own words and music, and producing and playing the guitar, keyboard and drums, she's also the number-one most-recognized female DJ in the world!

After connecting with Princess Superstar (otherwise known as Concetta Kirschner) I was blown away by yet another fascinating story of someone who has really pushed the envelope to become a strong business leader. It's no easy feat succeeding as a guitar-swinging, self-produced white female rapper in the hip-hop industry, especially when major labels that wanted to sign her told her to get rid of the guitar because it conflicted with her hip-hop style. She plays by her own rules and didn't buy it. Her lyrics push the envelope even further: "Got my boyfriend in the shower, I'm making six bucks an hour'" is just a small taste of how saucy the princess can be in her "Bad Babysitter" single, just one of her big hits. She's 'fast rhyming,' witty and playfully pornographic.

When I asked the Princess what personal philosophies she believes helped her succeed, her response was no surprise:

- Never, never, never give up. Even when you're exhausted.
- Believe in yourself. Fully.
- Know that you wouldn't be here if you weren't supposed to be.
- Get used to being alone and "freaked out scared!"

"In my pop dreamworld, she's bigger than Madonna and she spat in Britney's face. I applaud Concetta Kirschner's [Princess Superstar's] spectacular capacity for reinvention and self-creation because it's clear that musically she knows her shit, and lyrically she's sharper and funnier and freakier than all the Stefanis and Bedingfields and Christinas who seem like such pale shadows of her trailblazing wake."
– New Musical Express website (www.nme.com)

rphosis

What's in it for you? (Because this time it's not about your team!)

Once you start challenging your limits, you'll be pushing your life and living it to the max. Sure, you'll feel the benefits of applying this principle in the workplace but be ready to feel the affects across the rest of your life, too. Your world will change!

Once you start reaping the rewards of testing your limits, you'll realize it can be an addictive way of life. No mediocrity going on here – you will be growing, experiencing, learning, loving…living! Hey, that's what it's all about, isn't it?

So what's in it for you? Where do I start?

✓ Reinvention on demand

These days, the business world is moving so fast, you'd better be thinking 'what's in it for me?' And one of your best strategies to take care of number one and ensure you can keep up with change is your ability to reinvent yourself on-demand. Pushing your envelope is a principle that delivers those skills and that survival strategy. Practicing this principle will help you prepare and keep you on your toes at all times in order to head comfortably into unknown territory. That's what reinvention is all about.

> "I think you have to mix things up for longevity. It's also a healthy way to approach your job as an actor, because if you keep changing what you do, you not only exercise different muscles but you exercise different perspectives. That's a way to keep yourself alive creatively and career-wise, if the gods are with you. One of the hardest things for people, after doing something for a long time, is they get cynical. You've got to keep attention and curiosity in the mix.[6]"
>
> *– Willem Dafoe, Hollywood and theater actor*

I've learned to reinvent myself, shift gears and move comfortably from one world to another. I've organized military missions, led marketing teams and now written a book. What I'm talking about is the ability to not only manage a changing career path, but also to drive it and influence it and own it. If I knew then what I know now, I would never have thought that my career in the military could have led to where I am today. But as Steve Jobs said, you can only connect the dots looking back; you have to believe in yourself looking forward. Reinvention – and your ability to change the direction of your career direction or life on a dime – relies on that belief.

To make the most out of where you're heading, even if it is somewhat unknown, combine your personal strength and passions with a 'push your envelope' philosophy. Change your path from a linear forward progression to a three-dimensional experience!

✓ Grow big. Enjoy small

You will grow in many wonderful ways when you put this principle into practice, from learning who you are to the skills you never knew you had and the personal areas you want to keep working on. You will truly be in tune with yourself.

You will find that testing your limits and the resulting big achievements lead to valuing the free and simple things in life. In my case, it quickly became children, health, a dog and making sure I lived in a location that had, at least, a good radio station. I recently attended the Marketing Hall of Legends awards, attended by some CEOs, company leaders, mentors, and inspirational business and artistic stars. Almost every winner, including my former boss, Research In Motion CEO Jim Balsillie, thanked the most important people in their lives after receiving their awards – their children, their parents, their spouse. Big experiences always lead back to the simple things.

✓ New mindset. New you

Mind over matter. Your mind can set you free or it can hold you prisoner if you let it. If someone told you that they could train your mind to think more positively and confidently so you could achieve the things you want out of life, would you buy it? When you push your envelope and go beyond your safe limits of performance, your success and resulting confidence will lead to a new and powerful way of thinking.

metamo

> Getting even distracts from getting ahead.
>
> – *Unknown*

✓ **You're the CEO**

You may always work for a company that you love. Maybe you will shift gears a lot. Or you might just want to run your own business. It doesn't matter what the arrangement is, it's all about your mindset. And if you have the mindset to keep growing, taking on new challenges and trying new things, you'll be much more likely to run your own show instead of someone else making decisions for you. Here's what pushing my latest envelope, becoming an entrepreneur, has looked like for me:

	That was then	This is now
Career path	Join a big 'company' (military) and stay in it for 20 years	5 companies and 19 'jobs' later, now I run my own show
Where you work	Office, cubicles, heck, I even had a secretary for awhile!	Home office, on an airplane, in a hotel… anywhere
Where you meet	Conference rooms	Starbucks (something about the smell of java beans and mellow jazz in the background makes for great meeting ambience)
When you work	8ish to 5ish	Day or night… or weekends
Who you work with	Other corporate members, affiliates	A web of strategic partners and entrepreneurs
What you work for	Job security, promotions, pension, stock options, recognition	I get to own and create my day! I'm empowered, I'm the CEO. And yes, I'm exhausted, but fulfilled.
What you get at the end	A watch, a pension and hopefully some substantial assets	Ownership, for better or for worse, of the destiny I designed

Hindsight is 20/20

Burning bridges

Once you get used to pushing your envelope and taking yourself to new personal levels of achievement, it's only natural that you will start to take more ownership of your life and direction of your career. That will likely result in a personal sense of freedom. But you need to keep one thing in mind as you start moving on to bigger and better things: Be careful not to burn bridges.

The world is getting small. Really small, especially if you continue to work in one industry. And the higher up you go, the smaller it gets. You become more visible – you have more chance of bumping into people you've met, worked with or worked for in the past. Now they've become your client, your partner or boss.

It's never a good idea to cut off ties because you're moving on. 'Burning bridges' or blaming others is really unattractive and weakens your position as a confident individual and leader.

So as you gain momentum with your newfound personal power, as tempting as it may be to 'flip the bird' at the tyrant who used to run the company or team you worked for, ask yourself if you can rise above it. Even if you want to tear a strip off that jerk, save it. You may be partnering with him years later, or want to partner with the same organization he works for. And besides, the reality is that there are far more people out there who will be on your side, helpful and supportive along your career path. If you need to focus on something, focus on that. I'm not saying don't be true to yourself. But I am saying to think smart. Take that new sense of empowerment and channel it in a positive direction. Put your energy to work for you instead of against you!

What's next?

Wow. Now we're really getting close to where leadership can take you. Leadership can mean a lot of things. But leadership to me is more about instilling the power and passion within people to help them take themselves to the next level. To be able to bring people up with any wisdom, you have to go through your own personal experience of 'envelope pushing,' personal transformation and perseverance through change – lots of it. By getting good at taking yourself to the next level, you have developed the skills to bring others up with you. And you have really adopted the skills needed to lead through change.

Thriving in an environment of change is a key component of leadership today and it's very relevant. It will be part of your leadership reality so get used to it. Change can be a wonderful and welcome necessity or it can force you into some incredibly uncomfortable positions.

This chapter and the last one have a simple goal – to enable you to seize your leadership potential and do incredible things. In essence, to *turn the leader in you loose.* Leadership is a powerful personal enabler. And one incredible platform to launch your life on a new path.

metamo

ACTION PLAN

You are the CEO

1 BE BRAVE.

- Fear can be overwhelming. But tomorrow's another day and by then you could feel entirely different
- Get used to fear and make it work for you
- Find others who have 'been there.' Wisdom is good for the soul

2 NEVER GIVE UP.

- Commit to your choice
- Find a way. There's always a way
- Be prepared for continual challenges

3 BELIEVE AND IT WILL BECOME CONTAGIOUS.

- Take small steps to build belief in yourself
- Start shifting your own gears forward so you can connect your dots backwards

4 GO FOR THE PASSION NOT THE CASH.

rphosis

GET COMFORTABLE WITH BEING UNCOMFORTABLE

Help me make the most
of freedom and of pleasure
Nothing ever lasts forever
Everybody wants to rule the world

Everybody Wants To Rule the World, Tears for Fears

CHANGE

Never be the victim

Readiness

Anticipation

One step at a time

Going with the flow

Consummate optimism

Wake-up call

December 2005. I found myself in what looked like another war zone. And in many respects, it was. But this disaster wasn't man-made; it was caused by a powerful force of nature – Hurricane Katrina. Four months later, I was walking through the rubble of what remained of St. Bernard Parish, a suburb in New Orleans that had literally been submerged under the flood of water that had taken over the city for months. I looked up at a two-story home that had been picked up by some unknown force and dropped in its entirety in the middle of the road. I saw a car suspended from a nearby tree, gutters cluttered with remnants of people's lives, small broken toys, smashed picture frames, and pieces of clothing scattered everywhere. Ironically, the only piece of color in this dingy gray and washed-out wasteland was a string of green Mardi Gras beads hanging from a tree limb. This place was eerie, with no sign of any life. Office buildings were boarded up, restaurants were lifeless and most communities still had no power. Every tree was stripped of green. There was no grass. There were no birds, no bugs, no nothing. Everything was abandoned, vacant or gutted.

It looked like the end of the world.

> "From here, hell doesn't look so bad.[1]" – *Aaron Broussard, president, Jefferson Parish, Louisiana*

The devastation of this particular hurricane was enormous. *SitRep*, a publication from the Royal Canadian Military Institute, reported that the results, "in economic, social and environmental terms necessitated appropriations that initially surpassed US$2 billion per day." *SitRep* went on to say that "Katrina's final tally could easily exceed US$300 billion, a sum that is roughly equivalent to the amount invested by the United States during the last four years to secure Afghanistan and pacify Iraq."[2]

So there I was in New Orleans, 17 years later, in yet another 'war zone,' with the same thoughts going through my mind as when I served in the former Yugoslavia on a UN mission. Again, I trudged through the remnants of someone's life, now scattered about the street. Where are these families now? How are they coping? Have they found work to support themselves and their families? How do they start to pick up the pieces?

> "It's as if the entire Gulf Coast were obliterated by the worst kind of weapon you can imagine."
>
> *– U.S. President George W. Bush*

I had been invited on this quick three-day tour of the U.S. Gulf Coast and neighboring counties by my friend David Hughes, CEO of Habitat for Humanity Canada. David suggested I join him to gain insight into North America's latest mission-critical reality. The impact of the hurricane's destruction on people, communities, business and political leaders couldn't be more relevant.

With a career in the non-profit sector spanning several decades, David has led humanitarian teams in far-off places, for some incredible causes. In the past, his missions have focused on SOS Children's Village, an international organization in 132 countries around the world, aimed at helping orphans establish more permanent, stable, family-like environments. His mission this time was a lot closer to home – here in North America, impacting not only children but entire communities of people. He connected with the Habitat affiliates in the New Orleans vicinity to determine how best to offer a helping hand. The Gulf Coast Habitat teams and their resources were already stretched before Katrina, facing a mandate that had rapidly expanded. The current mandate of building 10 to 20 community homes in one year had suddenly grown to an overwhelming challenge of building 200 to 2000-plus homes in a year, following the hurricane.

LEADING THROUGH BIG CHANGE

Most of us may never have to lead through this level of devastation. Coming from a diverse leadership background, I have the utmost respect for global leaders who must lead in the midst of chaos and confusion. I have a special regard for those who dedicate their careers to providing that helping hand, be it to deliver an emergency response, food, shelter, medical support, or to encourage global peace.

> We have a strong brand at Habitat for Humanity. A strong and well-entrenched mission. But when faced with such a monumental change, there is great temptation to start over – start reinventing the wheel. However, in times of such great crisis, it's more important than ever to stay focused on what your 'core philosophy' really is. Only when you keep your original mission and vision on target can you transform successfully.
>
> *– David Hughes, CEO Habitat for Humanity Canada*

One thing we can all take away from 'imposed change' is that change is about transformation. And transformation can be a very positive thing. It can be the catalyst to bigger and better things, even though it's tough to swallow when you're in the thick of it.

> This is a desperate SOS.
>
> *Ray Nagin, mayor of New Orleans*

There's no doubt New Orleans Mayor Ray Nagin was in the thick of it when his city was left in ruins, and his huge challenge was not going to change in a hurry. I can only imagine how much sleep this man lost while the world looked on and the devastation dragged on. He faced enormous pressures running a city thrown into a state of catastrophe, where each and every one of his constituents had been severely impacted. How does one lead through a state of chaos, while your city spins out of control and morphs into a war zone, with looters and vandals sometimes running rampant? How does it feel to look on while residents watch helplessly as victims of the storm die around them? What does it feel like having the world's eyes upon you and your city, watching the nation's lack of emergency response while you're begging for support but not getting what you need? It must have been awful lonely at the top for Nagin.

GET OFF YOUR DUFFS

Faced with something as catastrophic as Hurricane Katrina, it would be easy to feel overwhelmed. Where do you begin to rebuild? How do frontline team leaders, city mayors and councillors, business leaders or Habitat local affiliates deal with this rapid change? How do you go from building five, 10 or 20 homes a year for a community to putting a dent in the construction of 15,000-plus homes, needed in your local area alone? With a lot of work and a lot of help – from everywhere. That's what Nagin relied on as his city remained helpless for weeks. In the days and weeks following the devastation, Nagin became a familiar face on national television stations, CNN and other big North American networks. In fact, scenes of him calmly responding to fist-waving and homeless New Orleanians, pleading for action months later, were common.

> The magnitude of what has landed upon us is monumental. This challenge has pushed our boundaries in ways we could never have imagined. But what is resulting from this devastation is a powerful regrowth of the Habitat model – we have revamped our funding models, leveraged our partnering programs and developed 'home in a box' kits to meet the needs – rapidly. And the fact that we have been on *Larry King Live* and talked with Katie Couric doesn't hurt our cause either!
>
> *– Ken Meinert, senior vice president, Operation Home Delivery, Habitat for Humanity International*

Now I stood at a press conference while Nagin announced some good news – the donation of funds by two world-renowned native musicians, Branford Marsalis and Harry Connick Jr., for the construction of a Musicians' Village. These generous donations would fund the development of 81 homes on a parcel of land acquired in the city's Upper 9th Ward – and the Habitat team would step in to provide its home-building expertise to help make the village a reality.

I had watched Nagin for months on TV, making desperate pleas for support and resources yet still continuing to bear the flack for the slow progress. I applauded 10 months later when Nagin refused to abandon the sinking ship and was re-elected as mayor. My hat goes off to this captain, who is obviously a leader with a lot of accountability. Here is a man who has stepped up to the plate, led through the good times as well as absolute chaos, and continues to stand firm behind a devastated city even though many consider it an absolute hell.

What kind of leader does it take to survive such chaos? I've seen many different styles of leaders, leading through chaos over the years. And Nagin, like most, has a style all his own. Cool under the pressure and not appearing to get too flustered even when the public or press pointed fingers. And demonstrating the ability to be cool under pressure is always a good sign. In the fleeting half-hour that I witnessed him in action, this leader appeared confident, even cocky, and certainly had a tendency to shoot from the hip when the press pushed him for answers on what his city was doing, in its state of rebuilding and economic hardship, for the upcoming Mardi Gras. But that cocky, from-the-hip approach seemed to work for Nagin.

So it was no surprise the rather brash advice he gave to constituents during his inaugural address. In typical Nagin style, he said: "This is The Big Easy, and sometimes we lay back a little too much. Get off your duffs."

And that's just what it will take: getting off our duffs. And making a difference – one house at a time. Every step counts.

GLOBAL REALITY

Take a step back. Look at the big picture and what is going on in the world around you. Hurricane Katrina is just one of many global events that have impacted us in the last five years.

In April 2000, the dot.com bubble burst – it didn't matter whether you worked in the industry or not; you were likely impacted by the industry's tumble. Stocks crashed and pension funds disappeared. There isn't a person out there with a 401K or RRSP who doesn't feel the pain of some of our blue-chip powerhouses going down the tubes. Another event, Sept.11, 2001, now what we commonly refer to as 9/11, saw a series of coordinated terrorist attacks against America, leaving approximately 3,000 people dead and bringing the United States, Canada and other countries together to fight terrorism. In 2002, SARS – an acute respiratory virus – was first reported in China and spread like wildfire over the next year across the globe and virtually crippled the city of Toronto, Canada. Travel and tourism, business, entertainment and health-care sectors all experienced huge hits while people and organizations pulled together to contain the virus. On Dec. 26, 2004, an Indian Ocean earthquake triggered the tsunami that hit one-quarter of the globe, killing hundreds of thousands of people and destroying villages, making it the deadliest tsunami ever recorded. In August 2005, Hurricane Katrina battered the coastlines of Mississippi, Alabama and Louisiana, turning out to be the costliest and one of the deadliest hurricanes in American history.

> "Tragedy has no walls. A tsunami in Indonesia, an earthquake in India, a monster hurricane in Louisiana – nothing connects us so quickly, so immediately, as the experience of loss.[3]"
>
> – *Chris Johns, editor-in-chief,* National Geographic

These accounts are not meant to bring you down, but rather to wake you up. Change is real. Perhaps you've been fortunate enough to have never experienced firsthand some of these devastating blows. For that reason, 'change' may look different to you, but it can happen on so many different levels – often quickly and brutally. On a more personal level, a family member may move across the country, go through a divorce or die. In the workplace, change can take the form of your boss getting fired or your company going through a restructuring process. In our technology-savvy world, through telecommunications, the Internet, and media coverage, we have become more connected with what's going on in the far corners of the Earth, in every aspect – geographically, politically, economically, industrially and socially. The world around us is now as much a part of our leadership reality as the cities we live in, and as the team that stands before you.

Change is guaranteed. No one is immune. As amazing as your job, team, or company might be, the one thing you'll need to plan for is change.

It's time to get off your duffs.

> "It would all be so easy if you had a map to the maze. If the same old routines worked. If they'd just stop moving 'the cheese.' But things keep changing. Be ready to change quickly and enjoy it again and again! They keep moving the cheese.[4]" – *Spencer Johnson, best-selling author of* Who Moved My Cheese?

ONE STEP AT A TIME

Change does not always come on schedule or happen in a way that's fair and paced. It only took a day to shatter the city of New Orleans and neighboring states, but it will take years to rebuild those communities. Even three months after Katrina, our visiting team of observers witnessed only small changes in the ravaged landscape. But where they did see big changes, however, was in how communities banded together to start the long and arduous process of rebuilding.

Today, the same resounding themes of how to survive and lead through change keep coming up:

> Change can be a **catalyst to the largest degree:**

Imposed changes triggered by Katrina are causing communities and international partners to rebuild communities and restore order.

> There is strength in **joining hands and partnering:**

There will always be someone there, willing to reach out with a helping hand.

> **Rebuilding happens one step at a time:**

Whether you're rebuilding communities or transforming businesses, in order to lead through change, you have to start somewhere and take the first step. Progress will only come after taking that first step.

The principle: Get comfortable with being uncomfortable

It ain't pretty. Leadership is tough. Katrina is leadership's worst-case scenario that I wouldn't wish on anyone.

Let this principle be your reality check. Change is inevitable so you might as well get comfortable with being uncomfortable. Life is often a bumpy ride, throwing changes at us faster when we least expect them. Just when you think you're getting things all figured out, they're going to change again. So plan on it.

> "When everything you do is wrong and you feel like
> you could barely survive
> When those around you are crumbling downwards
> buried in the sunset alive
> Thumbing your way to Vegas dirty, and screaming
> like you're back from hell
> Save your dreams and occupations 'cause it
> doesn't matter what you sell
> It ain't pretty!" – *"Pretty Vegas," INXS*

You might recall the mission-critical reality described earlier on in this book (Chapter v, "Mission Critical NOT Mission Impossible"). It's an environment that is notoriously fast, constantly changing and complex. It's ubiquitous. It's everywhere, and it's not reserved just for the business world.

The three types of change you will likely face in your future include the following:

- **Self-created** – it becomes a time to move on or do something really different with your career and life, so you decide to push your envelope
- **Necessary** – good news, growth-oriented change like expanding resources, scaling output, change in products and services. Or not-so-growth-oriented change, such as downsizing to meet market pressures or supply and demand
- **Mission critical** – change that doesn't just sneak up on you, but whacks you right in the side of the head. Crisis creates a sense of urgency and rapid results are required

We've already looked at self-created change in previous chapters. When you force change in your work or your life, what you're doing in effect is taking a big step toward 'pushing your envelope.' ◄◄ **Rewind** *to Chapter 12, "Push Your Envelope," to read more about propelling yourself to personal transformation.*

But it's important to understand the reality and impact of 'necessary' and the inevitable 'mission-critical' types of change that you will be leading in.

Change basically goes hand in hand with leadership and at the same time represents some powerful leadership necessities like:

- Breaking new ground
- Transforming
- Creating forward momentum
- Reaching potential

All of these things have something in common. They will make you uncomfortable, sometimes slightly uncomfortable; sometimes very uncomfortable. But you might as well get used to this reality.

Being uncomfortable is, at times, a reality in any leadership position. We're all impacted by our local environment and situation, but we're also affected by changes in the economy, shifts in politics and world events. Leading or not, these events cause change in our daily lives, travels, jobs and families. Health epidemics, hurricanes, terrorism, shifts in the economy…all of us have been impacted in some way or another at some level. Change causes disorientation. People can feel lost and confused. They don't know where or how to start again.

Change is inevitable. We all have choices around how we're going to get through it. You can choose to dig your heels into the ground, or you can move forward one step at a time. What's your choice going to be?

> "Fasten your seatbelts, it's going to be a bumpy ride![5]"
>
> – *Bette Davis as Margo Channing in* All About Eve

 **Change or revolution?**

Change will be uncomfortable, even when it's self-created. But through all of the discomfort, anxiety and turbulence, if you can focus on the 'new' – new doors that will open, bonds you will make and experiences you will gain – you might just get more comfortable with the uncomfortable. Consider it an 'inner revolution,' where you now realize that with the discomfort comes growth and bigger, better things.

"Although it might seem more like white-water rafting than drifting lazily in your canoe right now, it is important not to get distracted and lose perspective. Stop worrying about how to 'get it right.' What is needed is trust that the surging current of change will take you to where you really need to be. There's no point in attempting to predict outcomes because the scope of this revolution is far greater than what can be seen at this time."[6]

How to get comfortable with being uncomfortable

Some people are really good at being uncomfortable. They can roll with the punches, go with the flow. Then there are those who are going to stick their heels right in the dirt and put the brakes on. It's often understandable when you think about some of the discomfort change can bring: anxiety about jobs, worry about personal well-being, concern for the future. Who wants to go through all of that when things are good now, right?

As a leader during this decade, you'll need to go well beyond 'rolling with the punches.' You'll have to influence and lead through necessary, imposed changes. You'll need to learn to thrive in a bit of chaos and understand innately that change, even uncomfortable change, leads to transformation. And with transformation comes huge opportunity. You don't want to just go with the flow; you want to direct the flow if you can. You want to be the change agent – the leader who accepts that life is dynamic, and when things do change, you want to have the response and attitude that will influence others to come along.

Here are some steps you can take to get you and your team navigating through the ups and downs of your next mission:

1 Don't be the victim

> "Japanese children are given little Daruma dolls, weighted at the bottom so that they stand up if knocked over. Seven times down, eight times up.[7]"
>
> *– Japenese life lesson, symbolic of optimism, persistence and determination*

When you lead by example, you don't think or act like change is the end of the world, and it's likely your team won't either. The attitude to accept change and then grab the 'new world' by the horns and ride with it must start with you.

Over the years, I've shared some fairly consistent advice with my team: *Don't be the victim of change. Be an opportunist. Take advantage of the new doors that will open. If you don't like where things are today, hang tight because things are moving so fast that more change is just around the corner.*

With the rate of change in the industries I've worked in over the years, it's important for both me and my team members to adopt this mindset, allowing us the opportunity to go with the flow, deal with change, and grow professionally and personally. And it has led to some great personal transformations.

For instance, one particular 'don't be the victim' episode really sticks out for me. I was working for Ryder Integrated Logistics (a logistics company) and had convinced my leaders to promote me from operations manager to a customer-facing logistics role so that I could expand my career in a new direction. And it did, but in an entirely unpredictable way. I had been working on a North American logistics solution for one of our key electronics customers, and was asked by my senior logistics engineering boss to present my solution to our executive team, led by the general manager (GM) of the Canadian division of Ryder Integrated Logistics, a new solutions-based subsidiary of the parent company. After presenting the solution, the GM asked me to leave the room while the executive team deliberated on my proposal. My boss, however, interjected and insisted that I stay as I had been the key player on the project and, therefore, should participate in the discussion and decision-making process. Despite his brave efforts, the GM's response was a firm "No, she doesn't need to be a part of that executive discussion."

I'm not sure I've ever been so insulted and humiliated at the same time. I left that room feeling absolutely unvalued by our GM, not to mention belittled in front of the leadership team. Well, one of my strengths or weaknesses (depending on how you look at it) has always been having too much pride. So I went back to my desk and made up my mind to find a job in another company. After the meeting was over, my boss dropped by my office to apologize for the 'dismissal,' but it was too late. The steam train was rolling down the track.

Three weeks later, I had a job offer from Nortel Networks, who happened to be one of my previous clients and a company on the crest of an enormous high-tech wave. How exciting.

Thank goodness for the insult! I used it to my advantage to launch myself in an entirely new direction. No time to become a victim or feel undervalued. My new job was calling!

2 Create a 'tiger team'

You don't have to face challenging situations alone. One of the best ways of moving the team through change, influencing forward momentum and getting 'heel diggers' unstuck is to create a team of keeners who are unfazed by change or thrive in an environment in a state of motion. They are out there and they're on your team. Get them working on some immediate goals to start moving things forward.

Before you know it, the more resistant team members will come on board because it'll be tough for them not to get involved as they watch others break new ground. There is an energy and enthusiasm that comes with that new experience that is contagious. No one wants to be left in the dust. One of the most coveted positions when I worked at Nortel Networks in the Global Logistics team was to be on the 'tiger team.' This privileged band of globe-trotters was responsible for going into exotic and wonderful countries around the world to assess how to manage the intricate and complex process of moving and importing telecom gear. You think engineering and designing telecommunications is tough, you should try importing it after it's designed!

The team was created because Nortel was expanding rapidly and breaking into new markets. This elite team was rapidly pulled together with the tough mandate of coming up with these global logistics plans. All I knew was that I really wanted to be a part of that change and new direction, in any way I could.

I wanted to support change and get on board to move things forward with the team in whatever way possible to help them break new ground. Before I knew it, I was a full-fledged 'tiger' heading to South Africa, despite a dangerous travel advisory, to help our company establish a new logistics strategy in the blossoming market region of Africa.

Outside the corporate BOX

BEER AND THE BIG PICTURE

What do SARS, Avian influenza, the NHL strike and 9/11 all have in common? For Greg Sandwell, owner of the Honest Lawyer, a restaurant-bar-entertainment establishment, the answer is beer. Beer, and an impact on sales.

Sandwell and his loyal right-hand CEO, Renee Petrasovic, say, in its eight-year history, the Honest Lawyer team has had to roll with a lot of punches as global events have impacted their business. Located in four major Canadian markets, these corporate 'playgrounds' – otherwise known as 'restaurantainment' – feature food, beverages and themed entertainment for business teams. Who would have thought that restaurantainment would have been so impacted by mad cow disease, the hockey strike and almost every other national or global event that's taken place in the last five years?

But this team has its act together. Since 9/11, even though sales of food and beverages have dropped by 11 percent across the industry, according to Petrasovic, the Honest Lawyer has only seen a three percent drop and it's getting better every month. In fact, the company is expanding into new markets.

This dynamic executive duo attributes a couple of key principles to its success, leading a team of up to 300 through change:

- **Stay open-minded**

When the NHL strike affected the evening traffic flow for an entire sports season, this team did not drown in their beer. They expanded their market, promoting bar/bat mitzvahs, sweet-16 parties and stag and doe events to fill in the gap.

- **Communicate frequently but don't feed into the drama**

Internal changes to the team, like when this team had to remove its general manager, can shake up the team's foundation and promote a lot of gossip. Clear and consistent communication will keep everyone on the same page. Don't avoid it!

- **Have goals. Have a plan**

Like other strong leaders, the team at the Honest Lawyer knows that despite the level of success, there's always more they can achieve. Be goal-oriented, have a plan and communicate it, so your goals become the team's goals. Their motto: If we believe in ourselves, it's contagious – our team will believe in us.

This restaurantainment team has a great strategy when faced with change. *"You can win as a team or lose as a team. We choose to win."*

cha

3 Anticipate it! Change readiness

> "When I started out in business, I spent a great deal of time researching every detail that might be pertinent to the deal I was interested in making. I still do the same today. People often comment on how quickly I operate, but the reason I can move quickly is that I've done the background work first, which no one usually sees. I prepare myself thoroughly, and then when it is time to move ahead, I am ready to sprint." *– Donald Trump*

So how best can you and your team tackle change? Stay two steps ahead by anticipating it.

The best way to keep ahead is to prepare for it with a contingency plan. In fact, contingency planning is a strategy used by many businesses that operate in a fast-paced environment and have to deal with change on a daily basis. Having a backup plan is not an 'extra' you do, but a necessary step to success. Take live television producers, for instance. They survive and thrive in a world of last-minute changes, going with the flow, planning contingencies.

> "I still have grave doubts about the efficacy of making big plans in a world that is shifting gears at G-force speeds. Having said this, I can tell you that the ability at Transatlantic Marketing Group (TMG) to forge cohesive business plans and anticipate shifting market growth has been critical to the success we are currently experiencing.[8]"
> *– Heidi Lang, president and CEO of Transatlantic Marketing Group Inc.*

What's your plan B?

I got a TV producer's view on leading in a changing environment firsthand when I had the opportunity to sit in the trailer of an ESPN production team during the live show, *NFL Matchup,* an ESPN sports preview show that airs every week during the NFL season: "Everything can change. You can prepare forever but stuff still happens." The producer went on to explain that at a recent Miami Heat NBA game, Shaquille O'Neal didn't show up, which was unexpected. In a matter of seconds, the entire show's focus changed to reflect Shaq's absence. This producer's advice – go with the flow, always have a Plan B and then make sure you communicate it to your team. Tell everyone the new plan three times if you have to.

His philosophy is that if you believe that change can occur, it won't rattle you so much when change actually takes place. You can do your best to have a Plan B – you can plan for other camera shots or arrange pre-taped filler and background stories, but sometimes, no matter how much you prepare, you still might be caught off guard. And in those cases, being creative and thinking 'on the fly' is what's needed. In the case of Shaq's absence, a producer might be reorganizing his team or asking these questions: Shaq's not here? Okay, let's go with the new 'live' focus. *Where is he? Who can I turn to in the next few seconds or minutes to get some information on that new angle, live on air? Where do we have other cameras available to help fill in some of these gaps, or get answers to these live questions?*

I recently heard similar advice from a local television producer. Karen McLaughlin, producer of the cable network show *daytime,* described how she does contingency planning by go ing through these 'what-if' scenarios. When key talent doesn't show up to host the morning show, for example, that might mean that the producer or cameraman has to step in. Be prepared for the worst-case scenario. "While I'm taking walks at night I visualize the next day's show and then visualize what could go wrong and what I will do with zero time to spare." (For more information on Karen's role, see Chapter 03, page 100.)

If you don't already have a Plan B, you might have a team member map out a plan that details a new framework, with key points of what needs to be done if Plan A fails. If Plan A does fail, you already have a framework in place. Then inform the team in the event you need to use it.

Live television producers are often faced with no-shows or late-shows, and they have to adapt to those changes. Having a Plan B means asking yourself, if so-and-so doesn't show up, what do I do? What else can we air? What do we need to have in place in case we have to go to Plan B?

4 Kits, checklists and SOPs

How do you react quickly to change and get new or untrained resources moving in the right direction? Rapid reaction to any new situation is simplified through the use of templates or checklists that help define actions that need to be taken. You might have to jump in quickly or you might require new people to get up to speed fast. Team players can roll up their sleeves and 'dig in' with less supervision, and more quickly, when they have some frame of reference for what is required of them. Checklists and SOPs, or simple guidelines, are helpful in this regard.

You're better able to handle the fast changes and one-offs with some sort of structure. Airline pilots, military leaders, search and rescue teams and humanitarian teams like Doctors Without Borders or Habitat for Humanity all use these tools. There isn't a mission-critical team out there who would succeed without some sort of readiness plan. ◄◄ **Rewind** *to Chapter 10, "Executing Quick, Dirty and Sometimes Flawed," for more detail on checklists and SOPs.*

READINESS INTELLIGENCE

Rapid global response

How does Médecins Sans Frontières (MSF) respond so quickly and effectively to crises around the world? MSF has developed and produced pre-packaged disaster kits ready for transport within hours. Within 24 hours, with the support of pre-established logistical centers, emergency response equipment, such as surgical theaters or medical materials or pediatric care, is loaded on planes and flown into crisis areas around the world. Now that's fast. For more info, see www.msf.org.

The best way to manage feeling overwhelmed from change is to take one step at a time. There really is no other way to do it.

What is currently going on in your immediate world that might impact your team goals? Can you see where you need to go, long term? How about short term? What can you do within the next one, two or three days, or weeks? Identify some immediate solutions, no matter how small, despite the sometimes overwhelming tasks ahead of you. Once you start focusing on smaller steps that inch you forward in the right direction and help you experience some accomplishments, the overwhelming feelings can be replaced with a newfound energy and enthusiasm. ◄◄ **Rewind** *to Chapter 10, "Executing Quick, Dirty and Sometimes Flawed," for steps on how to take a new project and break it down into manageable chunks.*

CASE STUDY **Hope in a box**

In the small Bayou community of Thibodaux, Louisiana, Hurricane Katrina destroyed approximately 16,000 homes. Before Katrina, the local Habitat for Humanity affiliate had only built a maximum of 14 homes a year in previous years.

To fill in the need, Habitat for Humanity International headquarters in Americus, Georgia, responded with Operation Home Delivery, a rapid and unprecedented response program to build as many homes as possible along the Gulf Coast. Habitat affiliates across North America began pre-building housing components or 'house-in-a-box' kits, as they came to be known.

And at the local level, the Thibodaux Habitat team was rising to the challenge and expanding their vision. As I stood with my Canadian Habitat colleagues, we marvelled at what was now to become a Habitat job site for 86 homes. Jeanne, the local Habitat leader described how she had been looking desperately for some small parcel of land to start building efforts and, through no less than a miracle, discovered developed lots ready to go and a developer ready to partner and support Habitat's efforts. Her team's experience over the past few years had already been stretched. Now she was walking us through the plan to build 86 homes, an increase of almost six times the team's normal output. And this was just the beginning. Her small but powerful team of volunteers, regular staff and 'care-a-vanners' – volunteers who travel the continent to lend their building expertise – were developing plans to build more than 200 houses that year.

This small affiliate had a plan and mapped out its needs. This is where the Canadian team was able to step in and rapidly mobilize support for its U.S. colleagues.

Within days of our return to Canada, our Habitat team had a three-part plan to support this still-daunting scenario in Thibodaux:

1. ***Partner*** with the Thibodaux Habitat team as a 'sister' affiliate to contribute financially and purchase land for 86 homes;
2. Construct ***house-in-a-box kits,*** which provide pre-fabricated housing components for quick and easy assembly; and
3. Provide ***'mission experts'*** through volunteer teams and Team Canada expert missions to support the front lines in their efforts to rebuild the homes.

Three months later, the small Thibodaux team could see a ray of light with some small pockets of progress and forward momentum in tackling this gargantuan problem.

5 Diffuse the chatter. Keep everyone in the loop

Change will create anxiety, and anxiety increases people's propensity to try and rationalize what's going on, even if they don't have all the facts. So keep misinformation from spreading (misinformation which can cause even more anxiety). Personally, I like to tackle misinformation or gossip head-on, even if all I can replace it with is a vague response like, "I still don't know what the answer is." As the team at The Honest Lawyer says (see Outside the Corporate Box), don't feed into the drama!

RED FLAG **Nothing to say?**

Remember, one of the worst things you can do as a leader in times of change is to hide in your office. Communicate, communicate, communicate!

◄◄ **Rewind** *to Chapter 09, "Connect the Front Lines and the Big Picture" for great ideas on how to lead your team from the front using effective communication techniques.*

What's in it for you... and your team?

Nothing ever lasts forever.

Keep that in mind while you're busy trying to survive today's warp speed in business. The discomfort you might be feeling at that very minute will pass.

And the readiness or preparation in itself will only make your team stronger. You might have established some backup plans and a new direction you'll likely take if change hits. Or you might have created checklists and templates of your key functions so that anyone and everyone can step up to the plate if an unforeseen circumstance occurs. With these tools in place, everyone is prepared as best they can be. And everyone is equipped with the 'we can deal with it when it happens' mindset.

> "The best made plans don't survive first contact...."
>
> *– Clausewitz, military strategist*

You could very well end up 'flying by the seat of your pants' when change does hit, but preparing for it will help you and your team go with the flow as the ride gets bumpy. Your readiness and team preparation for 'whatever' will have the following positive impacts, even when things get ugly:

✓ **Keeping 'up' and in the loop**

When things are changing fast, keeping your team in the loop will keep motivation and morale at least somewhat buoyant. During rough times, you might not have much information to pass along, and I can't promise you that you won't be having some rough team meetings when communicating change and/or lack of new information to team members. The fact is that when you put people through the wringer, they are going to respond like they've been through the wringer – disoriented, unsure of whom to trust, and with low morale. But keeping the team in the loop, regardless of how they might react, is one small thing that managers can do to keep the team connected and moving through uncertain times. Keep talking to your team by conveying whatever scraps of organizational information you can provide them with. You'll be surprised how much better people feel about the entire situation and you as a leader when you take this simple step.

✓ You'll survive the right-angle turns

I had the opportunity to work with the CEO of Quattro Communications, an events management and public relations company, last year, while working as a high-tech consultant. Charlie Johnstone's team (who you read about in Chapter 01) was responsible for leading many very large annual events, one of which was the July 1st Canada Day party for the city of Toronto. The project team had prepared for months in advance to deliver 12 hours of outdoor entertainment for 150,000-plus Canadians, eager to celebrate the country's birthday. Johnstone and his team held meetings, developed communication strategies and worked with many different frontline leaders to manage and plan all the venues. From timely delivery of porta-potties to managing the concession stands to building outdoor stages for evening rock concerts, intricate planning and attention to detail were required. Johnstone's motto of planning all that you can and preparing to 'fly by the seat of your pants' comes from first-hand experience. (For example, he later learned after trying to get in touch with one of his leaders during the event that he was a little busy with a 'situation.' A donkey had broken loose from the petting zoo display and was running down the street!)

Any steps you can take to prepare your team for the unexpected will never be wasted. Planning, of any sort, creates an environment of clarity and focus. When things go amok, a cohesive unit makes it that much easier to make that right-angle turn.

✓ Become unstuck!

Lot of change, particularly if it's not positive (such as downsizing, layoffs, world catastrophes), can stop people in their tracks. It's a natural reaction to get stuck in anxiety and fear. Your job is to get and keep things moving forward, to move people through morale slumps, minimize chaos and reduce confusion. Planning provides a sense of direction and forward momentum. Having goals that people own will inject momentum right back into your 'stuck crowd.' Helping everyone see the way ahead, and then to see actual progress, works wonders.

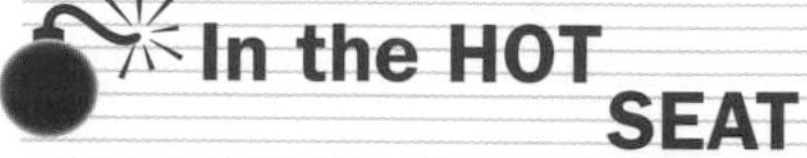

GETTING FOOD FAST TO HUNGER HOT SPOTS

You're the leader of an international 50-person team who has to get food to more than 500,000 people in a country hit hard by drought, HIV/AIDS and flooding. It's a country where life expectancy sits around 41 years, 54 percent of the population is below the national poverty line and 41 percent of children under five are suffering malnutrition.

Sound like a tough job? It's kept Barbara, a family friend, busy for the last decade as a leader with the United Nations World Food Programme, working in Eastern Africa getting food to the areas hardest hit by famine or 'hunger hot spots.'

In her line of work, change is the norm. In the past year alone, she has been responsible for leading the global supply chain (organizing the international transportation, warehousing and delivery) to get food to starving people in Kenya, Ethiopia, Sri Lanka (after the tsunami in December 2004) and, most recently, Mozambique. How does she survive and thrive in a role where she is impacted by what's going on in the world?

Here's how:

- **Have ruthless initiative** – Pursue new ideas to bring about change and be willing to take on whatever task is necessary to make it happen.
- **Have a high-quality team** – They are the backbone of your mission.
- **Keep asking yourself "what if?"** Just like a pilot asks himself or herself, "where can I put this aircraft down in an emergency?" you'll need to take a step back and ask yourself if are there things you have not considered that you should? What will your backup plan be?
- **Don't ever forget who you're here for** – The moment you start losing the belief in what you're doing is the moment you need to ask yourself what you are doing in the position.

Most of all, keep your eyes on the prize. Visible and tangible impact is worth tens of millions of dollars and will give you a sense of fulfillment. But the most precious thing a person can ever give is life.

Hindsight is 20/20

Bullies and ball-busters

The business world is full of 'yellers,' 'bullies' and 'ball-busters' (the female version of bullies). At the best of times, the mission-critical environment can bring out the worst in us. Tight timelines, no room for error and a lot of change can result in confusion and, let's face it, lots of stress!

Sometimes, when you're in a fast-paced situation, you have to take the bull by the horns. But be careful. There is a fine line between 'taking control' and making things happen and 'uncontrolled disrespectful outbursts.'

The latter has some serious repercussions and, depending on what you're leading, it can backfire. Instead of people being motivated and jumping on board to do whatever it takes, you can end up with a rebellion or a quiet mutiny. Tirades and yelling can only get you so far, even when it's a mission-critical project.

I once worked with a woman who was nicknamed (behind the scenes, of course) a 'ball-buster.' Sorry ladies, it's not the nicest term in the world. I witnessed her theatrics in meetings as she pounded her fist on the conference table, trying to create a sense of urgency for some new big initiative for the company. She must have thought she appeared tough, but she crossed the fine line of being assertive and instead came off as a bully.

Leaders like this tend to rant and rave and have finger-pointing tirades when things don't go their way. Or they'll shout at everyone without providing much direction because they don't know what to do when the going gets tough. Or even worse, they may belittle team members because it helps them feel bigger in an insecure environment.

Things will get stressful, and consensus management will get shoved aside for 'make it happen' decision-making when there's little time. But don't lose your head, because everyone else follows your cues.

What's next? Turn the leader in you loose!

Whatever it is that you want to do, it's out there waiting for you. It's now within your reach.

You've got the mindset. You've got the action plan. Now you just need to make it happen.

Where does your next opportunity lie? Big business? Your community? Starting your own company? Maybe working in another part of the world? Or maybe your next challenge is writing a book?

I hope you are excited because I sure am! There's so much to do and so little time to do it in. I can hardly wait for what leadership opportunites lie ahead.

Remember. Nothing ever lasts forever. And that's a really good thing because that means that bigger and better things lie just around the corner.

We all have a leader in us – we all have an incredible difference to make. So never forget, you are your own boss, you are in charge of your job, your career, your life. And you are the only CEO who really matters!

Because it's your life. Don't you forget it.

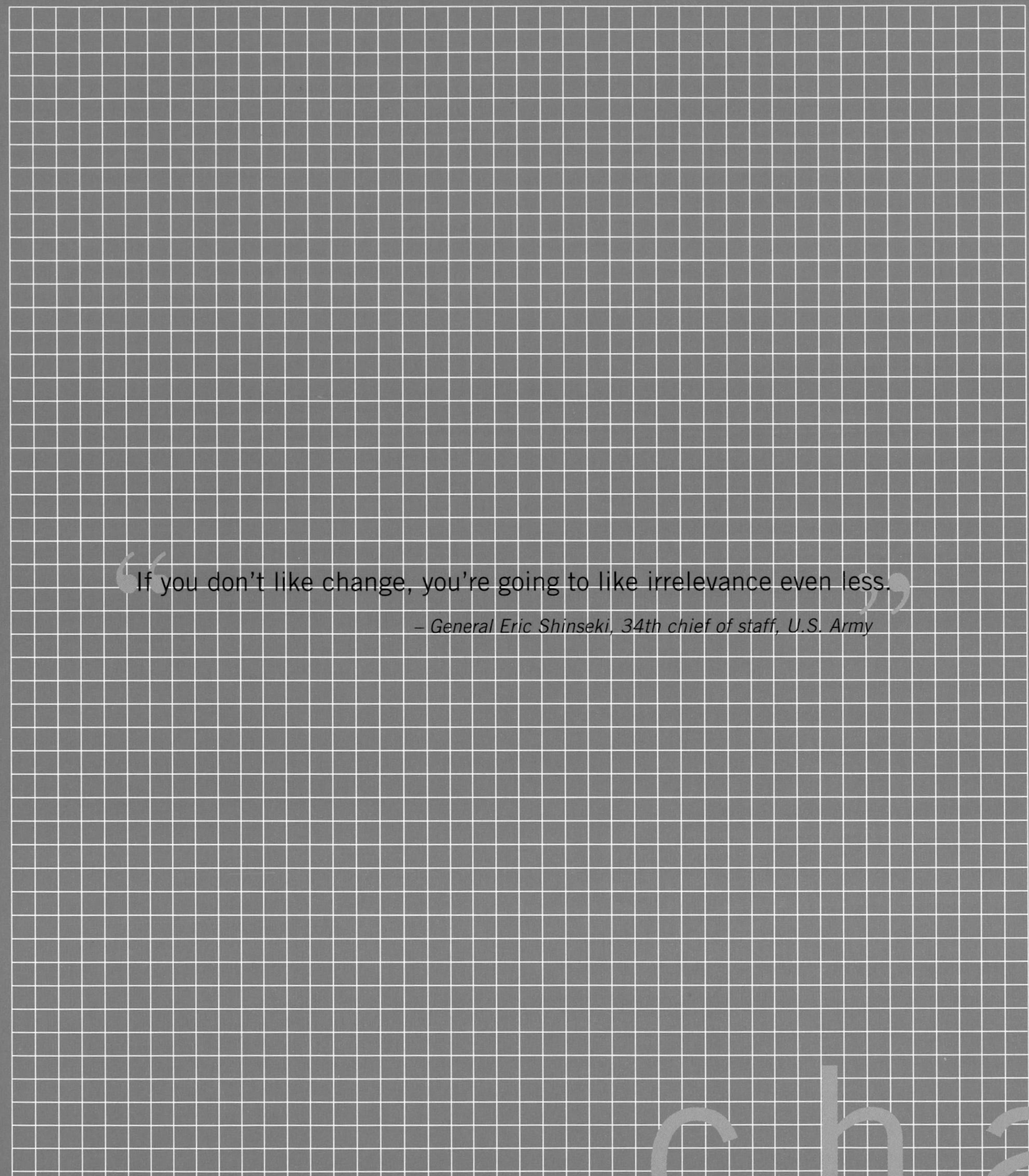

"If you don't like change, you're going to like irrelevance even less."

– General Eric Shinseki, 34th chief of staff, U.S. Army

ACTION PLAN

Turn the leader in you loose!

1 IT MIGHT NOT BE PRETTY.

- Don't be the victim. Don't let your team members be victims either
- Keep the gossip to a minimum. Keep your team in the loop and informed

2 CREATE A TIGER TEAM.

- Leverage team members who bounce back and take new direction with gusto
- Enlist 'change agents' to start creating some momentum and positive direction after a 'right-angle turn' has been imposed

3 WHAT'S YOUR PLAN B?

- Contingency planning will be your best friend. Use checklists and SOPs
- Good planning creates flexibility and agility to react fast and roll with the punches

4 BREAK NEW GROUND.

- Recognize that breaking new ground, dealing with rapid and imposed change or reaching your potential will invite uncertainty
- Remember, good and bad, all change brings transformation

nge

endnotes

Chapter i

1. Lewis MacKenzie, *Peacekeeper: The Road to Sarajevo* (Toronto: HarperCollins Publishers, 1994).

2. "Canada launches Operation Harmony," *Der Kanadier,* March 1992.

3. CBC, *Canada at Five,* "Female Van Doo Draws Attention in Sarajevo," March 16, 1992, http://archives.cbc.ca/IDCC-1-71-579-3020/conflict_war/van_doos/, accessed June 2006.

4. Reuters, "Peacekeepers Told Of Danger As Yugoslav Mission Starts," *The Toronto Star,* March 16, 1992.

5. Ibid.

6. General MacKenzie, "Canadian Eyes Only," CC ECMMY SECURE FAX, March 11, 1992.

7. *No Limits But The Sky* (Kansas City: Hallmark Books, 2002).

8. Booz Allen, "Annual CEO Succession Study," *Strategy + Business* (Summer 2005).

Chapter ii

1. Catherine Mossop, "Training & Development: Accelerating Leadership Development Through Mentoring," Perspective: *Your HR Information Source,* February 2005.

2. Andreas Priestland and Robert Hanig, "Developing First-Level Leaders," *Harvard Business Review,* June 2005.

3. *Apollo 13,* directed by Ron Howard, 1995 (Universal).

4. Deepak Chopra, *Seven Spiritual Laws of Success: A Practical Guide to the Fulfillment of Your Dreams* (Novato, CA: New World Library/Amber-Allen Publishing, 1995).

5. *A Bug's Life,* directed by John Lasseter and Andrew Stanton, 1998 (Disney/Pixar).

Chapter iii

1. Douglas Adams, *The Hitchhiker's Guide to the Galaxy* (London: Rosetta Books, 1979).

2. Thornton Wilder, *The Matchmaker* (New York: Harper, 1955).

3. Richard Branson, *Losing My Virginity* (New York: Three Rivers Press, 1998).

4. Kara Hull, "FedEx Founder Says Passion Breeds Success, *BGNews.com,* February 20, 2006, http://bgnews.com, accessed May 2005.

5. Chuck Salter, "Driving Ambition," *Fast Company* (May 2005).

6. United States Army, FM 22-100: *Army Leadership; Be, Know, Do,* Washington, 1999.

7. Pratap Parameswaran, *"'Just Do It': Nike's Magic Call to Action,"* (Business Times, February 9, 2000).

8. Antoine de Saint-Exupery, *The Little Prince,* trans. Richard Howard (Orlando: Harcourt, 1943).

Chapter iv

1. *Private Benjamin,* directed by Howard Zieff, 1980 (Warner Bros.).

2. Canadian Forces Publication 131 (1) para 405, *Principles of Leadership.*

3. United States Army, *FM 22-100: Army Leadership; Be, Know, Do,* forward, Washington, 1999.

4. Alan Deutschman, "Business the Branson Way," *Fast Company* (October 2004).

5. Dennis D. Dammerman, "Changing GE: Lesson's Learned From Along the Way," Lecture, Durland Memorial Lecture, Cornell University, Ithaca, April 1, 1998.

6. "Front & Center–Lessons in Leadership: Email Exchange Between the Bradley Professor and an Infantry Lieutenant," *ARMY Magazine* (June 2005).

7. "Indepth: Enron," *CBC News Online,* May 25, 2006, http://www.cbc.ca/news/background/enron/, accessed June 2006.

8. *Wikipedia,* s.v. "List Of Corporate Executives Charged With Crimes," http://en.wikipedia.org/wiki/List_of_corporate_executives_charged_with_crimes, accessed June 2006.

9. David Plotz, "Assessment: Conrad Black," *Slate,* August 31, 2001, http://www.slate.com/id/114605/, accessed June 2006.

10. Richard J. Newman, "Corporate Kleptocracy," *U.S. News.com,* September 13, 2004, http://www.usnews.com/usnews/biztech/articles/040913/13black.htm, accessed June 2006.

11. "Indepth: Sponsorship Scandal," *CBC News Online,* February 1, 2006, http://www.cbc.ca/news/background/groupaction/, accessed June 2006.

12. "Martha Stewart's Wild Ride," CNN.com, 2004, http://edition.cnn.com/CNN/Programs/people/shows/stewart/profile.html, accessed May 2006.

13. "In depth: Martha Stewart," *CBC News Online,* January

6, 2006, http://www.cbc.ca/news/background/stewart_martha/timeline.html, accessed June 2006.

14. "Forbes Rich List At Record Levels," *BBC News,* March 11, 2005, http://news.bbc.co.uk/1/hi/business/4337493.stm, accessed February 2006.

15. Todd Plitt, "Stewart Shares Business Rules," *USA Today,* October 10, 2005, http://usatoday.com/money/media/2005-10-10-martha-book-usat_x.htm?csp=N009, accessed June 2006.

16. Lisa de Moraes, "Martha Stewart's 'The Apprentice' Is No Perennial." *Washington Post,* November 15, 2005, http://www.washingtonpost.com/wp-dyn/content/article/2005/11/14/AR2005111401597.html, accessed June 2006.

17. Todd Plitt, "Stewart shares business rules," *USA Today,* October 10, 2005, http://usatoday.com/money/media/2005-10-10-martha-book-usat_x.htm?csp=N009, accessed June 2006.

Chapter v

1. Kevin Crowley, "Military or high-tech, it's all war," *The Record,* March 9, 2004.

2. Peter F. Drucker, "Management's New Paradigms," *Forbes.com,* October 5, 1998, http://www.forbes.com/forbes/1998/1005/6207152a.html/, accessed May 2006.

3. Daniel Michaels and Christopher J. Chipello, "Air Canada's Revival Recipe Is Its Other Units," *The Wall Street Journal,* April 25, 2006.

4. Air Canada, "Executive Biographies," Air Canada Website, http://www.aircanada.com/en/about/media/bio/milton.html, accessed May 2006.

5. Canadian Broadcasting Corporation. "Reinventing an Airline," The Canadian Broadcasting Corporation Digital Archives Website, http://archives.cbc.ca/IDC-1-73-1125-13325/politics_economy/air_canada/clip1, accessed May 2006.

6. Daniel Michaels and Christopher J. Chipello, "Air Canada's Revival."

7. Robert A. Milton and John Lawrence Reynolds, *Straight from the Top: The Truth about Air Canada* (Vancouver: Greystone Books, 2004).

8. Price Pritchett, *The Employee Handbook of New Work Habits for a Radically Changing World: 13 Ground Rules for Job Success in the Information Age* (Dallas: Pritchett & Associates Inc.).

9. MyungJong Hong, "World Class E-Commerce Strategies," research report prepared for the California Research Bureau, California, 2000.

10. Pritchett, *The Employee Handbook.*

11. Ibid.

12. *In Good Company,* directed by Paul Weitz, 2004 (Universal).

13. Barbara Moses, "The Challenges of Managing Gen Y," *The Globe and Mail,* March 11, 2005.

14. Job Service North Dakota, *North Dakota's Fountain of Youth: Is the Well Drying Up? A Report on North Dakota's Children.*

15. Virginia Galt, "The Generational Divide," *The Globe and Mail,* March 31, 2004, www.globeandmail.com, accessed May 30, 2006.

16. "Speed Merchants," *Academy Sharing Knowledge* (ASK), August 2002, http://appl.nasa.gov/ask/issues/11/features, accessed May 2006.

17. Ibid

Chapter 01

1. Isabel Matheson, "Corruption Besets Kenya Business," *BBC News,* January 25, 2005, http://news.bbc.co.uk/1/hi/world/africa/4206229.stm, accessed February 2006.

2. UNAIDS, *2004 Report on the Global Aids Epidemic, 2005.*

3. Stephen Lewis. Address, Official Opening of the XIII International Conference on AIDS and STIs in Africa, Nairobi, 21 September 2003.

4. Save the Children USA, "HIV/AIDS is a Children's Issue," Save the Children USA Website, http://www.savethechildren.org/health/hiv_aids/aids_childrens_issue.asp, accessed June 2006.

5. Margot Morrell, Alexandra Shackleton and Stephanie Capparell, *Shackleton's Way: Leadership Lesson's from the Great Antarctic Explorer* (Penguin Group USA, 2002).

6. Canadian Broadcasting Corporation, "Reinventing an Airline," *The CBC Digital Archives Website,* http://archives.cbc.ca/IDC-1-73-1125-13325/politics_economy/air_canada/clip1, accessed May 2006.

7. Roger Connors and Tom Smith, "Create a Culture of Accountability," *Bizlife* (December 2004).

endnotes

Chapter 02

1. Ma Deva Padma, Tao Oracle: *An Illuminated New Approach to the I Ching* (New York: St. Martin's Press; 2002).

Chapter 03

1. Canadian Department of National Defense, *NORAD,* Canadian Department of National Defense and Canadian Forces Website, http://www.forces.gc.ca, accessed February 2006.

2. "Wanna succeed? You better fail first!" Rediff.com, February 11, 2005, http://inhome.rediff.com/getahead/2005/feb/11success.htm, accessed March 2006.

3. Colin Powell, *The Leadership Secrets of Colin Powell* (McGraw-Hill Companies, 2003).

Chapter 04

1. Theeranuch Pusaksrikit, "Going Over the Edge For the Company," *The Nation,* January 6, 2004.

Therese Poletti, "Seagate Chief Executive an Amiably Aggressive Team Builders," *Mercury News,* August 8, 2005, http://siliconvalley.com/mld/siliconvalley/12331116.htm, accessed January 2006.

Therese Poletti, "CEO's Method for Creating Culture," *Mercury News,* August 8, 2005, http://siliconvalley.com/mld/siliconvalley/living/people/12331063.htm, accessed January 2006.

Chapter 05

1. *Kill Bill,* directed by Quentin Tarantino, 2003 (Miramax).

Chapter 06

1. Christie Hefner, "Thinking Outside the Box," *Media Studies Journal* (Spring/Summer 1996).

2. Ma Deva Padma, *Tao Oracle: An Illuminated New Approach to the I Ching.*

3. Andrew Findlay, "Blue Chip," *Up!* (November 2005).

4. Lululemon Athletica, "Lululemon Athletica Homepage," Lululemon Athletica Website, www.lululemon.com/culture/manifesto.php, accessed June 2006.

5. Rebecca Philps, "Vancouver Special: Lululemon's Mastermind," *Vancouver Magazine* (Feb. 2005), http://www.lululemon.com, accessed February 2006.

6. Lenny Kravitz, interview by Gordon Parks, June 2004, http://www.findarticles.com/p/articles/mi_m1285/is_5_34/ai_n6042972, accessed June 2006.

7. Michael A. Prospero, "Fast Talk – Voices from the Creative Front lines," *Fast Company* (December 2005).

8. Daniel Levi, *Group Dynamics for Teams* (California: Sage Publications Inc., 2001).

9. Ma Deva Padma, Tao Oracle: *An Illuminated New Approach to the I Ching.*

10. Daniel Levi, *Group Dynamics for Teams.*

Chapter 07

1. Kevin Roberts, *Lovemarks: The Future Beyond Brands.* (New York: Powerhouse Books, 2004).

2. David A. Heenan and Warren Bennis, *Co-leaders: The Power of Great Partnerships* (New York: John Wiley & Sons, Inc., 1999).

3. Wikipedia, s.v. "Steve Jobs," http://en.wikipedia.org/wiki/Steve-Jobs, accessed July 2006.

4. John Heider, *The Tao of Leadership: Lao Tzu's Tao Te Ching* Adapted for a New Age (Atlanta: Humanics New Age, 1985).

5. Ma Deva Padma, *Tao Oracle: An Illuminated New Approach to the I Ching.*

6. Knowledge@Wharton, "The Importance of Being Richard Branson," Informit.com, August 19, 2005, http://www.informit.com/articles/article.asp?p=393257, accessed June 2006.

Chapter 08

1. Cpt. David S. Davidson, USA Force XXI O/C, Team, *Troop Leading at the Platoon Level* (A misunderstood Art), http://call.army.mil, accessed June 2006.

2. Price Pritchett and Ron Pound, *A Survival Guide to the Stress of Organizational Change* (Dallas: Pritchett & Associates Inc., 1995).

3. Kevin Roberts, *Lovemarks: the Future Beyond Brands* (New York: Powerhouse Books, 2004).

4. The Official Formula 1 Website, "Understanding the Sport: Pit Stops," Formula 1 Website, http://www.formula1.com/insight/technicalinfo/11/694.html, accessed June 2006.

endnotes

endnotes

Chapter 09

1. “Time 100: Builder’s and Titans,” *Time,* April 18, 2005.

2. Nancy Gibbs and Nathan Thornburgh, “The Class of 9/11,” *Time,* Cdn. ed, May 30, 2005.

3. James D. Murphy, *Business is Combat* (New York: Regan Books, 2000).

4. IT Cortex, “Failure Causes: Statistics,” IT Cortex Website, http://www.it-cortex.com/Stat_Failure_Cause.htm, accessed May 2006.

5. “Effective Employee Communication Linked to Stronger Financial Performance,” Watson Wyatt press release (Washington, DC, November 8, 2005). From Watson Wyatt Website, http://www.watsonwyatt.com/us/news/press.asp?ID=15362, accessed June 2006.

6. Scott Kirsner, “Sweating in the Hot Zone,” *Fast Company* (October 2005).

7. “Seeds of Change: The Earth Charter and Human Potential.” An exhibition created by SGI and The Earth Charter Initiative, first shown at the World Summit on Sustainable Development (WSSD), Johnannesburg 2002. http://www.earthcharter.org/files/resources/Exhibition_cropped.pdf, accessed May 2006.

8. Bart Vanmaele, “The Re-Invention Tour,” Mad-eyes.net, http://www.mad-eyes.net/tours/re-invention-tour/index.htm, accessed May 2006.

9. *Be Cool,* directed by Gary Grey, 2005 (MGM).

Chapter 10

1. Ram Charan and Geoffrey Colvin, “Why CEOs Fail,” *Fortune Magazine,* June 21, 1999, http://money.cnn.com/magazines/fortune/fortune_archive/1999/06/21/261696/index.htm, accessed June 2006.

2. “Army Intelligence: Kelly Perdew’s Successful Transition,” *Military.com,* http://www.kellyperdew.com/presslinks/050217military.com.html?file=Perdew_Intro.htm&area=Reference, accessed June 2006.

3. Price Pritchett and Ron Pound, *A Survival Guide to the Stress of Organizational Change.*

Chapter 11

1. Deepak Chopra, *The Spontaneous Fulfillment of Desire* (New York: Harmony Books, 2003).

2. Virgin, “Richard’s Replies,” Virgin Website, http://www.virgin.com/aboutvirgin/allaboutvirgin/richardreplies/default.asp, accessed June 2006.

Chapter 12

1. Julie Lewis, ed., “What Does the Expression ‘To Push the Envelope’ Mean?”, *The Sydney Morning Herald,* October 15, 2005, http://www.smh.com.au/news/big-questions/what-does-the-expression-to-push-the-envelope-mean/2005/10/13/1128796638394.html, accessed June 2006.

2. Ma Deva Padma, *Tao Oracle: An Illuminated New Approach to the I Ching.*

3. Steve Jobs, “You’ve Got To Find What You Love,” commencement address, Stanford University, Stanford, 13 June 2005.

4. Lisa Deglìantoni, “Making Leaders and Mis-leaders,” *Psychology Today* (March/April 1996).

5. *Wikipedia,* s.v. “Frank Abagnale,” http://en.wikipedia.org/wiki/Frank_Abagnale, accessed June 2006.

6. Willem Dafoe, *Breathe Magazine,* interview by Aaron Gell, July 2005.

Chapter 13

1. *National Geographic, Special Edition, Katrina,* December 2006.

2. Peter Knaack, “Hurricane Katrina: Lessons Learned From a Continental Tragedy,” *Sitrep: A Publication of the Royal Canadian Military Institute* (January/February 2006).

3. Chris Johns, “In the Storm’s Wake: Giving Back,” *National Geographic Special Edition: Katrina,* December 2005.

4. Spencer Johnson, *Who Moved My Cheese?* (New York: G.P. Putnam’s Sons, 1998).

5. *All About Eve,* directed by Joseph L. Mankiewicz, 1950 (Twentieth Century Fox).

6. Ma Deva Padma, *Tao Oracle: An Illuminated New Approach to the I Ching.*

7. Robert Allen, *A Thousand Paths to Personal Power.* (London: MQ Publications Ltd, 2003.)

8. Heidi Lang, “The Road Ahead,” *PROFITguide.com,* 2000.

index

index

index

index

THANKS...for helping turn ideas into reality!

Sometime around 2002 or 2003, someone suggested that I consider writing a book. And then the magic began, as one by one, the people who were going to help make this plan a reality started showing up in my life.

David Chilton, my benchmark for success, has been a huge force behind the scenes, probably more than he knows. He has certainly hit the 'impact quotient' with me. (You can read more about this in Chapter 11.) David, your success is inspiring, but I'm most inspired by how much you give and how little you expect in return.

David introduced me to **Fina Scroppo**, who started out as my editor but quickly became so much more. Fina's experience and wisdom in what it takes to self-publish a book goes well beyond editing. She is a true leader in every sense, orchestrating people and timelines to help make this book a success. Couldn't have done this without you, Fina. Just think of all the places you can now use [JARGON] and [LINGO] like 'check your sixes' and FUBAR on your next project! Can't say I'm going to miss the CAPS in yellow highlights all over my chapters, though!

Leslee Mason-Gomes, our assistant editor. Thanks, Leslee, for helping to make this a 24/7 operation so that this book could launch on time.

Photographer extraordinaire – **Stan Switalski** – you are one hip photographer. You can 'spark the creativity' in everything – gears, ladders and people. Thanks for delivering that cool and creative look I was hoping for. You really hit the target.

Copy editor **Nancy Howden** and fact-checker **Tara Brouwer** for making sure my lack of attention to detail is less apparent to the reader. Thanks for your umpteen reviews as I wrote and rewrote stuff! I promise, if I ever do this again (don't worry, just kidding), I will be better at this! The devil's in the detail, right?

To **Joan Euler**, your enthusiasm and support in reaching out to the community to help make this book a success will not be forgotten!

And last but not least, a special thanks to **Lindsay Gibson** – my new director of marketing, events, finance, distribution and whatever else our small press and publishing company requires – with whom I have combined forces (there really is no other way). Lindsay, we've done this a few times before, but we are entering a whole new world. Hang on for the ride – this is going to be our best product launch (and subsequent martini party) ever!

Many, many, many thanks to all of you believers:

Jim Balsillie
Major Carolyn Boyd
Jan Chaplin
Brendan Crymble
Carl & Erica Crymble
Mark Davenport
Paul Doherty
Shawky Fahel
Steve Farlow
Craig Farrow
John Ferraro
Lieutenant-Colonel Norm *'Slider'* Gagne
Frank & Jaynne Gosling
Merril Hoge
David Hughes
Tom Hunter
Philip Kates
Iain Klugman
Alison Lafrance
Simon Lee
Major-General *(ret'd)* Lewis MacKenzie
Karen McLaughlin
Nathan McLaughlin
Peter McMenemy
Princess Superstar (Concetta Kirschner)
Don Morrison
Scott Neal
Jeremy O'Krafka
Andrew Pace
Renee Petrasovic
Sandi Pitcairn
Paula Quon-Redden
Serge Rancourt
Greg Sandwell
Ray Simonson
Andrew Smith
Ryan Stewart (2 Live Stews)
Joanne Thomas Yaccato
Barbara VanLogchem
Vince Washington

thanks

ORDER FORM

Check your local bookstore or retailer for **Hit the Ground *Leading!*** or order here.

Just fill out the form below and send it, along with your payment, to:

- Fax orders: 519-896-7893 • Online orders: www.iceleadership.com
- Telephone orders – have VISA or Mastercard ready:
  - Local: 519-893-5220 • Toll free: 1-866-397-3826

Please send ___ copies of **Hit the Ground *Leading!***

@ $32.95 CDN ea. ________

Shipping and handling:

$5.00 per book ________

Sales tax:

Canadian residents add 6% GST ________

TOTAL AMOUNT ENCLOSED: ________

Name (please print): ____

Signature (name as on card): ____

Address: ____

City: ________________ Province/State: ________________ Postal/Zip code: ________________

Telephone: (___) ________________

Payment:

__ Check __ Credit Card __VISA __ Mastercard

Card Number: ____________________ Name on Card: ____________________ Expiry Date: ______ / ______

We are a highly creative team and would love to work with you! Our company delivers a leadership and growth experience. If you are interested in purchasing volume orders of the book, developing a co-branded program or interested in our keynotes and workshops, please contact us.

ICE LEADERSHIP

integrate • communicate • execute

All inquiries should be addressed to:

ICE Publishing
2036 Hidden Valley Cres., Suite 1A, Kitchener, Ontario N2C 2R1
1-866-397-3826
www.iceleadership.com